>>COLLABORATE

>>COMMUNICATE

>>DELIVER

>>MANAGE

>>COORDINATE

>>SIMPLIFY

>>DEFINE

>>ORGANIZE

Web ReDesign | Workflow that Works©

>>ROADMAP TO REDESIGN: WORKFLOW FOR THE REAL WORLD

By Kelly Goto & Emily Cotler

WWW **CATEGORY:**INTERNET **COVERS:**WINDOWS AND MACINTOSH

WEB REDESIGN: WORKFLOW THAT WORKS.
©2002 KELLY GOTO AND EMILY COTLER. PUBLISHED BY NEW RIDERS PUBLISHING,
201 WEST 103RD STREET INDIANAPOLIS, IN 46290-9058. WWW.NEWRIDERS.COM

OPEN HERE

New
Riders

Web ReDesign | Workflow that Works

By Kelly Goto & Emily Cotler

New Riders

201 West 103rd Street
Indianapolis, IN 46290

International Standard Book Number:
0-7357-1062-7

Library of Congress Catalog Card Number:
00-108795

Printed in the United States of America

First Printing: August 2001

05   04   03   02   01   7   6   5   4   3   2   1

Interpretation of the printing code: The rightmost double-digit number is the year of the book's printing; the rightmost single-digit number is the number of the book's printing. For example, the printing code 01-1 shows that the first printing of the book occurred in 2001.

Trademarks

Warning and Disclaimer

Publisher
David Dwyer

Associate Publisher
Al Valvano

Executive Editors
Steve Weiss
Stephanie Wall

Product Marketing Manager
Kathy Malmloff

Managing Editor
Sarah Kearns

Acquisitions Editor
Linda Anne Bump

Development Editor
Audrey Doyle

Project Editor
Jake McFarland

Copy Editor
Amy Lepore

Technical Editor
Ellen Butchart

Cover Designer
Darren "Dag" Marzorati
with Serena Howeth

Interior Designer
Renée Frisbie

Compositor
Kim Scott

Proofreader
Debra Neel

Indexer
Becky Hornyak

Table of Contents

ABOUT THE AUTHORS

Kelly Goto is a sought-after lecturer and instructor on the topics of web development, information design, and user experience. Her sessions at conference after conference (and class after class) are invariably packed — Kelly has a knack for making the complex topic of workflow accessible, even engaging. Formerly an award-winning creative director at Idea Integration (www.idea.com), Kelly successfully managed the redesigns of many sites ranging from independent to corporate levels. In commercial design since the late 1980s (remember when PageMaker 1.0 was *the* design tool?), Kelly has acted as creative director, designer, and producer for many high-profile clients, including Warner Bros. Online, National Geographic Online, Adobe Corporation, Paramount Television, Macromedia Corporation, and Sony Pictures. Currently a principal at gotomedia, inc. (www.gotomedia.com), an online consultancy for user experience and interaction design, Kelly continues to focus on developing new techniques for collaborative development in digital media. When not tethered to her laptop, Kelly can be found trekking the Third World — where she does not check her email.

Emily Cotler is a graphic designer, web designer, journalist, and novelist. A designer since the late 1980s (remember rubdown lettering and stat camera separations?), she is in high demand for both web and print work. Focusing primarily on smaller sites for individual creative professionals and small enterprises, Emily specializes in creating (or re-creating, as the case may be) a positive web presence for smaller budgets. Her clients include *New York Times* best-selling authors Julia Quinn and Susan Andersen, and many small but thriving companies, including L.A.-based entertainment booking agency Artist Booking International, Denver-based technical writing firm Pomegranate Consulting, and Seattle-based Kira Stewart Photography. A regular contributor to *Publish Magazine* since 1998, Emily is known for her accessible style and readability — dry topics come alive, interesting topics come off the page. She currently has a 40-foot commute to Waxcreative Design (www.waxcreative.com) in Oakland, California, where she reigns as creative directrix. Her preferred method of escape from cyberspace includes a snowboard and a Colorado mountain.

Emily and Kelly, hard at work finishing this book, May 2001, Oakland, California.

Photo courtesy of deborah sherman photography.

ABOUT THE TECH EDITOR

Ellen Butchart manages design and user interface for the international team at Amazon.com, including oversight of all international sites and new country launches. She also has been the lead designer for the Amazon.com bookstore and has managed design for the Books, Music, Video, and DVD stores. Prior to joining Amazon, Ellen was creative director at MindCorps, an enterprise software development company in Seattle, and before that she was a CD-ROM producer at the Learning Company (where she produced reference products for the Compton's line) and at Knowledge Adventure, a children's software company in Los Angeles. In a prior career — and lifetime — she taught film studies at the University of Virginia and the University of Pennsylvania.

ACKNOWLEDGMENTS

We did not create this book by ourselves. Writing it in a Kelly-and-Emily-vacuum would have taken twice as long (at least) and resulted in a far less information-rich volume. We are indebted to many talented individuals, and many thanks are to be had…

Thanks to our families (especially Brian) and our friends who continued to love and humor us despite our constant unavailability and ubiquitous insertion of the words "The Book" into just about every conversation and excuse for asocial behavior.

Thanks to the editorial team at New Riders — Steve Weiss, David Dwyer, Linda Bump, Jennifer Eberhardt, Chris Nelson, Audrey Doyle, Ellen Butchart, Wil Cruz, Jake McFarland, and everyone else — your enthusiasm, attention to detail, and unfailing understanding were instrumental in shaping and producing this book.

Thanks to Steve Cotler, walking thesaurus, grammar god, voice police, and critical reviewer throughout the entire process — your unparalleled editorial assistance, generous-beyond-description availability, and blatant honesty made this book better (say very little more!).

Thanks to Chad Kassirer and Sean Dolan, wide-ranging experts in production and processes — your off-hours spent reviewing the material and contributing expertise are very appreciated.

Thanks to our book designers — Renée Frisbie, layout designer (your vision can be seen on every page), and Darren "Dag" Marzorati and Serena Howeth, cover designers (inspired, truly inspired) — you each outdid yourself… again. Thanks also to Kim Scott (layout production) for your amazing speed and attention to detail. And to Deb Sherman (photographer) — thanks for capturing the real, passionate-about-what-we-do Emily and Kelly rather than the harried, exhausted authors we had (temporarily) become.

Thanks to Thunder Lizard Productions, especially Steve Broback, Jim Heid, and Tobi Malina, for creating "conferences with content" and offering a venue for the development of the topic that became this book.

Thanks to *Publish Magazine*, especially Melissa Reyen, for enthusiasm and support — and for waiting for Emily for a year while this book took all her writing time.

Thanks to the San Francisco office of Idea Integration (formerly Red Eye Digital Media) — especially to Eric Tam for his undying loyalty and support, and also to Kevin Chavaree, Alon Salant, Thomas Chung, and Julie Bowdle. Special thanks to Serena Howeth, Eunice Moyle, Craig Drake, Alex Yra, Kian Nassiri, Rachel Kalman, and the rest of the Idea design staff for support and understanding when their creative director would disappear for days.

Thanks to the support team at, and associated with, Waxcreative Design — Brian Cogley, Kate Laux, Judyth Collin, Susan Asher, Don Asher, Julie Rozelle, Abi Cotler, and all the Waxcreative clients who agreed to somewhat longer than usual production schedules during the creation of this opus.

Thanks to Sheryl Hampton and Lisa Lopuck for your welcoming partnership and continued support. Thanks also to Eric Ott and Diana Smedley for your collaboration and continuous updates.

Thanks to the companies and colleagues that contributed material to this book: Phinney/Bischoff Design; Werkhaus Design; Idea Integration/San Francisco; Idea Integration/Houston; gotomedia, inc.; and Waxcreative Design.

Thanks — huge thanks — to all of this book's expert contributors: Jeffrey Veen for his insightful foreword, and also Leigh Duncan, Kate Gomoll, Jim Heid, Dr. Jakob Nielsen, Leslie Phinney, Ani Phyo, David Siegel, Eric Ward, Lynda Weinman, and the incomparable Jeffrey Zeldman (a.k.a. Theda Bara).

And Emily thanks Kelly and Kelly thanks Emily — mostly just for not killing each other inside the tunnel and for coming back into the sunlight as good friends.

DEDICATIONS

For the teachers who have inspired me — Henrietta Davis, Polly Bragg, and Bill Brown. And to my mom and dad — for a lifetime of learning, encouragement, and support.

— Kelly Goto

For my parents, Steve and Jane, who instilled in me the belief that I could accomplish almost anything in life so long as I worked hard and had a little luck...

And for Brian — whom I was lucky enough to meet — who showed me that I was already working hard enough and it was time for a little living.

— Emily Cotler

optimized our site to be easier to use and faster to load. We spent time understanding the new technologies and exploiting what they had to offer. Yet the email continued to come.

Eventually, we realized the obvious. Websites can and should respond to technological change and the maturing capabilities of those behind it. But ultimately, change comes from outside. It comes from asking two simple questions: What do my users want? And how are we going to deliver that?

As HotWired grew, we added sites like the HotBot search engine, Wired News, and a variety of other products that each provided a unique and decidedly different user experience. Later, we were subsumed by the vast web portal Lycos, and our potential audience multiplied to look more like television. Or, rather, more like the whole world than the technologically sophisticated slice that *Wired* attracted.

I wish we'd had a guide through all of this. What I would have given for a reference like this book, suggesting ways in which we could have minimized the pain and alienation that comes with constant experimentation. Things would have been different if we could have taken a measured approach to the evolution of our interfaces.

Ah, hindsight. With the past in such clear focus, it is easy to ask, "What if?" But with millions of sites today facing as many redesigns, I feel confident that the web can only get better. And with a book like this one — easy to follow, easy to read, and showing a typical project cycle with insider tips — it will happen a lot faster.

We've done a lot of work so far to make the web what it is. We've got a lot yet to do. I wish you the best of luck in your redesign projects, and may all your user feedback be good.

Jeffrey Veen
Author, *The Art & Science of Web Design*
(New Riders, 2001)
4 May 2001
San Francisco

Active in the internet community since 1987, Jeffrey Veen (www.veen.com) *is an internationally sought-after speaker, author, and user-experience consultant. As the Executive Interface Director for Wired Digital, he managed the look and feel of HotWired, the HotBot search engine, Wired News, and others. He specializes in the integration of content, graphic design, and technology from a user-centered perspective.*

PREFACE

We did not suddenly think, "Web ReDesign, now there's a topic for a book." The concepts behind this book evolved and were a direct result of the process methodology that was born out of Kelly's appearances at the Thunder Lizard conferences (www.thunderlizard.com) beginning in 1997. Kelly was then, and continues to be, on the Thunder Lizard roster at several conferences each year, where she lectures extensively on the topic of web design workflow in its many stages. As the market shifted from reengineering to redesigning, it became apparent that points specifically directed at redesigning websites needed to be addressed. And with every successive conference came The Question: "When are you going to write a book?" Kelly's PDF documents that accompany her lectures have always been widely and freely distributed, but clearly it wasn't enough, and by 1999 The Question was ever present. Then The Idea was born: Web ReDesign. But then The Idea sat. It was too big for one person.

The Kelly-and-Emily team came together over bagels and coffee. Emily, having attended one of Kelly's Thunder Lizard workflow sessions, interviewed her for an article for *Publish Magazine*, an industry periodical for which she had been writing for years. When Kelly read Emily's article, she realized that here was the co-conspirator who could help turn The Idea into The Book.

This book — a true collaborative endeavor — puts the topics of web management and workflow, information design, and usability all together under the umbrella of the timely topic of redesign. This process has been shared, modified, updated, streamlined, and simplified into what you see here today.

Kelly Goto (kelly@gotomedia.com)
Emily Cotler (emily@waxcreative.com)
Summer 2001

> The workflow of a project is exactly that:

a planned flow for the work involved.

Introduction

< W E B   R E D E S I G N :   W O R K F L O W   T H A T   W O R K S >

How To Use This Book

This book is a guide for web development methodology, with heavy emphasis on the additional and specialized needs of redesign projects. Our focus is workflow; our process — we call it the "Core Process" — is workflow that works. It is based on our experience and expertise, and it has been tested and used in the real world, on real projects, and has been refined accordingly.

The workflow of a project is exactly that: a planned flow for the work involved. It is a process that targets a goal step by step. This book is a roadmap that shows you how to proceed with minimal guesswork and budget-draining fuss. This book provides a complete, top-down view of a web re-design plan, presented in an accessible, usable format. This is about process; there is very little preaching here.

We do not put this methodology forth as something set in stone. You are not a dummy (and this is not a dummy book); you'll know when to follow and when to modify.

A TOOL SHED IN A BOOK

We've included tools in this book — tools you can use today, as in right now, as in *on your current project*. We offer checklists, surveys, worksheets, and forms to help you keep your project on track from initial planning through launch and beyond. Many of these tools are downloadable from this book's accompanying website (www.web-redesign.com). These tools, like the Core Process itself, have been tested, used, and refined.

We welcome your feedback on the tools.

HOW THIS BOOK IS ORGANIZED

The best way to use this book would be to read it from beginning to end before starting your next project. But who has the time?

With that in mind, this book is organized to be picked up and restarted and put down and skimmed over and browsed through and read in detail. We've included tips and pulled additional pertinent information into sidebars. We've repeated ourselves in

FOREWORD BY JEFFREY VEEN

You could say I've made something of a career out of redesigns.

When I first came to *Wired* magazine back in the prehistoric days of the web, I found myself immediately collaborating with some of the most amazing folks I'd ever met. Our goal was a modest one: to pioneer a new medium out of the collection of protocols and standards that was the web. Our secret, though, was that none of us really had a clue what we were doing.

This was 1994, after all. HTML was a collection of maybe two dozen tags. Mosaic was about the only browser anyone used, and it hadn't had its first birthday yet. Netscape, Internet Explorer, tables, frames, Java-Script, Cascading Style Sheets — all were yet to be conceived. We didn't have the term "e-commerce," nobody knew what an information architect was, and "dot com" was an artifact of domain names, not a new economy.

With so much uncertainty, we did what anyone would do in such a situation: We made things up as we went along. By that fall, we had built one of the first commercial sites on the web, HotWired.com, and had spun off from our parent company with the hopes of defining an entirely new medium. We threw the switch one morning at 9 a.m., popped open a bottle of champagne, and watched as our first few users made their way through our creation. We swelled with pride as traffic grew.

And then came the email.

"I can't find anything," they wrote. "What on earth do those icons mean?" "Why is this thing so *slow*?" Day after day, it became evident that this new medium offered a variety of new challenges, including the ease with which our audience could provide feedback — good and bad. We immediately hired someone to sort through all that mail, directing it to the proper eyes. But then we faced the real issue — actually doing something with all those comments. And thus began our first redesign.

Building a website is a lot like running a marathon. You go and go and finally, on the day of launch, you cross the finish line. There is a significant difference between a real-world race and a virtual web presence, though. On the web, the finish line is deceptive; once you cross it, you must start again from the beginning the next day. And you run again and again and again as you maintain and expand your site.

For the first couple years we spent working on our site, it felt like all we did was redesign. Shortly after we launched, Netscape released its first browser, and we suddenly realized our designs and interfaces might not look the same to all of our users. Later, as the browsers matured, each new release opened up new technological horizons, infinitely expanding the capabilities of our new medium. With so much change on the web, it only made sense to rebuild our site over and over again.

And we did. Each redesign of the HotWired.com site was a dramatic leap from where we'd been before. We

A Message from New Riders

As the reader of this book, you are our most important critic and commentator. We value your opinion and want to know what we're doing right, what we could do better, in what areas you'd like to see us publish, and any other words of wisdom you're willing to pass our way.

As Executive Editor at New Riders, I welcome your comments. You can fax, email, or write me directly to let me know what you did or didn't like about this book — as well as what we can do to make our books better. When you write, please be sure to include this book's title, ISBN, and author, as well as your name and phone or fax number. I will carefully review your comments and share them with the authors and editors who worked on the book.

Please note that I cannot help you with technical problems related to the topic of this book and that, due to the high volume of email I receive, I might not be able to reply to every message. Thanks.

Email: stephanie.wall@newriders.com
Mail: Stephanie Wall
Executive Editor
New Riders Publishing
201 West 103rd Street
Indianapolis, IN 46290 USA

Visit Our Website: www.newriders.com

On our website, you'll find information about our other books, the authors we partner with, book updates and file downloads, promotions, discussion boards for online interaction with other users and with technology experts, and a calendar of trade shows and other professional events with which we'll be involved. We hope to see you around.

Email Us from Our Website

Go to www.newriders.com and click on the Contact Us link if you:

- Have comments or questions about this book.
- Want to report errors that you have found in this book.
- Have a book proposal or are interested in writing for New Riders.
- Would like us to send you one of our author kits.
- Are an expert in a computer topic or technology and are interested in being a reviewer or technical editor.
- Want to find a distributor for our titles in your area.
- Are an educator/instructor who wants to preview New Riders books for classroom use. In the body/comments area, include your name, school, department, address, phone number, office days/hours, text currently in use, and enrollment in your department, along with your request for either desk/examination copies or additional information.

Call Us or Fax Us

You can reach us toll-free at 1-800-571-5840 + 0 (ask for New Riders). If outside the U.S., please call 1-317-581-3500 and ask for New Riders. If you prefer, you can fax us at 1-317-581-4663,
Attention: New Riders.

Technical Support

Although we encourage entry-level users to get as much as they can out of our books, keep in mind that our books are written assuming a non-beginner level of user-knowledge of the technology. This assumption is reflected in the brevity and shorthand nature of some of the tutorials.

New Riders will continually work to create clearly written, thoroughly tested and reviewed technology books of the highest educational caliber and creative design. We value our customers more than anything — that's why we're in this business — but we cannot guarantee to each of the thousands of you who buy and use our books that we will be able to work individually with you through tutorials or content with which you may have questions. We urge readers who need help in working through exercises or other material in our books — and who need this assistance immediately — to use as many of the resources that our technology and technical communities can provide, especially the many online user groups and list servers available.

<INTRODUCTION>   <TIPS>

places. We do this because we know you are probably reading in spurts and not necessarily in a linear fashion. We don't want you to miss out on anything.

The Core Process comprises five phases, presented in Chapters 3 through 7. In addition, we supplement the Core Process with a selection of expanded steps (in Chapters 8 and 9) that, depending on your time and budget, will help further round out your redesign process.

Most readers will want to use this book by familiarizing themselves with the overview (Chapter 2), reading the chapters, and reviewing the tools available. Then, while actually running your project, use the overview for reference and the chapters for detail. And, of course, utilize the many tools we provide during the course of your own production, including the checklists at the end of each chapter, to help keep you on track.

WHO IS THIS BOOK FOR?

This book is designed to streamline the process for everybody involved, not just the project manager and key decision-makers. Our goal is to put everybody — client and team alike — in the same frame of reference and have them all use the same terminology and understand the steps necessary for any web project. When we say any project, we really mean *any* — redesign or initial design, $10,000 budget or $100,000 budget. Truly, even if your project

is under or over this range, the Core Process will still be helpful.

When we say "core," we mean it. No matter the type of site being redesigned or the scope of the project itself, the Core Process remains essentially the same. Approaching any project in an organized and comprehensive manner will save time, budget, and headaches along the way.

Who Are You?

Whether you are a designer, an in-house webmaster, or a company owner trying to move your web presence to the next level, this book is for you. If you have ever felt frustrated because a web project was run inefficiently ("My client delivered site content five weeks late, yet the site launch date remained immovable."), this book is for you. If you are embarking on your first web project (from "This is the opportunity I have been waiting for" to "What am I going to do?"), whether taking over your company's website or being asked to build a department to do so, this book is for you.

This book is for every person — designer and nondesigner — who has ever lived through a workflow nightmare and wants to avoid it in the future. ("We went straight to visual design figuring we could deal with navigation and content at that stage. The result? Total disorganization and much backtracking.") Basically, everyone involved in any organizational capacity or responsible in any way for relaunching a site will benefit from this book.

Bonus

This book also works for straightforward website development in addition to redesign. The techniques and tools modify easily and provide a solid workflow for either. If you're designing a site for the first time, simply ignore the redesign parts and focus on the Core Process.

< W E B   R E D E S I G N :   W O R K F L O W   T H A T   W O R K S >

From the seasoned pro to the newbie, this book will help. If you already have significant experience, you will probably find yourself customizing the Core Process to fit your own project and your own existing processes. If you are a newbie, this is the place to start — the whole process is right here.

What Kind of Company Are You?

Are you a small to mid-size web development firm or a huge company with an existing intranet department? Perhaps you are a small corporation with a web department in-house or a mid-size company with an outside design firm contracted. Maybe you are a sprawling university system in which every department is using a different branding…

The Core Process outlined in this book applies to all of the above and then some. It truly is a one-process-fits-all workflow.

WHO IS THE CLIENT?

For the purposes of this book, "the client" is a somewhat schizophrenic, catch-all term. The client is one entity to the design house and a different entity — but not-so-entirely different — to the internal department.

If you are a design firm or web development company, the client is external — the company that contracted you. This is pretty straightforward client management.

For those of you in in-house departments, the client is internal — specifically, the person (or group) who is responsible for the content, the concept, and perhaps most importantly, granting approval. This is not necessarily the head of the internal web department; it might be a group including someone in marketing, someone in product development, a couple of VPs, and perhaps the CEO. Less straightforward client management.

The management of internal projects — specifically the presentation of deliverables — tends to be less formal than when you have a contracted outside client. As a result, organization and communication become even more important because lack of formality tends to open up cracks for things to fall through. Often, working internally leads to too many cooks without a clear idea of who is head chef or even what the recipe is. This is not uncommon with external clients either.

Throughout this book, we frequently reference "the client." Wherever we do so, we mean either the external or internal client — whomever is in the position to give project, budget, and design approvals. Even if you are your own client, know and accept that the client always requires managing. Some clients can be excellent to work with — totally organized and quick with responses. Other clients can sometimes be patience-trying and a drain on the project management budget. There are spots in this book where we specifically reference a situation for

< I N T R O D U C T I O N >

an in-house team with an internal client, or for a web development/design firm with an outside, contracted client. Only you can know how to interpret "the client" as it relates to you.

WHAT THIS BOOK IS NOT

No book can be everything to everybody. We focus on workflow and, at that, on a Core Process. With the goal of creating a basic (albeit comprehensive) book, we necessarily had to make the conscious decision to omit several facets of web development that were not strictly project management and workflow oriented.

This Book Is Not a Technical Manual

This book is not a step-by-step workflow for back-end implementation. If your site requires a backend database, e-commerce capability, dynamic content, and so on, you need an additional, parallel plan. The workflow for the redesign is this Core Process, this book. But backend development needs its own, totally separate workflow, and we simply don't go there (maybe next book).

Know Your Ends

Sites are developed in layers. All sites have a design/presentation layer — essentially everything the site user actually sees. Some sites have an application layer, where much of the functionality that the user interacts with resides (e.g., for registration, login, shopping cart transactions, personalization, etc.). The design/presentation layer and the application layer form the front-end of web development, as we know it, on the web today.

The application layer, being in the middle of the front-end and backend, sometimes crosses over between simple scripting (e.g., JavaScript, DHTML, CGI) and complex programming (e.g., for shopping carts, or secure transaction integration). It is the conduit and link between the front-end and backend of web development.

For sites with complex content retrieval systems, database architecture and massive engineering needs, a separate workflow is in order. This is the "backend" of web development.

For purposes of this book, however, "front-end" is the design/presentation layer only. We don't go anywhere near application development that requires engineering (maybe next book). "Backend" refers to everything behind the front-end, application layer included. Please note: *Not all sites have or need backend development, but 100 percent of websites have a front-end.* Because the Core Process addresses that which all websites have to deal with, backend is simply out of this book's scope.

We have no explanation as to why front-end is hyphenated and backend is not.

< W E B   R E D E S I G N :   W O R K F L O W   T H A T   W O R K S >

What this book does do in this regard, however, is provide an overview of the technical considerations that need to be clear and understood so you can evaluate the project's scope. This book provides you with surveys, suggestions, and tips, all geared towards helping you identify your overall technical needs. Our goal is to help you determine what these needs are and how realistic they might be so you can budget and plan for them. We also indicate points in the Core Process where the front-end and backend workflows meet, where the project managers for the two processes must confer.

We can tell you for certain — and we repeat it in several places because it is so very, very important — that whatever your technical requirements, whether significant backend or not, you will want to talk with your technical team — HTML production and engineering alike — throughout the project. And yes, that means from the get-go, all the way through the lifecycle of the redesign project.

This Book Is Not a How-To Design Manual

We address the workflow of a redesign project, not the specifics of design itself. We go into a cursory overview step by step of how the creative track is managed. For design graphics, we recommend Lynda Weinman's *Designing Web Graphics.3* (New Riders, 1999). For site design and production, try Jeffrey Veen's *The Art & Science of Web Design* (New Riders, 2001), Jeffrey Zeldman's *Taking Your Talent To The Web* (New Riders, 2001), or David Siegel's industry classic (still a great resource after all these years) *Creating Killer Web Sites* (Hayden Books, 1997). For more recommendations and links, consult www.web-redesign.com.

This Book Is Not a How-To Manual for Usability Testing

Again, this book is about workflow. Usability testing is definitely something we talk about — frequently. We believe very, very strongly in its value. We go into detail on the subject in Chapter 8, but primarily from a project management and workflow approach. For an in-depth background and philosophical approach, we suggest Jakob Neilson's *Designing Web Usability* (New Riders, 1999). For actual how-to, try Jeffrey Rubin's *Handbook of Usability Testing* (John Wiley & Sons, 1994). For more recommendations and links, consult www.web-redesign.com.

WWW.WEB-REDESIGN.COM

Unlike a companion CD, a website is a resource that can be updated, accessed, and actually *used*. The idea of creating a companion book site is not new. This one, however, comes with downloadable tools, references, and resource links. Throughout this book, we identify tools as being "downloadable from www.web-redesign.com." We are inviting you to take these tools and make them your own.

The website is not a replacement for the book.

< I N T R O D U C T I O N >

Even calling the website a supplement is a stretch. It is a resource. In addition to providing all the tools featured in the book, www.web-redesign.com will include links to related sources, updated information about us (where we are and what we are doing), and of course, a section that deals with errata and the publishing time lag.

In addition, we will feature new site redesigns, not as a contest but to see who is redesigning and why. We encourage you to submit your site redesign URLs and see if yours is the next to be promoted. Refer to the site for submission guidelines.

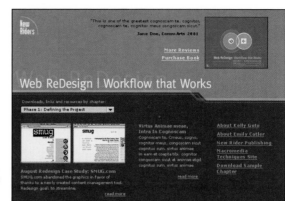

www.web-redesign.com
is hosted by Compass Communications, Inc.
(www.ccom.net).

< C A S E   S T U D Y >

Baby Center

Client: Baby Center
URL: www.babycenter.com
Design Team: In-house
Design Director (Original Design): Jonathan Tuttle
Project Manager (Original Design): John Stross

Design Director (Redesign): Allyson Appen
Associate Art Director (Redesign): Shannon Miller
Project Manager (Redesign): Alissa Cohen Reiter

BabyCenter.com focuses on providing pregnancy, infancy, and toddler information as well as offering maternity and baby products. The company's founding mission was to build the most complete resource on the internet for new and expectant parents.

< P R E V I O U S >

< C U R R E N T >

BABYCENTER.COM [OLD, OLDER, and OLDEST] went through several iterations as it evolved from a small startup to a full commerce and community site. Each redesign was based on evaluations of customers' needs. (1997–1999)

BABYCENTER [REDESIGNED] drives membership with prominent messaging and links. The redesigned site improves usability through a simplified design that retains several successful elements from the old site, including effective use of personalization. (2000)

Result: In-house expertise allows for quick response to users' needs and ongoing improvements, including increased personalization and content offerings.

> Successful redesign means no repeated mistakes, so follow

a proven path. Cover the gaps where items fall through and

don't lose sight of the customer — audience underlies it all.

Redesign accordingly.

Keys to a Successful Redesign   01

Keys to a Successful Redesign

WHY THIS BOOK RIGHT NOW?

Look anywhere on the web. How many sites that you visit with regularity have been redesigned in the last year or two? Several? Yes, we've noticed, too.

A startling number of websites will undergo a major redesign in the next 12 months. Some common goals are to "get it right this time," "redefine our online presence," or "catch up with our competition." Preemptively, and with an eye on the redesign wave and tightening economic conditions, web development teams working on new and redesigned sites are striving to make sure their projects won't have to be completely redone six to nine months out.

The pressure can be astounding. Companies like yours (and clients like ours) that met the original challenge of getting online in the past two, three, six years are now — frustratingly — hitting a wall. Not only are you having to scale, grow, and increase your internet initiative to stay current with your competition, you are having to hustle to do it, hurrying to hire a design firm (or a better design firm) or even build an in-house web department just to catch up. Time is not an ally. Despite an often-uncertain economy, business and the web are entwined. Beating your competition and staying on the leading edge means reevaluating, redesigning, and revamping what worked — or at least what *seemed* to work — yesterday.

Why this book right now? Because it is needed.

There are many good reasons to redesign. You inherited an old, mostly ineffective, brochure-ish site when you bought your company… You want to update your image with Flash or other media… You need e-commerce capabilities now that your services have expanded… You need a content management system… Your site is a navigational mess, and your site's users aren't getting where you want them to go… Your branding has fallen apart… You never really had branding in the first place… You want to bring the site in-house… Your company merged with another company, and neither site really explains what you do…

If any of the preceding applies to you (and these are just some of many examples), you are probably

<KEYS TO A SUCCESSFUL REDESIGN>

questioning what your next move should be. You may be somewhat unsure about how to go about doing this. What is the process?

There must be a process.

Meanwhile, the web waits for no one, not even you, and your competition might just be out-webbing you by a virtual mile.

Sounds like a tricky game. But it's not. It just takes strategy. It takes a plan — a solid workflow for your redesign. Think before you act; it's the only way. The one thing we can count on is that the web will continue to evolve. It will become smarter, more service-oriented, and more attuned to users' needs. The web will keep changing all the rules. You can count on that. And now, it's redesign or perish.

PRESENTING A WORKFLOW THAT WORKS

Many factors can derail or delay a project: unanticipated technical roadblocks, disorganized clients, poorly defined goals and schedules, sloppy budgeting. We have all experienced them, whether as a designer or a manager or both. "Designers are utterly starved for guidance on workflow," says Thunder Lizard Conference Chair Jim Heid. "Kelly is mobbed after her workflow sessions at our Web Design conferences, and her sessions are consistently among the highest-rated ones that we do. You can just tell that every designer in the room has lived through some kind of workflow nightmare, but Kelly shows how careful planning and organization can keep things on track."

Take Kelly's methodology, mix in a healthy dose of collaboration from Emily, and you have this book. After significant refinement over the course of many redesigns, *Workflow that Works* was born. This streamlined workflow plan for redesign is complete with tools we have used, revamped, reused, and so on, for designing and redesigning websites. These tools are instantly applicable and already tested and proven successful. Yes, instantly; you can use these tools today. We have some serious answers here — and we're sharing.

This book is a readable, understandable, *industry-needed* workflow plan. Call it a plan, call it a roadmap, call it a bible — we like to call it *Workflow that Works*, because that is what it is.

Why this book right now? Because the introduction of a cohesive web workflow plan — particularly one that addresses redesign — is more timely than ever, especially for in-house departments that don't work on website after website, or for small to mid-size firms without a solid methodology in place. Companies worldwide, every one with a site needing to be redesigned — most keep reinventing the wheel with each individual redesign project.

It doesn't need to be that hard. This book is a solution. This book will help.

< C H A P T E R   1 >

TEN EXPERT TIPS TO A SUCCESSFUL REDESIGN

Processes evolve. Over time and several redesigns, a few points screamed to be kept in mind: communicate with the client, be scalable, plan to plan, test your assumptions, analyze your current site, and so on. We ran these mini-philosophies by industry leaders and newbies alike. The result? Our collection of things to think about evolved into — drum roll, please — TEN EXPERT TIPS TO A SUCCESSFUL REDESIGN.

The 10 tips presented in this chapter cover many topics: planning, industry positioning, audience, usability, technology, content, scalability, and more. We will be addressing all of these and more in the pages that follow. This is by no means an exhaustive list; rather, it is a helpful group of things to keep in mind as you progress through the phases.

Redesign is happening. Address the need. And stay on track while you do it.

TIP 1 >

THINK BEFORE YOU ACT

Don't just put up a new site because you think you are behind the times. This is a common trap. Understand that there is more involved than simply designing a snazzier interface. Plan to plan. A logical workflow will help you cover all your bases.

TIP 2 >

IDENTIFY REDESIGN ISSUES AND GOALS

What is currently working on your site, and what needs to change in the redesign? Review customer service calls and emails — especially complaints. Conduct usability tests to identify specific redesign issues rather than speculate. Determine your goals and then execute accordingly.

TIP 6 >

BRING IN YOUR ENGINEER EARLY

Consulting with a technical engineer (for HMTL as well as application development and backend needs) early on in the process will save you time and headaches in the midst of your project. Your engineer will help you plan confidently and will clue you in at every step as to what is technologically feasible.

TIP 7 >

BELIEVE IN USABILITY TESTING

Redesign with your user in mind. Perform usability testing on both current and redesigned sites during the development process. Determine usability issues and seek to resolve them with redesign. Nothing gives you more honest feedback than watching someone go through your site. Can users use the new site? Watch and learn, and then apply.

< K E Y S   T O   A   S U C C E S S F U L   R E D E S I G N >

TIP 3 >

ANALYZE YOUR COMPETITION

View the industry objectively. Look at competitor sites and see what works. Compare features and services. See what works by actually using competitor sites and your current site, too. Understand how your site differentiates itself from the competition.

TIP 4 >

INVOLVE YOUR CURRENT AUDIENCE

Include your current user base in the redesign. Don't alienate your current audience with sudden change; communicate clearly why and when your site is changing.

TIP 5 >

DESIGN FOR USERS, NOT INVESTORS

If your site is not usable, your online presence risks failure. Too often, usability issues are clouded by the requirements of the advertiser or investor. Do not make the mistake of designing for the wrong audience. Know your audience. Take great pains to ensure that the needs of the user are compatible with your business objectives.

TIP 8 >

UNDERSTAND CONTENT DELIVERY REALITY

Content delivery is a top schedule buster in nearly all redesign projects. Have a dedicated, client-side point person who gathers, modifies, writes, and delivers content on time. Don't underestimate the need for a content delivery plan.

TIP 9 >

SET CLEAR EXPECTATIONS

Communication is key. Many times, a project starts beautifully and then breaks down due to misunderstandings and misinterpreted assumptions. Each document you produce should clearly outline your goals. Make sure all team members are always on the same page, speaking the same terminology.

TIP 10 >

THINK LONG TERM; FOCUS ON SHORT TERM

Don't try to do everything at once; you will drive yourself absolutely nuts. Redesign and launch in phases. In addition to allowing for realistic delivery goals, an iterative approach to launching also offers the chance for evaluation of the redesigned site so that changes can be incorporated.

<EXPERT TOPIC>   <CHAPTER 1>

LEIGH DUNCAN ON IDENTIFYING REDESIGN ISSUES AND STRATEGY

When companies cannot clearly articulate why they are redesigning their web presence — how their initiatives and expected business outcomes will change — their efforts often result in rework, expense, and partial or total failure. Ironically, even with larger businesses, this isn't uncommon. While "gut instinct" to redesign is often on target, it must supported by fact, analysis, and comprehensive strategy to lead to success.

Simply defined, strategy is the development of a clear action plan to "bridge the gap" between current state and future vision. Web redesign strategy, therefore, involves creating an organized plan to *improve* an existing site to better *serve* customers and *drive* desired business outcomes. Ultimately, good redesign strategy examines the underpinning technology, business model, institutional process, content structure, and brand positioning of a web initiative. It seeks to synchronize and optimize all efforts to better enable a site to inform, educate, engage, persuade, and sell to customers.

It's easy to become overwhelmed during a redesign. Rapid business changes and technology growth make juggling departmental, operational, developmental, content, creative, and other concerns a constant management challenge. However, regardless of the pulling needs, it is paramount to approach the project from one central position: the customer's perspective. Good redesign strategy starts here.

Developing a customer-centric perspective is the most important aspect to a successful redesign strategy and an organized project. This perspective requires all redesign participants to step back from detailed business considerations and approach customer need in a uniform fashion. A helpful way to do this is to simplify the site's audience segmentation into the site's **Primary Audience** (the most frequent users), **Secondary Audience** (the second-most important customer group), and **Tertiary Audience** (the remaining audience groups).

While this sounds simple, many companies find the exercise to be a challenge because it forces clear prioritization, articulation of behavior, and discussion of customer need. Once these basic segments are defined, it is much easier to map out a site based on weighted audience need and detailed business considerations. It also becomes much easier to manage other strategic exercises, such as the following:

- **Business plan review**
- **Current state assessment**
- **Future state vision**
- **Audience validation and testing**
- **Content and services planning**
- **Creative brief/design strategy**
- **Technical implementation approach**
- **Marketing and business planning**

These exercises, though not an exhaustive list, outline some strategic next steps for redesign and illustrate how customer-centric focus sets the stage for the practical evaluation of business, technical, and design concerns. Once the stage is set for website redesign, any project manager is better empowered to move forward with confidence.

Leigh Duncan, a 10-year industry veteran (most recently as an e-commerce Manager with KPMG Consulting) with a depth of knowledge in multiplatform e-commerce, has provided e-business strategy, marketing, design, and content management counsel to world-class clients including Target Corporation, Proctor & Gamble, Chevron, 1-800-FLOWERS, and America Online.

< C A S E   S T U D Y >

Smug

Client: Smug
URL: www.smug.com
Design Team: fearless.net, New York
Publisher: Leslie Harpold
Budget: Zero dollars and two favors

Smug is a long-running, noncommercial humor 'zine published monthly by editor/designer Leslie Harpold. Launched in 1996, the site has roots in the do-it-yourself print publishing scene of the late 1980s and early 1990s. Over the years, Smug has published some of the most clever writing found on the web.

< P R E V I O U S >   < C U R R E N T >

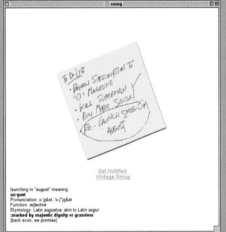

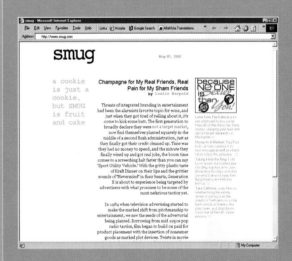

SMUG.COM [OLD] utilized icons to indicate the different areas for stories and writing samples. A series of simple links indicated archived material in chronological order.

SMUG.COM [OLD] ANNOUNCING NEW SMUG.COM [REDESIGNED] ran this humorous splash page announcement for months prior to launching their redesign. The options presented were entry into the existing site, or an email link that offers notification of when the redesign gets launched.

SMUG.COM [REDESIGNED] abandons graphics in favor of simplification, thanks to a newly created content management tool. The redesign goal: to streamline the maintenance process as the online 'zine went from monthly to biweekly updates.

Result: Streamlined updating.

> The Core Process: a comprehensive plan

for all types of teams, all kinds of

companies, and all kinds of budgets.

One Process Fits All   02

Seeing is comprehending. Presenting a visual of the Core Process: all five phases, each consisting of three interwoven and/or parallel tracks. This comprehensive flowchart illustrates how the Core Process — from start to finish — is really a roadmap of the workflow of redesigning a website (ignore the redesign aspects and it works for initial web development as well). Use this chart as both a starting point and as a reference.

In addition to this visual representation, we offer a detailed list of action items in the pages that follow in this chapter. The flowchart and the action item lists correspond, but are not identical. Yet each approach is helpful.

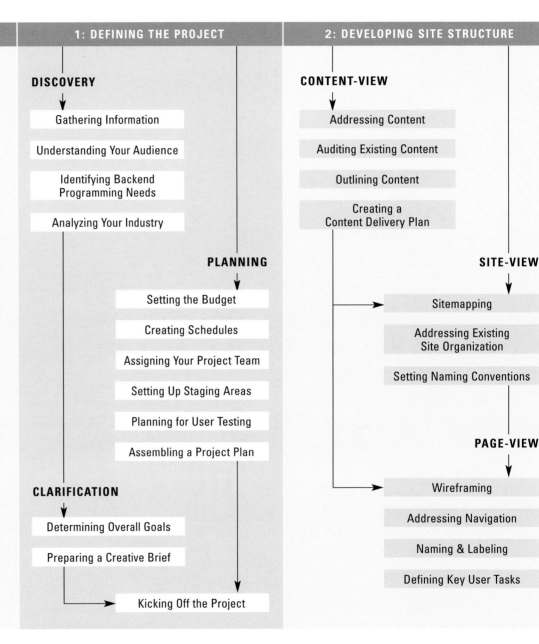

1: DEFINING THE PROJECT

DISCOVERY

Gathering Information

Understanding Your Audience

Identifying Backend Programming Needs

Analyzing Your Industry

PLANNING

Setting the Budget

Creating Schedules

Assigning Your Project Team

Setting Up Staging Areas

Planning for User Testing

Assembling a Project Plan

CLARIFICATION

Determining Overall Goals

Preparing a Creative Brief

Kicking Off the Project

2: DEVELOPING SITE STRUCTURE

CONTENT-VIEW

Addressing Content

Auditing Existing Content

Outlining Content

Creating a Content Delivery Plan

SITE-VIEW

Sitemapping

Addressing Existing Site Organization

Setting Naming Conventions

PAGE-VIEW

Wireframing

Addressing Navigation

Naming & Labeling

Defining Key User Tasks

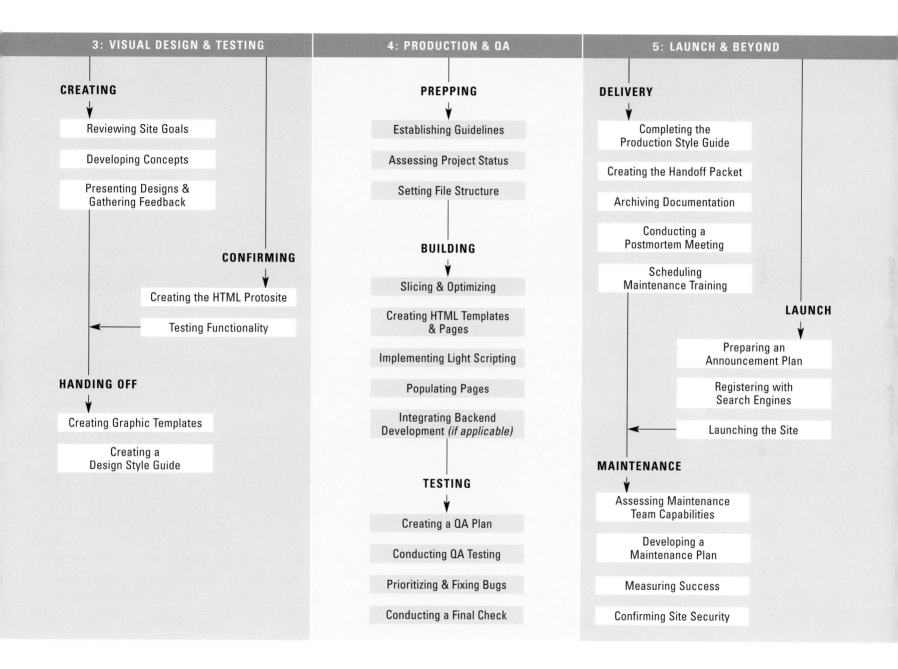

3: VISUAL DESIGN & TESTING

CREATING

Reviewing Site Goals

Developing Concepts

Presenting Designs &
Gathering Feedback

CONFIRMING

Creating the HTML Protosite

Testing Functionality

HANDING OFF

Creating Graphic Templates

Creating a
Design Style Guide

4: PRODUCTION & QA

PREPPING

Establishing Guidelines

Assessing Project Status

Setting File Structure

BUILDING

Slicing & Optimizing

Creating HTML Templates
& Pages

Implementing Light Scripting

Populating Pages

Integrating Backend
Development *(if applicable)*

TESTING

Creating a QA Plan

Conducting QA Testing

Prioritizing & Fixing Bugs

Conducting a Final Check

5: LAUNCH & BEYOND

DELIVERY

Completing the
Production Style Guide

Creating the Handoff Packet

Archiving Documentation

Conducting a
Postmortem Meeting

Scheduling
Maintenance Training

LAUNCH

Preparing an
Announcement Plan

Registering with
Search Engines

Launching the Site

MAINTENANCE

Assessing Maintenance
Team Capabilities

Developing a
Maintenance Plan

Measuring Success

Confirming Site Security

< C H A P T E R 2 >

One Process Fits All

A single, comprehensive workflow that can be incorporated and adapted by all web development teams. A set of core steps that apply to all projects. One process — the Core Process — in five sequential phases. One process fits all, with a focused emphasis geared especially toward the specific needs of redesign presented in this chapter in overview format.

The Core Process can be followed by all types of teams, for all kinds of companies, and with all kinds of budgets. Flash or HTML, complex functionality or nothing more involved than simple JavaScript rollovers, redesigned site or brand new web presence... every site shares common construction requirements. All web projects need to be thoroughly planned and defined. All need to have their content organized and structure blueprinted. All need to be designed aesthetically. All need to be built. All need to be launched. All sites. Every last one.

The Core Process takes you through these necessary steps. We describe what you should do (necessary), what you can do (extra), and what you should watch out for. We also highly recommend two additional processes — testing for usability (see Chapter 8: Testing for Usability) and analyzing your competition (see Chapter 9: Analyzing Your Competition). Should time and budget allow, your adaptation of the Core Process should incorporate these processes as well.

What follows in this chapter is the Cliff Notes version of the Core Process — an overview. But just like your English teacher in high school used to say, *"Do not rely on the overview alone!"* There is no detail here, no description of why and how. We provide that information in the chapters to come. We include tools there, and charts, and helpful lists. While subsequent chapters are comprehensive, this chapter is a concise overview. Refer to it and use it to familiarize yourself with the Core Process. Each project is unique, of course, and every team and budget has different demands pressed upon it, so variation will obviously be at your discretion.

< ONE PROCESS FITS ALL >

PHASE 1: DEFINING THE PROJECT

This first phase of the Core Process is all about gathering and analyzing the information necessary to clearly identify the scope of the project and then prepare for kickoff. You will start by asking a lot of questions (relax, we'll give you the questions), and you will amass a lot of data — data that you will use to shape and communicate the expectations of the project. No matter the size or scope of the project, the need to plan is ever present.

In Phase 1, you literally set the stage for your redesign. Many of the items that get addressed here affect every phase, and a few, like knowing your audience, figure into every step. When defining project scope, you must have an understanding of everything from budget to maintenance.

Phase 1 is the biggest phase of the Core Process. The work you do here will define the entire project — every move you make and every deliverable you create.

DISCOVERY	CLARIFICATION	PLANNING

Discovery

Spend as much time as possible understanding the company, the outgoing site, and the redesign project. Gather information and ask questions. Learn about the audience. Analyze the current site and compare it to the competition, both on- and offline.

Become an "expert user" in the client's business. Develop an understanding of the strategy behind the site and what the value is for the user.

> **DISCOVERY**
>
> > Distributing/Collecting/Analyzing Surveys
>
> > Collecting Existing Materials from the Client
>
> > Understanding Your Audience
>
> > Identifying Your Audience's Technical Capabilities
>
> > Identifying Backend Programming Needs
>
> > Analyzing Your Industry

> Distributing/Collecting/Analyzing Surveys

Gather information. The Client Survey and the Maintenance Survey should be handed to the client at the project's outset. They are concise and comprehensive questionnaires that prompt the client into articulating expectations. The data collected will aid in gaining insight into the audience and goals of the site. Both surveys appear in full in this book and are downloadable from www.web-redesign.com.

> Collecting Existing Materials from the Client

Request materials: brochures, annual reports, collateral, sample products, and so on. Go on a tour of the facility, store, and/or existing site. Understand the client's current marketing materials and general marketing plan.

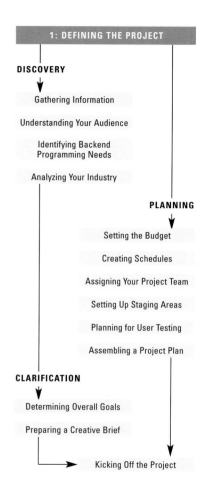

1: DEFINING THE PROJECT

DISCOVERY

Gathering Information

Understanding Your Audience

Identifying Backend
Programming Needs

Analyzing Your Industry

PLANNING

Setting the Budget

Creating Schedules

Assigning Your Project Team

Setting Up Staging Areas

Planning for User Testing

Assembling a Project Plan

CLARIFICATION

Determining Overall Goals

Preparing a Creative Brief

Kicking Off the Project

<TIPS>   <CHAPTER 2>

Prepare for Scope Creep

Understand the concept of "Scope Creep" and how it will affect your project. The slow, inevitable swelling of a project's scope from something defined to something significantly bigger, Scope Creep happens with almost every project. Little things add up. Beware of seemingly casual client requests for small changes. Scope Creep is subtle; you usually don't recognize that it is happening. At your kick-off meeting, define Scope Creep to both your client and your team and explain how keeping careful tabs on the schedule, deliverables, and process will help keep the project on target. See Phase 1 for more on Scope Creep.

> Understanding Your Audience

Use the data gathered from the Client Survey to get a strong sense of who your users are, why they will come to the site, and what tasks they will be performing. Define your target audience and any secondary audiences, too. Create a user profile. Keep in mind that you may need to profile more than one target group.

> Identifying Your Audience's Technical Capabilities

Once you know your users, you need to know what kind of site they can access. From platform to connectivity speed, types of programming languages to plug-ins, determine your audience's abilities. An extensive survey, the Client Spec Sheet, should be given to the client shortly after project kick-off. The Client Spec Sheet is a production item. Part of it appears in Phase 4, and it is downloadable in full from www.web-redesign.com.

> Identifying Backend Programming Needs

This is an only-if-it-applies step. A straightforward tool, the Expanded Tech Check asks the client a few questions. If any are these are answered "yes," your project needs backend programming, and an additional workflow will have to be employed. See this book's Introduction for a definition of "backend" as we use it. The Expanded Tech Check can be downloaded from www.web-redesign.com.

> Analyzing Your Industry

Analyze the client's industry to see what the competition is doing on- and offline. The goal is to become an "expert customer" in the client's field. Visit multiple sites, perform tasks, call customer service, and see what is successful and what is frustrating. For a detailed description of an extended process, see Chapter 9.

Clarification: Determine Overall Goals

Now that you have the data you need, extract the "essence" of the site and determine the site's goals. Identify the main goals of the redesign, including answering the question, "Why are we redesigning?" Goals might include increasing traffic, decreasing calls to customer service, streamlining sales, improving navigation, achieving a different look, and so on.

CLARIFICATION: DETERMINE OVERALL GOALS

> Preparing a Creative Brief

> Preparing a Creative Brief

The creative brief is a summary of overall visual and conceptual goals. The document restates the target audience, user experience goals, and communication strategy. It also lists the proposed style and tone of the redesigned site. The client signs off on the creative brief, and it is used extensively by the team. Use the provided worksheet as a guideline when

< O N E   P R O C E S S   F I T S   A L L >   < T I P S >

writing the creative brief. The creative brief worksheet is downloadable from www.web-redesign.com.

Planning

There's no shortage of administrative tasks here: budget, schedule, team assignment, and more, each focusing on another defining aspect of the project. Now that the goals of the site have been defined, you can actually plot the course of action for the development of the redesign. The documents you generate in this stage become components of your project plan.

> PLANNING
>
> > Setting Your Budget
>
> > Establishing Means of Time Tracking
>
> > Creating Schedules
>
> > Assigning Your Project Team
>
> > Setting Up Staging Areas
>
> > Planning for User Testing
>
> > Assembling Your Project Plan
>
> > Kicking Off the Project

> Setting Your Budget

Of all administrative tasks, budgeting naturally comes first because it defines the size, boundaries, and feasibility of a project. Although the budget usually depends on what the client has to spend, actual costs get based on hours. Take a realistic view of the resources, time allocation, and deliverables. Use the budget tracker tool to aid in the estimating and tracking process. You can see this tool in Phase 1 or download it at www.web-redesign.com.

> Establishing Means of Time Tracking

Have a reliable method in place to track time — and then really do it. Track actual against projected hours. When you actually track hours, you are able to see when a project is going out of scope. There are many methods of tracking time — some work and some lack. Find one that works for you. We suggest a couple in Phase 1.

> Creating Schedules

People respond to deadlines. Establish them in two ways: first in an overview schedule and then in a detailed, date-by-date schedule. Both the overview (a broad-scope look at the project that enables you and your client to see the big picture) and the detailed schedule (complete with deliverables, approval reviews, and due dates) communicate a sense of urgency. Base your schedule on ours (shown in Phase 1).

> Assigning Your Project Team

Select your team. When identifying individual roles, understand that people often wear multiple hats, so clarify responsibilities for each team member. Maintain clear communication with all team members throughout the process. Major project roles are listed in Phase 1.

Track Your Hours

In general, organizations that track their hours—and usually know where their budget stands and how it is being utilized—are profitable. Those that don't track their hours either aren't profitable or are lucky. Establish a method for tracking hours... and then actually, truly, diligently track those hours. Time tracking is critical for both design firms and in-house departments; it helps you track profitability and keep team members accountable for their projected hours (and your projected budget). For more on tracking time, see Phase 1.

Get Signed Approvals

Nothing makes a client more accountable than a signature on paper. Here's a good rule to live by: If it discusses scope, budget, or schedule, get it signed. Establish one contact from the client side who has final sign-off. Email approvals are a good start, but follow up with a hard copy to protect yourself — get a physical signature via fax whenever possible. For every project, create a project folder (or a physical binder) to house all signed documentation: contracts, briefs, the initial proposal and subsequent revisions, the approved sitemap, visual design directions, and so on. Clients sometimes suffer from short-term memory loss. Gently remind them of things they have approved and dates they have agreed to throughout the process. For more on documentation, see Phase 1.

> Setting Up Staging Areas

A staging area acts as a hub of communication. Whether you call it a "client site" or a "project site," create a project-specific URL for posting current material for review. This client staging area should be kept current, be easy to maintain, and contain very simple navigation. Create a different area as a place for the team to work. This team development area is not for client viewing.

> Planning for User Testing

Decide what form of user testing your project will employ. There are many valid forms of feedback (focus groups, online surveys, and so on), but usability testing differs in that it shows what users *actually* do, not what they think they *might* do. In Phase 1, we present the different forms of user testing. For more on usability testing, see Chapter 8.

> Assembling Your Project Plan

Documentation requirements vary from project to project. A project plan contains the budget, schedule, creative brief, technical documentation, and any other information that sets the scope for the project. The presentation varies, as does the page count; these most often depend on the formality of the project you are working on. A list of suggested project plan components appears in Phase 1.

> Kicking Off the Project

A face-to-face meeting is an appropriate opportunity to actually kick off the project. Bring the client together with the team and review discovery materials (if any were gathered), align expectations, and establish project scope. Set a clear means of communication and a standing weekly meeting or conference call for the duration of the project.

< O N E   P R O C E S S   F I T S   A L L >

PHASE 2: DEVELOPING SITE STRUCTURE

With Phase 2, the actual hands-on work begins. Developing site structure is all about content and information strategy — determining how to organize information so that site users can find it quickly and easily. Whether working on a brand new site or a redesign, whether the budget is $5,000 or $250,000, the need for a logical structure is a constant across all websites. Yes, the client is anxious to see the look and feel of the redesign, but devising a solid, well-thought-out plan will lay the foundation for everything to come — including the visual design.

CONTENT-VIEW	SITE-VIEW	PAGE-VIEW

Content-View

Without good, relevant content, your site won't be compelling. Content and structure are intertwined — you cannot create one without defining the other. Division and categorization of pages is necessarily determined by content, and the way in which you organize a site's content defines the backbone for the structuring process.

> **CONTENT-VIEW**
>
> \> Addressing and Organizing Content
>
> \> Auditing Existing Content
>
> \> Outlining Content
>
> \> Creating a Content Delivery Plan

> Addressing and Organizing Content

Content should be addressed as early as possible. Start organizing the content conceptually and examining it from a user's perspective. What content would site users logically expect to see together? Contract or assign a dedicated person to the role of content management, preferably on the client side.

> Auditing Existing Content

Be careful not to fall into the trap of using old content just because it is available and easier. A content audit is a thorough review of all existing material: copy, images, diagrams, media, and so on. It is an excellent and necessary opportunity to determine what content should get carried over and incorporated into the redesign and what should be tossed.

> Outlining Content

Use the simple, familiar, Roman-numeral-outline format to further organize your content. Determine content sections, including new material. You can expect the client to provide the outline, though you may have to guide and urge. You don't have to have all the content written/revamped/received, but you do need to know what is coming.

> Creating a Content Delivery Plan

A Content Delivery Plan clarifies what content is due when — existing, revamped, and new content alike. Responsibility for copy, images, and other necessary elements is assigned. Due dates are

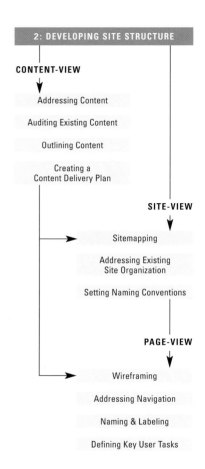

2: DEVELOPING SITE STRUCTURE

CONTENT-VIEW

Addressing Content

Auditing Existing Content

Outlining Content

Creating a
Content Delivery Plan

SITE-VIEW

Sitemapping

Addressing Existing
Site Organization

Setting Naming Conventions

PAGE-VIEW

Wireframing

Addressing Navigation

Naming & Labeling

Defining Key User Tasks

<TIPS>   < CHAPTER 2>

Combat Content Delay

Late content is the number one reason for project delay. Why? The task
itself and the resources needed to
complete said task are severely
underestimated. Accept it. Plan for
it. Charge for it. One way to combat
content tardiness is to HIRE A
CONTENT MANAGER: a person to
manage and oversee the entire
content-delivery process. A second
way is to CREATE A CONTENT
DELIVERY PLAN. This is a schedule
that outlines realistic dates for
delivery according to readiness.
See Phase 2 for more on content.

established. Here's a content truth: Content will in-
evitably be late, but this plan will help.

Site-View

Being able to see the whole site at once is an important perspective while structuring. In much the same
way that a house needs to be architecturally blueprinted, a site also needs to have its structure drawn.
This information will translate into a sitemap,
which will serve as the backbone for the entire site.

SITE-VIEW

> Sitemapping

> Addressing Existing Site Organization

> Setting Naming Conventions

> Sitemapping

The sitemap shows proposed links and main navigation. It works with the content outline (but not in
place of it). If the sitemap changes, it should be updated, reapproved, and redistributed. The sitemap
we discuss in this book outlines content, organization, and some functionality, but does not replace a
technical or functional schematic.

> Addressing Existing Site Organization

As you create the sitemap, take a look at the current
site's organization from a user's perspective. How
can it be changed to be more intuitive? Examine a

site map of the current site and then of the planned
redesign. Compare the two. Make sure you are truly
fixing flow issues in your redesign.

> Setting Naming Conventions

All files, whether assets or pages, must have some
sort of methodology to their naming. There is no
correct or industry-standard way to name them, so
pick a method and establish it with your team —
then be consistent. Apply naming conventions to
your sitemap and Content Delivery Plan for ultimate
organization.

Page-View

Structuring a site from a Page-View is a lot like
storyboarding. With content addressed and the
sitemap created, you can look carefully at the site on
a page-by-page basis. By examining what goes on
what page and how the pages work with one another, you can confidently take the organized content and present it in a way that is meaningful and
logical to the user.

PAGE-VIEW

> Wireframing

> Addressing Navigation

> Naming and Labeling

> Defining Key User Paths

< O N E   P R O C E S S   F I T S   A L L >

> Wireframing

A wireframe is a purely informational, nondesigned layout that outlines content, primary and secondary navigation, and light functionality. By putting all the page elements down on paper, you can see what you are building before you start designing. Plus, looking at wireframes in relation to each other (interactive wireframes) gives you an idea of page flow. For a handy list of what to include in wireframes, see Phase 2.

> Addressing Navigation

Navigation connects the user with the content. Buttons, links, and graphics can be used to maintain a sense of place, offering users familiarity: Where are they in the site? Where do they need to go? How do they get back to where they were? Redesign project leaders should be aware of the tendency to rely on the old site's navigation. Examples of different navigational models appear in Phase 2.

> Naming and Labeling

The naming of buttons and labels, including the tone of the wording, should be consistent throughout the site. Determine at this stage what type of cues (icons and/or text) will be necessary to support the naming, labeling, and navigation. Consistency here is key.

> Defining Key User Paths

If your site does not require the user to actually perform any tasks (for example, fill out a form, log in, make a purchase), you can skip this step. But if the user's experience includes tasks, identify the task's path and build wireframes for each page in the path. With these interactive wireframes, you can check page flow and judge the validity of the path. For an example of a real user path in both wireframes and screenshots, see Phase 2.

PHASE 3: VISUAL DESIGN AND TESTING

The visual design, the look and feel, the graphic interface — it's the first experience the user has with the site. Even before users know if the site is easy to use, they see what it looks like. Designing the visual face of any site is exciting, and in Phase 3, designers finally get to be creative. At this stage, all design elements are created based on the established information design and the tone and goals set forth in the creative brief. The design is then approved, refined, and tested.

Production designers also start working during Phase 3. They begin to test functionality and assumptions. By developing a Protosite, they can confirm navigation and content organization.

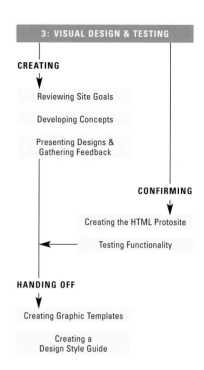

3: VISUAL DESIGN & TESTING

CREATING

Reviewing Site Goals

Developing Concepts

Presenting Designs & Gathering Feedback

CONFIRMING

Creating the HTML Protosite

Testing Functionality

HANDING OFF

Creating Graphic Templates

Creating a Design Style Guide

<TIPS>   <CHAPTER 2>

Visual design and testing, whether through the development of a Protosite or through straight functionality testing, work toward the same goal on all sites — to create an overall interactive design that meets the needs of the user and that will smoothly translate to HTML.

CREATING   CONFIRMING   HANDING OFF

Creating

Finding the balance between creative expression and technical constraints is challenging. Visual design is not just about creating a pretty interface; it is about matching users' needs with solutions on multiple levels. Even if the design is compelling, if it is difficult to use, it is unsuccessful.

> CREATING
>
> > Reviewing Site Goals
>
> > Developing Concepts
>
> > Presenting Designs and Gathering Feedback

> Reviewing Site Goals

Visual design should not be done in a vacuum. Review site goals and technical specs. Reread the creative brief; refamiliarize yourself with the audience. Aim to design for your audience, not for any designer's ego.

> Developing Concepts

Conceptual brainstorming involves coming up with visual solutions that function and that meet overall site objectives. Visual designers start experimenting with colors and layouts, thumbnails and sketches. The production team is also involved; all concepts should be passed by development to confirm feasibility before being presented to the client.

> Presenting Designs and Gathering Feedback

Present the client with a few rounds of designs, each refining the previous. Set clear expectations; control the client and avoid "endless tweaking syndrome." If the client pulls toward a direction not originally stated in the creative brief, be prepared for additional billing. Refine the agreed-upon design until it is approved. Get client approval in writing.

Confirming

During the visual design phase, take time to confirm the content, page flow, navigation, and proposed functionality developed in Phase 2. Without doing this, moving on to HTML production is a risk. Involve the production designers at all points — from initial sketches through presentations — to ensure that the designs are producible.

> CONFIRMING
>
> > Creating the Protosite
>
> > Testing Functionality

<ONE PROCESS FITS ALL>

> Creating the Protosite

While designing, have your production team start with an HTML click-thru. This "Protosite" enables you to examine content, navigation, and page flow. Establish whether your informational model makes sense. In other words, can someone actually go through your site as planned? In some cases, this Protosite will turn into your actual site.

> Testing Functionality

For special needs, such as pop-up screens, DHTML pull-down menus, frames, and other elements involving light scripting, conduct advance testing against multiple browsers and platforms before the designs are formalized. This minimizes the risk of major issues appearing during production.

Handing Off

Once the look and feel is refined and approved, it needs to be applied across multiple pages, and then each of those pages must be prepped for optimization and HTML production.

> **HANDING OFF**
>
> > Creating Graphic Templates
>
> > Creating a Design Style Guide

> Creating Graphic Templates

The transition from final, approved design to production takes form in a handoff of graphic templates. These files call out all functionality (including on/off/over states) and contain placeholders or dummy text for content — all the information that production needs to translate the visual design into HTML.

> Creating a Design Style Guide

For the purposes of ongoing production, design, and maintenance, a Style Guide is an excellent reference document. The Design Style Guide lists established standards for fonts, colors, headers, and many other treatments to help maintain the integrity of the design. A chart of recommended Design Style Guide components appears in Phase 3 along with a visual example.

PHASE 4: PRODUCTION AND QA

Phase 4 is where you put together all the pieces and make them work. Everything comes together at this point. Production merges content, design, and HTML and/or Flash production into the completed site. Phase 4 sees the backend technical implementation (if applicable). This is also the time when you should conduct quality assurance (QA) testing on your site. Test the site against your requirements. Test for HTML fluidity. Run QA. Identify the bugs, prioritize the fixes, and then fix them. Get user feedback and iron out the kinks. Launch is imminent.

PREPPING   BUILDING   TESTING

4: PRODUCTION & QA

PREPPING

Establishing Guidelines

Assessing Project Status

Setting File Structure

BUILDING

Slicing & Optimizing

Creating HTML Templates & Pages

Implementing Light Scripting

Populating Pages

Integrating Backend Development *(if applicable)*

TESTING

Creating a QA Plan

Conducting QA Testing

Prioritizing & Fixing Bugs

Conducting a Final Check

<TIPS>   <CHAPTER 2>

Incorporate Usability Testing

Of all forms of user feedback, the data collected from usability testing is the most valuable because it measures not how you *think* your users will behave, but rather how an individual user *actually* navigates, finds information, and interacts with your website. Results are immediate and indisputable. By conducting informal testing throughout the development process, you can test assumptions and make decisions, thus refining your site's information design, navigation, naming and labeling, and visual design along the way. Incorporate usability testing into your process. For more on usability testing, see Chapter 8.

Prepping

Before starting actual production, take time to re-address the original expectations and scope of the project. Review the audience's technical specifications, confirm that graphic templates are ready to be handed over, check content status, and prepare for the work of the actual building stage.

PREPPING

> Establishing Guidelines

> Assessing Project Status

> Setting File Structure

> Establishing Guidelines

Specific questions regarding browser, platform, technology, and file structure need to be answered early in the Core Process, long before production begins and ideally right after the project kicks off. The Client Spec Sheet is a survey for the client's key technical person to answer. The answers provide the production team with all necessary parameters for establishing guidelines. The Client Spec Sheet is long and detailed. It appears in part in Phase 4 and can be downloaded in full at www.web-redesign.com.

> Assessing Project Status

Projects often change midstream. Assess your project with regard to time, budget, scope, and expectations. How many hours did you budget for, and how many hours have you used so far? Compare your original projections to the current reality. Now, before building actually begins, is the time to add resources or to ask for additional budget if there have been miscalculations and/or additional wish items or unforeseen technology glitches.

> Setting File Structure

Start clean. Chances are the old site's folder structure is a mess. When determining what naming convention and organization work best for the project, keep future maintenance and scalability in mind. Even for dynamic sites, there are still static pages to consider. Know in advance of starting production how the files will be named, saved, and archived.

Building

HTML production is ready to begin in earnest. If all questions are answered and all details already addressed, this can be a very streamlined process. If not, it can be costly. The goal is to code each HTML page only once. Maintaining clear standards for HTML production is extremely important, especially when working with a team of HTML production designers. Strive for consistency. Test and troubleshoot along the way.

< O N E   P R O C E S S   F I T S   A L L >   < T I P S >

> **BUILDING**
>
> \> Slicing and Optimizing Graphics
>
> \> Creating HTML Templates and Pages
>
> \> Implementing Light Scripting
>
> \> Populating Individual Pages
>
> \> Integrating Complex Functionality

> Slicing and Optimizing Graphics

Translating graphic files into HTML pages is a challenge and a skill. Here is where the production designers actually cut up, or slice, the graphic templates into individual GIFs and JPGs that will turn into the flat graphics, animations, and rollovers that will compose the HTML templates and pages. Strive to keep page sizes down. Use flat colors and filled cells whenever possible.

> Creating HTML Templates and Pages

All sites, whether static or dynamic, start with an HTML template. This master page, or set of masters, will be used to create the rest of the site. If the site will be built in static HTML pages, this is the start of actual HTML site production. Light scripting of globals is coded at this step, and invisible content that is global is also included here.

> Implementing Light Scripting

"Light" means do-it-yourself scripting in JavaScript or DHTML. Features such as rollovers, forms, pull-down menus, pop-up windows, frames… need to be implemented in the HTML templates (or in an individual page if the feature is for that page only) and tested at this time.

> Populating Individual Pages

If content isn't in, you can't populate your pages. This is a spot in the Core Process where flow clogs. Content is due, but chances are it will be late, and this creates a domino effect that often adds days and dollars to the production schedule. Avoid this. Stay on top of content delivery and set clear and realistic deadlines that can (and should) be adhered to.

> Integrating Complex Functionality

If your project involves backend engineering, you'll need help from a more technically minded book. Backend and application implementation is a whole other ball of wax, and we are not addressing said wax here. We are, however, citing where this engineering begins to integrate with production: here, toward the end of the building stage of Phase 4.

Include Invisible Content

While building the individual pages and populating them, add the invisible content to the pages (for globals, add the information when building the HTML templates). Invisible content includes ALT, META, and TITLE tags and is often left (if not forgotten) until production is well underway. Some invisible content is a deliverable from the client, but mostly production designers decide. As a result, naming conventions are necessary.

Testing

You've built your site; now make sure it works. Quality assurance testing is simply the exhaustive checking of your site for bugs and against the original specifications outlined in Phase 1. You tested at various stages up to this point. Now that the site is built, it is time to test it as a whole. Whether your testing is formal or informal, using a test plan or just "winging it," there are tools, resources, and expert-level firms that can make QA a breeze.

> TESTING
>
> > Creating a QA Plan
> > Conducting QA Testing
> > Prioritizing and Fixing Bugs
> > Conducting a Final Check

> Creating a QA Plan

From informal to semiformal to full testing, there should be a plan in place. A QA test plan specifies the methodology used to test against browsers, platforms, and technical specifications. Resources, schedule, equipment, and assumptions are listed, along with a plan for bug tracking and fixes prior to release. In Phase 4, you can find a tidy list of items to include for a core QA plan.

> Conducting QA Testing

QA testing should be conducted in multiple stages. Internal testing comes first (sometimes called alpha testing) and then beta testing, hopefully on the actual server (before launch if you have access, or after going live if not a soft launch). Testing levels depend on budget, time, resources, and expertise. The main aim of QA is to identify bugs. If you have a separate, formal QA team, it will *only* track the bugs. The production team needs to fix them.

> Prioritizing and Fixing Bugs

Establishing a method of tracking, prioritizing, and fixing bugs will make the process run much smoother. Determine priorities and monitor and recheck fixes prior to launch. A list of items to note when bug reporting is available in Phase 4, as are suggestions for downloadable helpful tools available online for in-house QA teams.

> Conducting a Final Check

You're ready to go "live." All testing and fixes have been completed on the staging server (or hidden URL). Before moving the site to the live server, however, a last check should be conducted on design, content, production, and functionality. Also make sure the client has signed off on the site. The final check, in detail, is listed at the end of Phase 4.

< O N E   P R O C E S S   F I T S   A L L >

PHASE 5: LAUNCH AND BEYOND

Getting to this phase means you are ready to go live with your redesign. Congratulations! Launching your site is a major milestone, but you're not done yet. This phase covers what you need to think about before, during, and after your site goes live. It is about gathering loose ends and wrapping the project up before the site moves into the next phase of production: ongoing maintenance.

Phase 5 is where the distinction sharpens between in-house teams and external web development firms. Although we don't go into this distinction here in the overview, in Phase 5 we are careful to note where the responsibilities of the different teams usually begin and end.

DELIVERY	LAUNCH	MAINTENANCE

Delivery

Most projects have one team designing and building and another team managing the ongoing maintenance. The transition between a site-in-development and a site-in-maintenance is usually determined by launch. During this transition, one team hands off all design and production files to the other team for ongoing design, production, and updating.

DELIVERY

> Completing the Production Style Guide

> Creating the Handoff Packet

> Tracking and Archiving Documentation

> Conducting a Postmortem Meeting

> Scheduling Maintenance Training

> Completing the Production Style Guide

After launch, production-specific guidelines are added to the Style Guide started in Phase 3. The Production Style Guide should include code information for HTML tags, attributes, and definitions of graphic elements — all information necessary for one production designer to hand off to another. A chart of recommended Production Style Guide components appears in Phase 5, along with a visual example.

> Creating the Handoff Packet

All relevant design and production materials should be organized and put into a packet for distribution to the client and the maintenance team. See Phase 5 for a list of suggested handoff materials.

> Tracking and Archiving Documentation

All documents (electronic and hard copy) having to do with project scope changes, budget issues, and client approvals should be saved. Hard copies of the

5: LAUNCH & BEYOND

DELIVERY

Completing the
Production Style Guide

Creating the Handoff Packet

Archiving Documentation

Conducting a
Postmortem Meeting

Scheduling
Maintenance Training

LAUNCH

Preparing an
Announcement Plan

Registering with
Search Engines

Launching the Site

MAINTENANCE

Assessing Maintenance
Team Capabilities

Developing a
Maintenance Plan

Measuring Success

Confirming Site Security

<TIPS>   <CHAPTER 2>

Conduct a Competitive Analysis

Analyzing both your industry and your competition can help you better understand how your site rates. Review the main features and usability of a cross-section of competitive sites. An informal analysis conducted from the user's point of view allows for a greater understanding of features, services, and ease of use. Further formal research and analysis can allow for an in-depth look into the client and the industry, coming with a higher budget and utilizing greater expertise. A competitive analysis should be part of the Discovery process, no matter the level of your approach. For more on conducting a competitive analysis, see Chapter 9.

initial contract, proposal, project plan, and any other relevant documentation should be filed and archived. Cull and organize. A suggested archival list can be found in Phase 5.

> Conducting a Postmortem Meeting

Every project is a learning experience. The postmortem meeting is a chance for all key players to get together and constructively rehash the project. Seeing what worked and what could be improved on the next time around — this is the goal.

> Scheduling Maintenance Training

Some training for the maintenance team is almost always needed. This is usually accompanied by specific guidelines outlined in the Style Guides. For larger sites and in-house teams, this maintenance may include additional phases of ongoing application development, content management systems, and relaunches.

Launch

With QA testing completed and production frozen, you are ready to announce the live site. Most likely, there are still some bugs to be fixed, but the site has been given the "go" for public viewing. While the actual launch is really nothing more than a blip in the project timeline, a few factors requiring much more time and resources should accompany the upload.

> **LAUNCH**

> Preparing an Announcement Plan

> Registering with Search Engines

> Launching the Site

> Preparing an Announcement Plan

An announcement strategy has been planned long in advance of the launch date — usually by an in-house or outside marketing team. Hopefully, that plan includes notifying your existing audience in advance of the site's redesign to encourage buy-in and feedback. As outside factors may be involved, make sure there is clear communication as to the site's readiness and launch status before any major advertising is started.

> Registering with Search Engines

Even if your site is already listed in search engines, plan to resubmit after the redesign launch. Use the META Data Creation Tool in Phase 5 to help create effective keywords and title tags. Also, don't miss Phase 5's four surefire ways to hide from search engines — so you can make sure you don't.

> Launching the Site

Pull the switch. You're live. Congratulations! Plan to upload the site during nonpeak hours to allow for troubleshooting of last-minute snafus. Have a

< ONE PROCESS FITS ALL >

temporary home page in place during the transfer between old and new sites. Larger sites may re-launch in phases because upload and testing may take several hours over several days. Have a roll-back ready in case of major problems.

Maintenance

Make sure a team is in place for content creation, HTML production, and any necessary visual design changes. How often will the site update? Daily? Monthly? How will you be archiving material? Who will be maintaining the site? How savvy is that person? You filled out the Maintenance Survey at the beginning of the project in order to plan, now it is time to assess, reassess, and transition into a whole new workflow: maintenance.

MAINTENANCE

> Assessing Maintenance Team Capability

> Developing a Maintenance Plan

> Measuring the Success of the Site

> Confirming Site Security

> Assessing Maintenance Team Capability

The individual(s) responsible for updating needs to have a high enough level of skill to handle the maintenance of the redesigned site. The web development team should assess the abilities of the maintenance team against the complexity of the redesigned site. Advise the client if the team is understaffed, under-skilled, or over-resourced.

> Developing a Maintenance Plan

Determine the frequency and details of maintenance updates. Create a spreadsheet or official plan outlining the sections and content that will be updated on a daily/weekly/monthly/quarterly basis. Set deadlines that include a regular check of the site against the standards set in the Style Guide.

> Measuring the Success of the Site

Now that you have launched, it is time to track and measure results. Does your new site actually improve on your original redesign goals? Have sales increased? Have calls to customer service decreased? Having both qualitative and quantitative feedback on usage and customer satisfaction helps you analyze your redesign's success.

> Confirming Site Security

Site security is a very specialized field, and we don't go into it in depth, but in Phase 5, we do present a list of things to consider as you plan for your redesign's security. Hackers are relentless; it helps to safeguard.

< C H A P T E R 2 >

CHAPTER SUMMARY

This overview offers a singular panorama of the entire workflow — you can actually see the entire Core Process from start to finish. It is often helpful, especially when in Phase 1, to see everything still to come. When you are building your budget, you can look through the pages of this chapter and budget by task, ticking off each one in each phase as you allocate hours. When you are scheduling, you can see all the steps laid out in list format and gain a better timeline view. For project management, being able to see the next several steps at any point in the process can be valuable as far as staying on top of your team.

Finally, this chapter is sort of a summary, but instead of following the main subject, we present it here at the beginning. This way, you can familiarize yourself with the Core Process and then read about it in detail. We believe it is more helpful this way.

< C A S E   S T U D Y >

LiquidMedium

Client: LiquidMedium
URL: www.liquidmedium.com
Design Team (Redesign): Idea Integration, SF
Creative Director: Kelly Goto
Art Director: Serena Howeth

Designer: Kian Nassiri
Production Lead: Manny Frietas
Maintenance Team (Update on Redesign):
LiquidMedium in-house

LiquidMedium manages the entire process of the human capital supply-chain, from sourcing and procurement to the placement and management of staffing resources.

< P R E V I O U S >   < C U R R E N T >

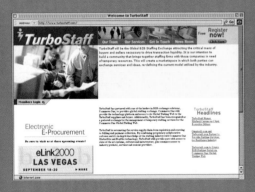

TURBOSTAFF.COM [OLD] was corporate, dated, and no longer reflected the goals of the company. It was time for both a rebranding and a site redesign.

LIQUIDMEDIUM.COM [REDESIGNED] has a new logo, identity, and branding. The look is fresh and updated; still corporate but not stiff. (2000)

LIQUIDMEDIUM.COM [UPDATED] slowly evolved into a new site. After going in-house for maintenance, the site added content and new sections. Within six months, it looked very different. (2001)

Result: More apparent navigation and prominent placement of company partnerships.

> Project scope: the proposed definition of project

boundaries from all angles, including budget, schedule,

creative vision, technical needs, and overall size.

Phase 1: Defining the Project

< C H A P T E R 3 >

Phase 1: Defining the Project

Getting started can be daunting, and actually starting a web redesign project is no exception. So much to do... where to begin? Although you — and maybe even the client — may have a general understanding of what will be involved in getting the project done, the details and process of starting a redesign project can be elusive. The first part of this first phase is all about getting ready to get started and about gathering information.

This chapter will help you set the stage, plan, and prep. Here we focus on developing methods of communicating expectations and making sure there are no mistaken assumptions. We include a lot of handy tools designed to help you help your client provide you with the necessary information you need to define goals, objectives, budgets, timelines, and of course, the audience. (Don't miss this one; defining your audience is one of the most important and overlooked preparatory points in any web development project.)

Please note that this chapter outlines the workflow steps necessary for *defining* a project. We do not go into *getting* a project. We present workflow, not business development. But because it is often necessary to define quite a bit of the project in order to get it, there is a great deal of information here that is potentially helpful.

WHAT THIS CHAPTER COVERS		
DISCOVERY	**CLARIFICATION**	**PLANNING**
› Gathering Information	› Determining Overall Goals	› Creating a Project Plan
› Understanding Your Audience	› Preparing a Creative Brief	› Setting the Budget
› Analyzing Your Industry		› Creating Schedules
		› Assigning Your Project Team
		› Setting Up Staging Areas
		› Planning for User Testing
		› Kicking Off the Project

Discovery is an industry-wide term that can mean several things. It can have a budget (often in the significant five figures) and a plan all its own. We have simplified the Discovery process so that it is accessible across a range of projects and pricing.

<PHASE 1: DEFINING THE PROJECT>

We have divided this first phase of the Core Process into three tracks: **Discovery**, **Clarification**, and **Planning**. Through a series of surveys, discussion, and research, **Discovery** leads to understanding three critical things: the client's online goals, the audience and its needs and online capabilities, and the industry and the competition as it relates to the web. Discovery is all about gathering information and asking a lot of questions. The answers will serve as a reference for nearly every step that follows.

Clarification and **Planning** each consist of taking the information gathered and putting it together into documentation — the former into a creative brief and the latter into schedules, budgets, team rosters, and testing plans. This documentation is designed to communicate several topics clearly and concisely to both client and team:

- What are the client's wishes and goals? What is the proposed plan to carry these out?
- How much is the entire project going to cost, how is that cost broken down, and how many hours are allocated to each individual task?
- Who are the team members, and what are their responsibilities?
- What are the client's responsibilities?
- What are the deliverables, and when are they due?
- How will the site be tested against user needs?
- What are the long-range goals for the site?

At the end of this defining phase, all materials get distributed at the kick-off meeting, attended by all team and key client members. The goal is to communicate clearly, to keep the members of the team aligned with the same goals and terminology during the life of the project, and to make sure no one is ever left guessing as to what comes next or when what's next is due.

GATHERING INFORMATION

Discovery is a thinking process. Its purpose is to allow team members to put themselves in the minds of the site's users and to understand as much as possible about the target audience(s), the company, the outgoing site, and the redesign project. To start, you need information. You need to discover all you can about the project, the client, the client's industry, and the intended audience. There are a lot of questions to ask; the surveys will get you going.

Discovery can take one week or many weeks, depending — as usual — on budget and approach. The Discovery team can be one person or a posse of researchers. Regardless, Discovery starts with the Client Survey.

The Client Survey

Clients usually have clear *business* objectives, but they are notorious for not having clear *site* objectives. And why expect them to? They are neither designers nor web experts.

<
> DISCOVERY
> > Gathering Information
> > Understanding Your Audience
> > Analyzing Your Industry

< C H A P T E R 3 >

Client input is the foundation on which successful websites are built. This survey will help you articulate and identify the overall goals of your site redesign, including specific questions regarding message, audience, content, look and feel, and functionality. Each key decision-maker should fill out his or her own survey, answer each of the questions in a thorough but brief and clear manner, and add any additional notes or comments at the end of the survey. When finished, all compiled information should be emailed back to the project manager on the web development team.

This survey is available for download at www.web-redesign.com >>>

THE CLIENT SURVEY

General Information

1. What is the name of your company and your current (or intended) URL?

2. Who are the primary contacts from your organization and who has final approval on the project? Please list names, titles, email addresses, and phone numbers.

3. What is your intended launch date for the new site? Are there any outside considerations that might affect the schedule (for example, PR launch, tradeshow, annual report)?

4. Do you have a specific budget range already established for this project? Can this project be divided into phases to accommodate budget and timing constraints?

Current Site

1. Do you feel your current site promotes a favorable user experience? Why or why not?

2. What specific areas of your current site do you feel are successful? Why are they successful?

3. What shortcomings exist with the current site, and what three things would you change on the site today if you could?

4. Have you conducted usability tests or gathered user feedback for your current site? If so, how long ago? Please include any reports or findings.

5. How important is it to maintain your current look and feel, logo, and branding?

Reasons for Redesign

1. What are the main reasons you are redesigning your site (new business model, outdated site, expanded services, different audience)?

2. What are your primary online business objectives with the site redesign? What are your secondary objectives? (Examples include increased sales, marketing/branding awareness, and fewer customer service calls.) Please discuss both long- and short-term goals.

3. What is the main business problem you hope to solve with the site redesign? How will you measure the success of the solution?

4. What existing strategy (both on- and offline) is in place to meet the new business objectives?

Audience/Desired Action

1. Describe a typical user coming to your site. How often is the user online, and what does he generally use the web for? How old is the user and what does he do for a living? (Use as much detail as possible in profiling your target user. Profile more than one type if appropriate.)

2. What is the primary "action" the user should take when coming to your site (make a purchase, become a member, search for information)?

3. What are the key reasons why the target user chooses your company's products and/or services (cost, service, value)?

< P H A S E   1 :   D E F I N I N G   T H E   P R O J E C T >

4. How many people (as far as you can tell) access your site on a daily, weekly, or monthly basis? How do you measure usage? Do you forecast usage to increase after the site launch and by how much?

Perception

1. Use a few adjectives to describe how the user should perceive the new site. (Examples include prestigious, friendly, corporate, fun, forward thinking, innovative, and cutting edge.) Is this different than the current image perception?

2. How is your company currently perceived offline? Do you want to carry the same kind of message through your website?

3. How does your company differentiate itself from competitors? Do you think your current audience differentiates you from your competition? Please list competitor URLs.

4. List the URLs of any sites you find compelling. What specifically do you like about these sites?

Content

1. Will this site use existing content from the current site? If so, what is the source, who is responsible for approval, and has the content been audited? If not, will you be creating content in-house or using an outside provider?

2. What is the basic structure of the content, and how is it organized? Is it a complete overhaul of the current site or an expansion?

3. Describe visual elements or content that should be utilized from your current site or marketing materials (logo, color scheme, navigation, naming conventions, and so on).

4. How will the content of this site (along with functionality and navigation) expand or differ from your current site? Do you have an existing sitemap for the outgoing site structure? Do you already have a sitemap or outline for the proposed redesign?

Technology

1. What is your target platform and browser (if you know)?

2. Are there specific technologies (Flash, DHTML, JavaScript, Real Audio) that you would like to use in the site? If so, how will they enhance the user experience? Please describe in detail.

3. Will you have database functionality (dynamic content generation, search capabilities, personalization/login)? Do you already have a database in place? Please describe it in detail, including specific information regarding existing programs and software.

4. Will you have a need for secured transactions (e-commerce)? Do you already offer transactions online? Please describe in detail.

5. Will you require other specific programming needs (such as personalization or search capability)? Please describe in detail.

Marketing/Updating

1. How do most people find out about your current website? What methods of distributing the URL already exist within the company?

2. Briefly, what are your short-term marketing plans (specifically, for the site redesign and the 12 months following launch)?

3. Do you have an existing or planned marketing strategy in mind to promote this site redesign? If so, please describe.

4. Do you intend to keep the site updated? If so, how often? Who is responsible for updating and providing content?

Additional Notes/Comments

Please take as much space as you need.

_____

_____

_____

_____

_____

_____

< T I P S >   < C H A P T E R 3 >

Unifying Goals

Do key players in the client's company have differing opinions and
goals for the redesign? This is usually a red flag indicating that the
client is experiencing an internal
tug-of-war or is suffering from a
significant level of disorganization.
Depending on the source of the dispute, it is possible that data collected from a round of usability tests on
the outgoing site and/or on some
competitor sites might help client
personnel agree on common goals.
Real users will clearly demonstrate
what is working and what isn't.
Understand, however, that user-
based feedback, while incredibly
insightful, is not a substitute for
having clear business objectives.

For more on usability testing, see
Chapter 8: Testing for Usability.
For more on competitive analyses,
see Chapter 9: Analyzing Your
Competition.

By asking clients the right questions, you coach them into thinking through their redesign project in a different way and thus guide them into aligning their business objectives with the constantly chang-ing, evolving, and demanding web.

The Client Survey (available for download from www.web-redesign.com) should be a straightfor-ward distribute/collect/analyze process, with the analysis sometimes requiring emails or phone calls between you and the client for clarification. Distrib-ution of the survey is the very first thing to do with a redesign project — with *any* web development pro-ject. Encourage feedback within a short timeframe.

Recommend to the primary client contact that the Client Survey be distributed to all key client deci-sion-makers. Many organizations have several key players, and feedback from several sources usually gives a broader feel for any project. It is the client's responsibility to manage this distribution and then process each set of client answers into one response for the development team to use. If you are heading an internal team, it is probably your responsibility to manage the Client Survey's distribution, collec-tion, and consolidation. Having only one response to the Client Survey is particularly important be-cause when working with several individuals you will get several opinions. The client, as a unit, must be aligned with common goals.

Customizing the Client Survey

The Client Survey can be — and in fact, should be — customized to be client or industry specific. If you are in-house and you know the company and in-dustry well, certain basic questions can be elimi-nated and more in-depth questions added. In fact, if you are the project manager on an internal team, you may be filling out the survey yourself.

All projects will differ in size, scope, and focus. The Client Survey asks for in-depth, but basic, in-formation necessary for general site redesign. Using the Client Survey as a base, determine whether any additional information is required to understand the specific goals of the project. Don't overwhelm the client with dozens of extra questions, however. If the client glazes over, it's likely you won't get even the basic information you need.

Analyzing the Client Survey

Once analyzed, the client-answered survey serves many purposes. You will refer to it regularly, espe-cially to define site goals and to build schedules, the budget, and the all-important creative brief. It is, quite simply, the project's springboard.

< PHASE 1: DEFINING THE PROJECT >

< TIPS >

The Client Survey as a Screening Tool

We've all had nightmare clients. Unreasonably demanding, capricious, unreachable, unrealistic, cheap... Use the Client Survey as an interviewing or screening tool for prospective clients as soon as a project presents itself. Because clients have to complete the survey and return it, this makes them accountable. The ones who take the time to answer your questions in a thoughtful, well-organized manner are likely to put proper thought into the creation of a site and have the makings of a good client. Clients who fit a number of red flag client characteristics (see chart below) are sometimes better left alone. If you have the luxury of choice, screen and choose projects and clients wisely.

GOOD CLIENT	RED FLAG CLIENT
A good client has some of the following attributes:	This is not necessarily a nightmare client, but here are some things to watch out for:
• Is goal-oriented: focused on the big picture	• Has a "get-it-up-quick" attitude with unrealistic schedule requests
• Answers the Client Survey in a clear and detailed manner	• Doesn't know what the content should be but wants it to "look cool"
• Supplies a Request for Proposal (RFP) or a clear outline of goals and scope	• Asks to create a demo site, says "the real one will come later"
• Understands the web environment and the development process	• Cannot give final approval or is not putting you in touch with the decision-makers
• Gives final sign-off and approval	• Doesn't have time to fill out the survey
• Is in agreement on deliverables, schedule, and budget	• Small budget, swift deadline
• Is responsive to email and phone calls	• Nonresponsive, cannot make decisions, does not email or call back in a timely manner
• Has a team-oriented approach	• Indecisive, changes mind frequently
• Gets you content on time	• Wants to handle the creative aspects to "save money"
• Is part of the solution instead of the problem	

Include the Client

Working in partnership with the client to define the project — establishing the budget, timeline, schedule, visual style, technical needs, content, basic structure, target audience, and the site's primary message — is a good tactical move. When clients are involved, they acquire a sense of ownership in their redesign, they make themselves available, and they help more. Be observant, however. Client assistance is invaluable, but some people meddle while they "help." Nonetheless, if clients *feel* involved, chances are you will receive what you need from them when you need it. Dedication and commitment in a team-oriented environment is better than an "us versus them" attitude.

< C H A P T E R 3 >

EXAMPLES OF ADDITIONAL CLIENT SURVEY QUESTIONS

If the redesign project will include an identity overhaul, ask the client about its current branding system. Here are some sample questions:

1. What specifically do you want to communicate with your logo? What kind of emotional response should the customer feel?

2. List or attach logos you like and explain why.

3. What colors and imagery convey the personality and tone of your company?

4. Will a tagline be part of the logo? What should the tagline convey?

If promoting the site is a specific redesign issue/goal, try some of these additional questions:

1. What methods of promoting your URL do you currently utilize outside your own organization both online and off? Are they generating traffic?

2. How will you keep users coming back to your site? And how can you encourage your current users to solicit new users?

3. What are your short-, medium-, and long-term goals to increase traffic and awareness of your site?

When you are finished analyzing the Client Survey, you should have clarity on several points, concepts, and ideas:

- **Site goals.** What are the overall goals of the site redesign? What is the primary business problem that will be solved (for example, increase traffic, increase sales)? What other goals will be achieved (for example, decrease calls to customer service, create a more user-centric site)?

- **Audience.** What are your audience demographics and user profiles? A sample demographic includes occupation, age, gender, online frequency, connection speed, and online habits (what sites users visit and why, how often they purchase online, how web-

savvy they are). It also includes their type of computer, their browser, and where they live. A user profile takes that demographic and puts a real name and persona to it.

- **Redesign Issues.** What are the redesign issues and goals? Have a clear understanding of old site vs. new site in terms of usability, tone, perception, and message. Some examples of uses for this list: to help create the creative brief, to review at the kick-off meeting, and as a check-off list during subsequent phases of development.

- **Tone.** What is the client's desired tone and audience perception? Sophisticated? Sleek? Fun? Credible? Dependable? Inexpensive? Have a clear interpretation of this; you need it to write the creative brief.

< P H A S E   1 :   D E F I N I N G   T H E   P R O J E C T >

- **Scope.** What are the project boundaries from all angles including budget, schedule, creative vision, technical needs, and overall size (as clearly defined as possible with existing knowledge)? You cannot create a budget without knowing this.

- **Maintenance.** What is the client's vision for future site updates? Formulate a basic idea of how often and to what degree the site will be updated. The Maintenance Survey will provide additional data.

- **Contacts.** Who is involved on the project? Start a contact list for both the client and development teams. This should contain all client contact names, email addresses, telephone and fax numbers, and snail mail address (for deliveries and billing). Plan to keep this list updated and available on the password-protected client staging site (discussed later in this chapter).

The Maintenance Survey

It may seem premature to address site maintenance this early in the redesign process, and the client might even balk at another comprehensive survey (hopefully not, however, because there is another one coming up regarding audience technology capabilities). Knowing who is going to maintain the site, how often the client plans to update it, as well as the level of growth planned in the first 12 months following launch are all questions that need to be addressed as early as possible for one compelling reason: You need to plan around the projections made. Many things will be affected by maintenance, including site structure and organization, folder and file structure, and the often-complex world of content management. Please note that the Maintenance Survey (available for download from www. web-redesign.com) does not need to be filled out and analyzed prior to the project's kick-off, but it is an issue to consider as early as the Developing Site Structure phase, which follows Defining the Project.

The client should answer the questions as thoroughly as possible, and the project manager should then use the results from this survey as a guide. By addressing these questions at the beginning of the project, you are able to plan in advance for maintenance needs once your redesign is live.

< C H A P T E R   3 >

This survey is designed to help you determine how your site maintenance will be addressed after launch. Answer the following questions briefly and clearly and to the best of your knowledge. When you are finished, email all compiled information back to the project manager on the web development team.

This survey is available for download at www.web-redesign.com >>>

THE MAINTENANCE SURVEY

General Information

1. What areas of the redesigned site will be updated (for example, news, photos, horoscopes, products, reviews) and how often (for example, daily, weekly, monthly, quarterly, annually)?

2. Describe the maintenance team and individual responsibilities and time allocation, if known. (Full time? Part time? Split jobs?)

3. How will the site be updated? Will you be inputting content manually into HTML files? Will you be using a content management system to dynamically update and deploy content (useful, for example, in the management of e-commerce inventory or text-publishing databases)? If using a content management system, please describe in detail.

4. Who is responsible for maintaining the site from a technical standpoint, and what is this person's technical expertise level? What experience and capabilities does he or she have? Will the person require training?

5. Who is responsible for making graphic changes on the site? Will the person be using existing design templates when making changes or additions? What is his or her design expertise level?

Content Creation

1. Who is responsible for creating the content for the site? Is this person able to dedicate part- or full-time resources to content creation?

2. Who is responsible for approving look-and-feel changes (as the site expands) to ensure that the quality of the site is maintained?

3. How often will new sections or areas be added to the site? Will they be based on the existing site's template or be independent sections?

Production Expertise

1. What technological expertise is necessary to update the site (basic HTML knowledge, light scripting knowledge)?

2. Is there an automated process of changing content on the home page (an automatic refresh of images or text each time a person comes to the site, a randomly generated quote, or a date change)?

Promotion

1. How will the user know the site has been updated? Will there be email announcements or specials tied into the site updates?

2. Who is responsible for continued search engine and keyword updates and submissions? How often will keywords and META tags be revised?

<PHASE 1: DEFINING THE PROJECT>   <TIPS>

UNDERSTANDING YOUR AUDIENCE

The web is all about the user. What needs, capabilities, wants, and fickle characteristics of your user will you need to know? All of them (or at the very least, as many as possible). But because speculation is not credible here, do some sleuthing.

Use the Client Survey to gather initial data so you can get a strong sense of who your users are, why they are coming to the site, and what tasks they will be performing. A typical user demographic description includes occupation, age, gender, online frequency, connection speed, and online habits (what sites they visit and why, how often they purchase online, how web savvy they are). The description also includes their type of computer, their browser, and where they live. Keep in mind that you may need to profile more than one target group (with multiple audiences, create separate user profiles).

Use this general demographic information to create a general profile, which will be used as the audience profile in the creative brief. This should be a concise paragraph about each user, including typical tasks the user might perform on the site. Here is an example of a general profile:

> "Typical user is a university student between the ages of 18 and 22, who accesses the web on a daily basis. S/he is extremely web savvy and completes online purchases for books, CDs, DVDs, and gifts regularly — 2 or 3 times per month. S/he has high-speed internet access both at the dorm and at the library, most often using the library computers for research and the dorm computer for personal correspondence. Typical tasks on the site include searching for authors, titles, and products to purchase. S/he has a user name and password and is able to complete purchases quickly and easily."

If you have the resources, we highly recommend building a few detailed, individual profiles [3.1]. To achieve this, you may need to interview both the client and a few actual users to gain a real-world view of the actual target audience. The results will be worth the effort.

Most sites draw several distinctly definable user types. You may need to create more than one general profile.

Request Existing Material

The client may have existing research about the target audience and market. Ask questions. Gather as much information as possible. Keep in mind, however, that the client's business model may have changed in a year's time, so the provided information may no longer be relevant.

< CHAPTER 3 >

Paige McCormick

Paige McCormick

Paige McCormick is an elementary art teacher, artist, and girls' Little League Track coach in Portland, Oregon. She is 35 years old and lives in Northwest Portland near Forest Park with her dog Ruth Ann (Ruthie).

Paige owns her house and spends a great deal of time fixing it and gardening. She has a very busy and active lifestyle. When not working, Paige spends her time outdoors running, mountain biking, and playing with Ruthie.

Paige is an enthusiastic dog owner and goes out of her way to provide for her dog. She has given up on stuffed animal toys — they're so cute, but Ruthie guts them immediately and eats the fiberfill. Paige casually studies dog behavior and training techniques. She enjoys living near Forest Park because it provides an excellent place for Ruthie to chase squirrels.

Paige has a 56K modem but is thinking about upgrading to DSL service soon. She uses a Mac G3 and considers herself very computer savvy. She does a significant amount of her shopping online, which she finds saves her a great deal of time, although sometimes the shipping is a deterrent. She appreciates the automatic monthly deliveries of dog food.

She loves smaller pet shops that specialize in items that appeal to her aesthetics and dislikes large warehouse-style pet stores such as PetClub, although she admits they provide necessities at a reasonable price.

< 3.1

This sample user profile gives a detailed description of a typical user. Also called a "persona," this document can be as brief or as detailed as your information, creativity, and time allow.

Outlining Technical Requirements

What technological "latests and greatests" will your redesign project require? This is, without question, one of most significant factors in defining the project. A redesign project that is front-end only — even if it is extensive in scope — is a very different project from one that also includes dynamic content and security capabilities. It is not unusual for clients to want all the bells and whistles without understanding the associated costs. Analyzing both basic and backend technology needs will gather the data necessary to show where client expectations do not match reality [3.2].

Because the client may have (and often does have) unrealistic expectations, it is the project manager's responsibility to make sure the client understands not only the fundamentals of redesigning the website, but also how each choice and decision that is made impacts both the scope and therefore the budget of the project.

Please remember that this book is not a step-by-step workflow for backend implementation. If your site requires a backend database, e-commerce capability, dynamic content, and so on, you need an additional, parallel plan. For more information on what this book does not cover, please refer to the book's introduction.

3.2 >

Clients often have only a vague idea of what features actually cost. Once true costs and timing are communicated, clients frequently adjust their technical expectations.

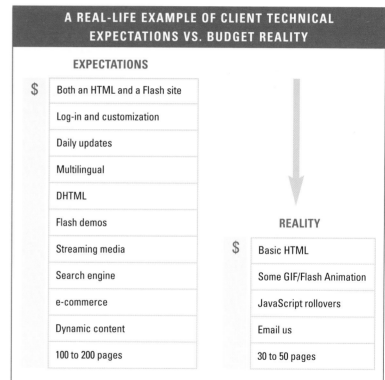

A REAL-LIFE EXAMPLE OF CLIENT TECHNICAL EXPECTATIONS VS. BUDGET REALITY

EXPECTATIONS

$ | Both an HTML and a Flash site

Log-in and customization

Daily updates

Multilingual

DHTML

Flash demos

Streaming media

Search engine

e-commerce

Dynamic content

100 to 200 pages

REALITY

$ | Basic HTML

Some GIF/Flash Animation

JavaScript rollovers

Email us

30 to 50 pages

< EXPERT TOPIC > <CHAPTER 3>

KATE GOMOLL ON USER PROFILING

Designers and developers need to keep real people in their minds as they design. Reality TV has been so successful because real people are endlessly fascinated by the unexpected things that other real people actually do and say. As you define your audience, if you can write a story about an actual person — complete with pictures, hobbies, quirks, product preferences, pet peeves, and details about that person's daily life — the designers and developers will actually read it and, more importantly, absorb it.

Typically, companies run focus groups or conduct market surveys to learn about the potential users of their products. The results from this research are traditionally presented in summary reports that describe user goals, needs, and desires in terms of percentages and trends. While this information is useful for overall product planning and marketing, it often isn't specific enough for product designers and web developers.

The summary reports that most research departments create are an abstract representation of people. They are usually a discussion of trends and market breakdowns, lacking any details about individual customers. But designers and developers need details when they create a product. Details about users' motivations, frustrations, and desires help the development team make important and strategic decisions. There will always be disagreement over how a new or redesigned product should look and work. But when you have profiles of real users at your fingertips, the arguments shift from "I would never do that" or "My Mom would hate that" to arguments about actual users like Paige [3.1]. Suddenly, team members are asking whether Paige would require instant-on functionality or whether Paige would be turned off by an advertising banner. The designers use the data in the profiles to help make sensible design tradeoffs.

I'm not saying that you shouldn't conduct research using a decent sample size or that you should stop doing focus groups and conducting surveys. But often, schedules don't allow even the most minimal research. Still, if time is spent figuring out what types of users fall into the target market group and then visiting at least one person from each of the market segments, very useful profiles can result. Sometimes teams will launch a grassroots profiling effort — even when it's not in the budget — simply because designers need them! Designers simply can't do their jobs without knowing specific information about the potential users.

What kinds of information should you include in your profiles?

- **Basic demographics**
- **Day-in-the-life stories**
- **Photographs of people, their environments, their tools**
- **Likes and dislikes**
- **Observational data**
- **Product usage patterns**
- **Frustrations with your product or similar products**
- **Product-related desires**

Because these profiles are only useful if people want to read them, take the time to write a compelling narrative; make each person you profile memorable. Use the details you collect from users to develop each person as a character. If you have the time and budget, create profiles for many potential users. Then roll them up to create just a few composite

<PHASE 1: DEFINING THE PROJECT>

<TIPS>

characters to represent the user segments. These profiles, also called personas, will become shorthand descriptions for the user segments that your product serves. The key to successful user profiling is to work from actual user data, not hypothetical, made-up stories. You'll find that the truth really is stranger — and more revealing — than fiction.

Kate Gomoll is President of Gomoll Research & Design, Inc. (www.gomolldesign.com), *a consulting company that specializes in user experience design. The company's recent clients include DirecTV, Charles Schwab, WebTV, Hewlett-Packard, Internet Appliance Network, and Compaq. Kate has published chapters on user observation in* The Art of Human Computer Interface Design *(Addison-Wesley, 1990) and* The Macintosh Human Interface Guidelines *(Addison-Wesley, 1992). A nationally recognized expert in the field of software interface design and usability, Kate teaches customer research methods at conferences and workshops worldwide. She also taught user-centered design workshops through UCLA Extension for many years. Prior to starting her consulting business, Kate was an interface designer in the Advanced Technology Group at Apple Computer.*

Understanding Audience Capabilities

It comes down to this question: Who is the client willing to leave behind? Some sites depend on appealing to all audiences. If your targeted audience is everybody-with-a-computer-and-then-some, users with older technologies must be accommodated, and bandwidth requirements must be kept low. Many web users have small monitors, use older browsers, and still connect with slower modems — these users may be as valuable to the client as those with a T1 connection and the absolute latest browsers. High-bandwidth requirements would frustrate and alienate someone on a slow modem and would probably cause that user to abort the page load. Result: lost business.

High or low bandwidth? Most clients will know which group they want to target. It is your job as project manager to determine what that audience can accept technically and then scope the project accordingly.

When catering to high-bandwidth users, the client wants to show all the latest and greatest with little concern for who gets left behind. Clients want an audience that supports all their high-end technologies (full Flash, the very latest browsers, and so on). These sites tend to be experimental and artistically cutting edge, like the Altoids Too Hot site [3.3].

Bandwidth?

For the purposes of this book, we employ a rather narrow definition of the term "bandwidth." We define bandwidth in terms of capability (that is, download size over time, browser versions, plug-ins, and so on). Therefore, when we say "high-bandwidth user," we are referring to users on the latest browser versions that can handle a high-byte download at a quick speed (that is, T1- or DSL-enabled users on relatively new machines). The same site that downloads quickly to a high-bandwidth user downloads slowly to a low-bandwidth user (that is, modem users on machines over two years old).

High bandwidth does not necessarily mean web savvy. Many machines come packaged with all the latest plug-ins and browsers and are purchased by people with very little online experience. Remember also that many web neophytes go online through high-bandwidth company networks.

< CHAPTER 3 >

< **3.3**

High bandwidth:
www.toohot.com loads in
seconds with a DSL con-
nection, but it takes over
a minute to download for
users with a modem. It ani-
mates all the way through.

< **3.4**

Low bandwidth:
www.amazon.com
downloads in a snap, even
on modems, and contains
no specialized functionality.
It is even accessible to
audiences on 3.0 browsers.

Sites that need to be accessible to anyone (including the budding wireless market), anywhere (even where DSL is unavailable), must appeal to a low-bandwidth-capable audience. These are mass market and global audiences. These sites load quickly even on modems (we are no longer targeting 14.4 modem speeds and hardly considering 28.8; one must draw the line somewhere). These sites don't require any special technologies or plug-ins and they work on small screens and old browsers. Examples include www.amazon.com **[3.4]**.

Most companies want to shoot for a widely targeted audience, one that includes users on both modem and higher-speed connections. These companies don't want to lose the users needing low-bandwidth access, but they want to accommodate some higher technology and appeal to users who can and do appreciate what high bandwidth can allow. The site for the movie trilogy *Lord of The Rings* **[3.5]** accomplishes this by loading a Flash site, but offering a straight HTML option. Some sites, like www.macromedia.com, even take the choice away from the audience and incorporate a browser sniffer that automatically directs users to the site they can access.

Analyzing Audience Capabilities

Once you know who your audience is, start determining what its technical capabilities are. You are looking for specifics about whom you want to reach and whom you can leave behind. What percentage of your audience is still connected via modem? What percentage of your audience has 17-inch or bigger monitors, and can you afford to shortchange users of 15-inch monitors? What percentage of your audience has downloaded the latest Flash plug-in? At what browser level is most of your audience? What bandwidth can these people comfortably handle? (Does the client even care? Maybe not, if the purpose of the site is merely to display.)

Determining this information is no simple task. Historically, educated speculation has been employed: "My demographic is San Francisco professionals. Chances are they have at least a T1 connection." This type of guesswork is good if your demographic is that specific. Luckily, because you are redesigning, it is possible that the server has all kinds of statistics in its logs. Resources on the web? Not too many that are reliable or up-to-date. www.hitbox.com and www.statmarket.com are two resources that help match a demographic to a statistic, but both sites are accessible through paid subscription only.

Your goal is to identify your target audience's technical capabilities — including download size, modem speed, and browser compatibility — so you can set standards for the team to work within. These standards must be in alignment with the expectations of the client. Chances are, however, these expectations may need adjusting. The client wants to

3.5 >

Aiming to satisfy both high and low is usually achieved by making concessions to each. www.lordoftherings.net loads a home page that contains some Flash, while offering a link to the HTML site. Users without high-bandwidth capability can choose to wait for the Flash site or easily access the HTML site. The desire to utilize Flash is compromised only slightly with this appeal-to-all setup.

<TIPS>

<CHAPTER 3>

Bring In Your Technical Expert Early

Whether a straightforward front-end or a technical behemoth, now is the time to bring in the technical experts. Involving key tech personnel early, especially as the project is being defined, will help troubleshoot — even eliminate — issues along the way.

offer streaming QuickTime movies to a modem-enabled audience? Not compatible. Keep in mind that your key client contact may not be the best person to answer these questions. Interviewing the client's technical team, if there is one, will probably yield better results. Depending on *your* expertise, you may want your tech lead to talk to your client's tech lead.

Determining Technical Needs

Use the Expanded Tech-Check worksheet (available for download from www.web-redesign.com) to determine what, if any, backend programming needs you have. When you have completed this simple worksheet, you will know whether you need to implement a separate workflow for backend development. Either way, front-end only or front-end and backend together, the completed Expanded Tech-Check worksheet is a good thing to have on hand as reference for your team.

Tech Spec

Creating a written specifications document that details and itemizes how a conceived site will function is a must-do for most large websites (a less comprehensive version will do for smaller sites). Most often called a Technical Specification, or a Tech Spec, this document requires input and sign-off from all project decision-makers — both team and client — and is a necessary step to ensure that everyone is using the same terminology and has an identical understanding of the site's plans. A Tech Spec should delineate all the technology planned for whatever functionality is dependent on a database or other complex transactions. This means that if your site has an existing backend structure or has one planned that needs to be incorporated into your front-end redesign, you should have a Tech Spec.

But because our methodology, the Core Process, focuses only on that which applies to all web redesign projects (and all websites need a front-end, whereas only some require a backend), we decided to keep advanced technical discussions to a minimum. We are merely mentioning it here because it is one of those points of interaction between the backend and front-end workflows. The Tech Spec is a document that both teams use as reference throughout the project. Because it is a technical blueprint of the site, the Tech Spec spells everything out — every last point of user interaction that requires anything more advanced than a hotlink — and whoever reads it can get a clear picture of the planned site.

<PHASE 1: DEFINING THE PROJECT>

THE EXPANDED TECH-CHECK

These questions will help determine larger-scale technology issues that may include high-level programming and backend development needs. This is used initially as a checkpoint at a very basic level to identify client expectations. When you are finished, email all compiled information back to the project manager on the web development team.

1. Please identify whether you currently use any of the following features on your site. Describe in as much detail as possible. (Check all that apply and describe briefly below.)

   ☐ Search engine
   ☐ Personalization (login/cookie set)
   ☐ Registration
   ☐ Security features
   ☐ Survey/voting tools
   ☐ Email newsletter distribution
   ☐ Other _____

   _____

   _____

2. List any other features that you hope to add to your site, now or in the future.

   _____

   _____

   _____

3. Are there or will there be any e-commerce transactions on the site (secure transactions, interface with inventory database, and fulfillment)?

   ☐ Yes (Please describe in detail below.)
   ☐ No

   _____

   _____

4. Is there or will there be login, registration, and/or personalization incorporated?

   ☐ Yes (Please describe in detail below.)
   ☐ No

   _____

   _____

5. Do you currently or will you in the future use a content management system (useful, for example, in the management of e-commerce inventory or text-publishing databases) to dynamically update and deploy content?

   ☐ Yes (Please describe in detail below.)
   ☐ No

   _____

   _____

   _____

6. Does the site need to integrate with any preexisting database system? If so, what kind of database is currently being used (FileMaker, Access, SQL Server)?

   _____

   _____

7. Will you be using any scripts or code that have already been established? Are they server-side or client-side (if known)?

   ☐ Yes (Please describe in detail below.)
   ☐ No

   _____

   _____

8. Please list names and contact information for the current tech lead and any third-party vendors/providers that we may need to talk with to gather additional details.

   _____

   _____

   _____

If you answered "yes" to any of the preceding Expanded Tech-Check questions, you will need to begin a separate workflow track of development, engineering, and execution.

LESLIE PHINNEY ON BRANDING AND THE DISCOVERY PROCESS

Brand continues to be the latest buzzword. From Nike to Intel, it seems like everyone is talking about the importance of branding. Far from a passing fad, the power of branding is something designers have recognized and helped shape for years.

At the most basic level, branding is the art/science of identification, of positioning exactly what differentiates a company's product or service. A brand encapsulates the key features of a product or service — its image, use, and price — in an easily recognized and interesting form. In short, it's the end user's entire experience.

Branding for the web incorporates the same basic principles, while adding to them an understanding of the particular needs and accessibility to a much wider audience base. Messages on the web move even faster than an advertising spot, but knowing the strengths of a brand and maximizing them through design and effective writing remain equally important no matter the media.

For a company redesigning its web presence, the most important branding issue is maintaining the equity that currently exists for the brand if it already has a strong personality, or enacting the necessary steps toward developing the brand with a strong focus on applications for the web.

It is important to keep in mind whom the target audience is, what kind of technology it is using, how much it is tuned in to the internet, and its online habits. Researching these criteria may be easier for an established brand that is going through a refresh process — but even so, a company with either a new or established brand cannot afford to assume anything without doing some homework. The marketing issues and strategies aren't a whole lot different than they were 10 years ago. It's just that consumers have more options now — and the time a product or service has to make an impact is getting shorter. The main issue, then, is really knowing your brand's personality, its benefits and differentiators — and then letting a great design team go to work.

Whether it's a design firm, an ad agency, or a public relations consultant, a creative service partner must get behind the brand and see it for its worth now and its potential later. Be very wary of any partner that churns out beautiful designs after one telephone conversation with your marketing department. It is imperative that you have a process, a way to extract information on your product or service and turn it into a reliable, innovative brand.

Leslie Phinney of Phinney/Bischoff Design House in Seattle (www.pbdh.com) *has been working with both Northwest and international clients to develop strategic marketing collateral, including brand development, for 20 years. When the internet really began to emerge about seven years ago, PBDH was one of the first Seattle firms to add an interactive design wing. The firm has been continually adding to its interactive capabilities and now designs and builds more than a dozen dynamic sites for clients each year.*

< PHASE 1: DEFINING THE PROJECT>

ANALYZING YOUR INDUSTRY

Some projects have the luxury of a contracted or in-house marketing team. These researchers run exhaustive market and audience research and in-depth competitive analyses. An analysis this extensive, however, is not usually an option for most projects in which budget is a real consideration. No matter the budget level, however, spend time looking at the competition and the industry. Look at the current, outgoing site's features and learn about the online features that competitors use — what is working? What isn't? All this will greatly help you learn about your audience. With this information, you will be better armed to re-create and redesign a successful website.

You can do a cursory analysis, but we highly recommend expanding Phase 1 by conducting a competitive analysis. See Chapter 9 for a detailed discussion of methodology for this process.

DISCOVERY SUMMARY

Discovery is an information-gathering process meant to dig deep into the details of what is important to a client's business, target audience, and industry. Scope and depth of research and inquiry will differ from project to project, but the results are the same: valuable data. The more information you gather, interpret, and comprehend, the more prepared you will be to execute a site on budget and on target.

Keep in mind that parts of the Discovery process (such as user profiling and competitive analysis), specifically those that may require additional budget allocation, may not be completed before moving into other aspects of defining the project. In fact, they might not even be done before the kick-off meeting.

To help you make certain you covered all the key points in the Discovery process, use the Discovery Check-Off List on the next page as a guide.

< C H A P T E R 3 >

DISCOVERY CHECK-OFF LIST

To help ensure that you have all the information you need to move forward, use this check-off list to make sure you touch on all aspects of the company, industry, and audience.

1. Company/Client

☐ Distribute the Client Survey to all key decision-makers and align expectations for primary goals, target audience(s), desired tone, and so on.

☐ Gather existing company information, marketing materials, studies, existing research, and printed materials and reports.

☐ Follow up with email or phone interviews and determine reasons for the change (current issues, possible solutions, and specific goals for redesign).

2. Industry

☐ Research the client's industry on- and offline. Use traditional research methods (the library, online searches, the phone book) as well as paid research methods (Jupiter Research, Gartner, and so on) if the budget allows.

☐ Research industry-specific publications, news-groups, subscribed materials, organizations, whitepapers, and so on.

3. Strategy/Marketing/Branding

☐ Gather information on current and planned marketing and advertising efforts (on- and offline advertising, placement, strategy).

☐ Understand marketing strategy and measurable goals, both short and long term. (An immediate goal might be to sign up new customers. A long-term goal might be to create a global brand recognized worldwide.)

☐ Understand branding strategy, desired perception, message/tone, and approach (current thinking and desired thinking).

4. Current Site

☐ Conduct usability testing and analysis of the current site. Determine what is working and what is not working with the site (navigation, content, functionality).

☐ Gather existing quantitative data. Using logs and marketing data, what types of purchasing habits and traffic patterns exist?

☐ Gather qualitative data. Using customer feedback and customer service data, what do customers like and dislike about the current site? What areas are successful and why?

☐ Gather technical/functionality specifications. Have a general understanding of how the current site functions and the specific technologies involved.

☐ Conduct a content audit. What is relevant and not relevant on the site? How effective is the current content to meeting the overall site goals?

5. Competition

☐ Identify primary and secondary competition, both on- and offline (from client and team research).

☐ Conduct a formal or informal competitive features analysis (see Chapter 9).

☐ Identify main features and differentiators for each site and/or company.

6. Audience

☐ Define the primary target audience(s) (from the client and Client Survey).

☐ Gather demographic information about the target audience(s) (occupation, gender, income, online and offline habits, connection speeds, browser and platform specifications).

☐ Create user profiles and user tasks (showing lifestyle, work and home environment, income range, occupation, internet usage, and typical tasks performed on the client site).

☐ Create user scenarios (specific situations for the target user to complete or engage in an online task or transaction).

7. Products/Services

☐ Identify and familiarize yourself with what the company offers in products or services.

☐ Understand buying habits — factors that enable the potential customer to become a paying or registered customer.

☐ Determine effectiveness of customer service. Is it helpful or not?

8. Other

☐ Use any additional areas specific to your client or industry that may give additional insight and information to your research.

DETERMINING OVERALL GOALS

"What is the goal of this redesign?" "Why are we re-designing?" "What will the redesigned site accomplish that the present site doesn't?" You *need* answers to these questions. Don't get sidetracked, though. You are not yet looking for the answer to "How are we going to redesign the site?" You'll figure that out when you build your project plan. For now, you are seeking to identify specific goals. Review the Client Survey. What did the client list as its goals? Were the goals specific? In conversation with the client, were any other goals mentioned? Pull these together and create a list of overall goals.

Here are some possible client goals:

- **To increase traffic**
- **To increase sales**
- **To highlight a new product**
- **To make a dynamic, content-driven site**
- **To decrease calls to customer service**
- **To create intuitive navigation**
- **To streamline browsing and purchasing**
- **To create a scalable structure for future growth**

What are goals, however, without a way to measure whether they have been reached? How will the client determine whether the site has met the stated goals upon launch? Take your list of goals and sort them into primary, secondary, and tertiary priorities. Identify ways in which you can determine whether these goals have been met post-launch (for example, a statistical increase in purchase process completion). To determine the site's success, suggest that the client identify both measurable goals and milestones, and do so both quantitatively and qualitatively. Redesigned sites should be able to compare statistics to the old site. Make a note of these measurable goals and revisit them in Phase 5: Launch and Beyond when maintenance is readdressed.

PREPARING A CREATIVE BRIEF

An effective way to make sure you understand what someone has said to you is to repeat it back to the person clearly and concisely. In addition to being the basis for understanding the overall tone, goals, and direction of a project, the creative brief restates the client's wishes by organizing the answers from the Client Survey. List the overall site goals in the creative brief. This will serve to align both the team and the client under the same terminology. With everyone talking the same language and working toward the same goals, the project has an excellent chance of staying on target.

Take thoughtful time when preparing the creative brief (**[3.6]** is a generic sample) because you and your team will be referring to it throughout the project, but don't sweat over it for weeks. It is a short and simple statement of site objectives, from overall

CLARIFICATION

> Determining Overall Goals

> Preparing a Creative Brief

< C H A P T E R 3 >

EntertainXYZ Website Redesign
Creative Brief

<date> <version>

Project Summary:

EntertainXYZ is an award-winning, on-air branding agency that provides innovative solutions for the film and television industry. Known only to a niche community in the local industry, EntertainXYZ is seeking a redefined online presence and identity to promote the company's unique approach and vision to a global audience. Additionally, EntertainXYZ would like to promote additional capabilities including print and interactive identity campaigns. The existing website is a brochure site with outdated content and an old client list. Immediate goals include advancing marketing and promotion of the company via the site at Promax, the industry's major showcase tradeshow. In addition, a significant goal is to re-create the site so that it is scalable and easy to update. Long term, the EntertainXYZ site will be a tool and a resource for clients and the company, with the eventual build out of a client communication area and a corporate intranet.

Target Audience:

EntertainXYZ's typical website visitor is a VP of marketing for a high-profile television studio. He is considered "old school" and has been in the industry for more than 20 years, starting from initial television production and set design. He has an interest in technology but rarely uses his computer for anything but email, a calendar, and contact information. He is on a shared studio T-1 network connection, and when online, he uses the Netscape 4.0 browser — the one that came with the computer and has not been updated. He is online rarely and usually only when directed to the web. He looks at competitive studio advertising, marketing, and promotional efforts and, when away from work, never goes online.

Perception/Tone/Guidelines:

1. Dynamic, experienced, contemporary, exciting, fun, communicative.
2. Elegant, semicorporate, high production value, high visibility.
3. Use current EntertainXYZ marketing and branding efforts in a new and different way.
4. Information should have a fresh and conversational tone.
5. Easy to navigate and find information.

Communication Strategy:

The website redesign will provide direct communication methods including film and television show profiles, featured articles, and company information. In the first phase of development, the site will feature an easy-to-update portfolio and client list with additional capabilities highlighted. In the next phase of development, a password-protected client area will be added for current projects and communication, as well as an internal company intranet that will be used to facilitate internal communication and company news.

Competitive Positioning:

EntertainXYZ has many competitors in the development community, mostly smaller shops with many partners who say they "do it all." Highlighting the quality of production and development projects, the high-level project and client list, and the overall attention to detail and breakthrough branding and positioning efforts will separate EntertainXYZ from its competition. Attention to overall marketing strategy will also help differentiate the website in the industry's eye.

Single-Minded Message: Innovative communication

_____   _____
Signature   Date

goals to targeted audience to user perception. It should identify — among other things — style, audience, and message. In addition, the creative brief sets the project's tone (how people should perceive the site and the company).

The creative brief should articulate visual and conceptual goals for the new site, both independent of and in comparison to the existing site. This document should be nonvisual — no sketches or layouts — and it should be short (only one to two pages) to ensure that it actually gets read. It can be as informal as an email or formal enough to be included in a bound report. No matter the form or format, it needs to be client approved. Get it signed.

Pull information you need from the answered Client Survey and from your various meetings thus far with the client. Use the Creative Brief Worksheet to help build the framework for your creative brief. Further questioning may be necessary.

< **3.6**

Sample Creative Brief.

The client's marketing department may have already developed a creative brief. Ask around. Be aware that a client-provided creative brief does not replace one created by the redesign team.

THE CREATIVE BRIEF WORKSHEET

Answering the questions on this worksheet will effectively build the skeleton for your creative brief. The information gathered in the Discovery process (Client Survey, research, interviews) will provide you with the answers.

Project Summary: State general project information, goals, and relevant background information for the site redesign. This paragraph should be a statement overview of the project as a whole.

1. What is the basic overview of the project? Briefly include background information if relevant.

2. What is the single purpose of the new site?

3. What are the secondary goals of the new site?

4. What are the long-term goals?

Audience Profile: Profile the target audience. Provide enough detail to enhance everyone's understanding of who the audience is. Include some user demographic information. Your goal with this section is to answer the following: Who is the target? What do these people care about? And what do they do online on a daily basis?

1. Who is your target audience? Choose a typical user and profile in detail. Include occupation, age range, gender, online frequency, online activities, and any other relevant information. Profile more than one if applicable.

2. What is a typical task the user might perform on the new site? (For example, register, log on, search for information, buy a specific product, send their email address, call for more information.)

Perception/Tone/Guidelines: How should your target audience to respond to your new online presence?

1. What does the target audience think and feel about the company and the current website?

2. What do we want them to think and feel?

3. How will this new website help achieve this goal?

4. What adjectives can be used to describe the way the website and the company should be perceived by the target audience?

5. What are some specific visual goals the site should convey?

Communication Strategy: How will we convince the target audience?

1. What is the overall message you are trying to convey to your target audience? (For example, cost-effective, secure, reliable, efficient.)

2. How will you convey the overall message? (For example, effective messaging through copy, directed path towards goal, specific offer on home page.)

3. Identify stages of development (if appropriate) used to execute goals.

4. How will you measure the success of the redesigned site?

Competitive Positioning: How you are different from your competition and the factors that will make you a success.

1. How is your company or your web presence different from your competition?

2. What specifically sets your compnay apart from your competition?

3. What areas of the current site are successful and why?

Targeted Message: State a single-minded word or phrase that will appropriately describe the site once it is launched.

<<< This worksheet is available for download at www.web-redesign.com >>>

CREATING A PROJECT PLAN

With all Discovery data collected and site goals defined, you can move confidently into the creation of a project plan. There are separate and distinct aspects of the project to plan, but when you have finished, you will have assembled several deliverable documents that help define the project and plot the course of action for the development of the site design. Compiled, these documents form your project plan. Larger companies put far more effort and resources into these documents (which can swell in size up to 100 or more pages), but we live in the real world. What we present here are the key items that make up the Core Process — the minimum amount of planning and organization necessary for a project's success.

Sometimes referred to as a "scope document" or a "project charter," the project plan should contain at least the following (each of which is described in detail elsewhere in this chapter and is listed here in suggested order):

- **Project overview**
- **Schedule (including deliverables and methodology)**
- **Budget breakdown**
- **Creative brief**
- **Target audience information**
  - **User profiles**
  - **Audience technical capabilities**
- **User testing plan**
- **Details and assumptions**
- **A line for a signature (VERY IMPORTANT)**

Proposal or Project Plan?

We're not offering marketing, sales, or business-development advice here. The Core Process assumes you have the project already. We hardly touch proposals and don't go into writing one at all (maybe next book). With that disclaimed…

What is the difference between a proposal and a project plan? Both are used to define the project, outline overall goals, and announce the plan of action. Both contain a budget and a schedule with deliverables clearly defined. But as far as the Core Process is concerned, the main difference is this: The proposal is a skeletal overview, or starting point, and is dealt with before you have a signed contract. The project plan goes much deeper into details and execution strategy. It comes after the signed contract.

< PHASE 1: DEFINING THE PROJECT >

The project plan protects both the team and the client. It spells everything out and forms a referential starting point for the project. By agreeing to the contents of the project plan, the client acknowledges that it understands what the team is preparing to undertake on its behalf.

The project plan is a deliverable. It can be submitted to the client, along with a legally binding contract and initial invoice. Once the project officially starts, any changes to this document will result in an additional charge (AC), so take care when listing needs and details. With a client signature on the project plan or proposal (whichever you create), the clock can be started.

Details and Assumptions

At the end of the plan, near where a signature is required (where the client is sure to be paying attention), include a list of Details and Assumptions [3.7]. The Details and Assumptions list is concise and confirms specific items that often are inadvertently subject to independent thinking (which is a flowery way of saying: "Stuff the client thinks it can

Make sure the client approves and signs off on the project plan. Nothing creates accountability more than a signature on paper.

3.7 >

Use this sample Details and Assumptions list as a guide. As these are only examples, you should modify as your project requires. Be as descriptive as possible. Note that although the Details and Assumptions list can be included in a contract (and therefore be part of a legally binding agreement), on its own, it does not substitute for a legal contract. It is for clarification and reference only.

Details and Assumptions

- This project includes concept development, design and layout, production, and programming for the <client/project> website.

- The structure and hierarchy of the site will be based on client-provided information, with feedback and direction from <web development firm> when creating site architecture.

- The client will provide all text content in electronic format on disk as well as a proofed hard copy. Video and audio material will be provided in digital format, ready for online use. Production and schedule are based on receiving all content by a targeted date specified elsewhere in writing. Late delivery will directly impact budget and schedule.

- Production of the site includes creation and optimization of all files/images and HTML coding for up to <___> pages. This site contains light scripting that only includes JavaScript rollovers. The site will be created to exist on a UNIX or NT server and will be compliant with Netscape 3.0+ and I.E. 3.0+ for both Mac and PC.

- This project is scheduled and estimated for a 10-week turnaround, starting <date>. Because development team resources are available in a predetermined window only, the project is not scheduled past <date>. Factors that increase or decrease the production schedule (for example, late content, additional features added) may incur additional charges as applicable.

- The estimated budget is based on existing information. Once criteria and direction of the site are finalized, additional costs may apply for custom application development and other programming needs.

<TIPS>   <CHAPTER 3>

When to Invoice?

Invoicing expectations should be established prior to the start of work. A normal payment schedule is 30% upon approval of the proposal or project plan, 30% upon approval of the visual look and feel, and the remainder upon delivery of the final site. Be clear that any additional charges will be clearly identified and approved at any point in the development process where they apply and that those charges will be added to the final invoice.

assume or randomly change, like the schedule."). Its main purpose is to protect the team, primarily against arguments concerning scope. It achieves this by clearly identifying the boundaries of the project in an easy-to-read-and-interpret list format. Perhaps these three items appear in your Details and Assumptions list:

- **This site will contain 20 to 25 pages.**

- **This project is scheduled to be completed in 11 weeks.**

- **All stock photography/illustration fees are the responsibility of the client and are not included in the budget. Obtaining any/all usage rights for stock work are the responsibility of the client.**

If midway through the project the client wants to add 15 pages but not pay for it, the client can't argue that it was 40 pages the team had agreed to create. Or if client disorganization causes the content to be three weeks late, resulting in a longer schedule or hours of overtime, the team has a point of reference

for increasing the budget. The more detail you provide, the more protected you are (this is especially important for web development firms).

SETTING THE BUDGET

Estimating web development projects can be especially challenging due to the myriad variables involved and the alarming propensity for "Scope Creep." It takes practice and experience to predict how long each phase and task will take. Underestimate and you end up not even covering your overhead. Yes, it is possible to invoice $50,000 and still lose money. Know this much to be true: Everything will take longer than you think, especially project management. Build cushions. Cover yourself.

The project's budget will define the actual scope of the project; the words "depending on budget" will dictate how much time and resources you can allocate to any individual task. Of all administrative tasks, this one naturally comes first because it defines the size, boundaries, and feasibility of a project.

Budget Reality #1: We Charge What We Can

Most companies charge what they can. While individual projects are dependent on the team's experience, client expectations, and current market conditions, all the following should also be considered: availability and resources, overhead and outside costs, technology and backend programming, timing and expectations, and documentation.

Budget Reality #2: It Comes Down to Hours

Estimating can be based on task, by team, or through guessing (not recommended). Whatever your methodology and regardless of budget presentation (whether fixed cost, projected range, or based entirely on time and materials used), when all formula is stripped away, it comes down to one thing: hours. As a result, tracking time is crucial for staying within budget.

<PHASE 1: DEFINING THE PROJECT>   <TIPS>

And keep in mind that a $25,000 budget handled wisely can yield a far more effective redesign than an $80,000 budget mishandled.

Understanding Scope Creep

Scope Creep is the slow, inevitable migration of a website from a straightforward, comprehensible project to an out-of-control nightmare. Seemingly insignificant modifications and unplanned extra time spent handholding and babysitting your client lead to budgetary increases and time delays. Little things add up. Scope Creep is subtle; you seldom realize it is happening. At your kick-off meeting, define Scope Creep to both client and team and explain how the various schedules and delivery plans all work together to keep the project on target.

Help avoid Scope Creep by having a very clear list of deliverables. Establish and state unequivocally in the Details and Assumptions list of the proposal or the project plan that client-initiated changes mean budget increases. It will help to refer to these written statements if the client suffers from selective memory loss.

Keep meticulous track of hours and all client-initiated changes. As soon as you see that you are going over budget, ask yourself and your team why. Does the client send seemingly casual emails, asking for little changes and minor additions? Does the client send 10 emails a day instead of streamlining into one concise communication? Worse, is the client emailing suggestions, instructions, and/or

requests to the production designer or visual designer, bypassing the project manager altogether? Are you receiving content, feedback, and sign-offs when these items are due and needed, or are you having to chase after them? All of this contributes to Scope Creep. A certain amount is expected, but it is the project manager's job to educate the client and clearly define what is within budget and what is out of scope. You can produce an amazingly successful redesign, but if you go way over budget and do not account for it, you're not going to feel great about losing money on the project no matter how many accolades it garners.

Avoid Scope Creep. Make it your mantra.

Estimating: What and How to Charge

Estimating projects is a developed skill. We can offer some suggestions that will help improve your forecasts, but it will mostly depend on your ability to properly estimate scope (how big is the project really?) and client management (how much time will it take to educate and control the client?). Start with the basics; determine your timeframe and resources and then do the math. How many hours will you allocate to each task? Who will make up your team? What deliverables will be due? Forecast realistic hours necessary to complete the goals. Be baldly honest: Can the project even be done before the launch date? Work backwards from launch. You may find that you need to increase resources and negotiate with the client for additional funds.

Fixed Bid Concerns

Many clients request a fixed bid. If you do submit a fixed price, it is the responsibility of the project manager and the team to keep the project scope under control. This means being firm about client-requested "small" changes and keeping track of time to ensure that the project stays within the budgeted hours or — on a more depressing note — at least being aware that you are working in the red or at a reduced rate.

Marking Up

Multiply your total by a percentage to allow for contingencies and overhead costs. A 10% to 20% markup is standard protective padding. A 50% to 100% markup is often applied to cover overhead such as rent, phones, administrative tasks, and sometimes the ugly necessity of legal fees.

< CHAPTER 3 >

PHASES OF DEVELOPMENT

PHASES OF DEVELOPMENT	low range 150 hr total		medium range 300 hr total			high range 800 hr total			

Phase 1: Defining the Project

Conduct the Discovery process. Define overall goals. Write the creative brief. Create a budget and schedules. List deliverables. Put together a team. Develop user profiles. Determine a user testing plan. Outline technical requirements. Build staging areas. Kick off the project.

- low range: project manager 50 hrs
- medium range: project manager 100 hrs; usability test 20 hrs
- high range: project manager 200 hrs; info design 100 hrs; strat/brand/analysis 60 hrs; usability test 60 hrs

Phase 2: Developing Site Structure

Develop site structure, navigation, and page flow. Begin information design and wireframing. Begin content acquisition.

- low range: info design 10 hrs; usability test 5 hrs
- medium range: info design 30 hrs
- high range: design 180 hrs

Phase 3: Visual Design and Testing

Develop visual design, combining conceptual direction, tone and functionality, and look and feel. Identify branding, copy flow, and incorporation of content. Create an HTML Protosite and test for usability.

- low range: design 40 hrs
- medium range: design 60 hrs

Phase 4: Production and QA

Graphic optimization, HTML production, and light scripting completed. Test for usability. Run QA testing and debug the site. Freeze content.

- low range: art & HTML prod 40 hrs; QA 5 hrs
- medium range: art & HTML prod 60 hrs; QA 20 hrs; progr/javascr 10 hrs
- high range: art & HTML prod 100 hrs; progr/javascr 40 hrs; QA 60 hrs

Phase 5: Launch and Beyond

Debugged site is ready for launch. Address maintenance and marketing. Have a celebration. Have a post-mortem meeting.

< 3.8 >

A typical breakdown of hours for three sizes of projects. This is only an example; each project will differ based on size, scope, expectations, and deliverables.

<PHASE 1: DEFINING THE PROJECT>

See the chart provided [3.8] illustrating a typical allocation of hours for three different sizes of projects, each running on the five-phased Core Process. Take notice of how much of the total resources project management takes. With this conceptual, phase view of your project understood, you can then break it into weeks on a spreadsheet [3.9].

3.9 >

This budgeting time tracker is a straightforward Microsoft Excel spreadsheet that takes each role and sets up an hourly charge, estimated hours, and a weekly tally. This spreadsheet can also be used for weekly time tracking against budget projections. This example shows a typical eight-week breakdown with a small team in place. (A blank form is available for download at www.web-redesign.com.)

team member/role	rate	wk 1	wk 2	wk 3	wk 4	wk 5	wk 6	wk 7	wk 8	wk 9	wk 10	wk 11	wk 12	total hrs	total $
project management	$50.00	40	40	40	40	40	40	40	40					320	$16,000.00
art direction	$50.00	12	12	40	40	40	20	20	20					204	$10,200.00
information design	$50.00	12	40	40	20									112	$5,600.00
														0	$0.00
art production	$35.00	2		20	20	40	40	40	40					202	$7,070.00
														0	$0.00
														0	$0.00
														0	$0.00
														0	$0.00
														0	$0.00
														0	$0.00
														0	$0.00
														0	$0.00
														0	$0.00
[hours]		66	92	140	120	120	100	100	100	0	0	0	0	[total]	$38,870.00

Documentation

Here's a good rule of thumb: If the client signed it, save it. Email approvals are a good start, but follow up with a hard copy to protect yourself — get a physical signature via fax whenever possible. For every project, create a project folder (or a physical binder) to house all signed documentation: contracts, briefs, the initial proposal and subsequent revisions, approved sitemap, visual design directions, and so on.

You don't have to three-hole punch and save every email, but you should print all emails relating to budget, scope, sign-off, and especially requests for changes, and have them at your fingertips. Save everything electronically as well. Avoid messy files and lost documents; start organized and stay that way.

All the forms, briefs, and schedules are key to both keeping the project streamlined and maintaining your credibility. Most documents can be as abbreviated as an email or as formal as a written, multipage report complete with 8×10 color glossy pictures with circles and arrows and a paragraph on the back of each one. The importance of each piece of documentation lies in clarity of communication, not necessarily in the extravagance of delivery. However, sometimes more documentation *is* smart, especially if you have a capricious client or an inconsistent team.

< CHAPTER 3 >

Often, with an experienced and set team in place, it is most effective to estimate by team member. (For example, "Kate usually needs about 40 hours for information design on a site of this size and complexity.") This method might apply better to a web development firm.

Sometimes it is easier to break a project down by task rather than by the time needed for each role. (For example, "This project will probably take between 30 and 40 hours for information design.") Whether estimating by team or by task, use whichever method helps the client understand the total cost.

Blank estimating forms are available for download at www.web-redesign.com >>>

ESTIMATING METHODS

Estimate by Team

Who is on your team and how much time will they be spending on the project? Take each role (remember, some team members wear multiple hats), determine an hourly rate, and multiply by the hours or days that each role requires [3.10].

Add a 10% to 50% markup to allow for contingencies and overhead. In the end, provide your client a range of pricing based on your totals.

Team Member	$ Rate	Est. Hours	Days	Subtotal	X % overhead	TOTAL
Project Manager	$50	200	25 days	$10,000		
Art Director	$50	20	2.5 days	$1,000		
Designer	$40	40	5 days	$1,600		
Usability Specialist	$50	30	5 days	$1,500		
Production Designer	$40	40	5 days	$1,600		
Programmer	$60	10	1.25 days	$ 600		
Copywriter	$35	40	5 days	$1,400		
QA Lead	$25	12	1.5 days	$ 300		
				$18,000	50%	$27,000.00

< 3.10 >

Estimate by Team.

Estimate by Task

Break the project into appropriate tasks and give time estimates to each task in terms of days and weeks. Apply rates depending on the type of task: creative, production, programming, admin/management [3.11].

Add a 10% to 50% markup to allow for contingencies and overhead. In the end, provide your client a range of pricing based on your totals.

Task	Est. Hours	$ Per Hr	Days	Subtotal	X % overhead	TOTAL
Project Definition	40	$50	5 days	$2,000		
Information Design	40	$50	5 days	$2,000		
Visual Design	60	$50	7.5 days	$3,000		
Flash Animation	20	$50	2.5 days	$1,000		
Production	80	$40	10 days	$3,200		
Programming	10	$60	1.25 days	$ 600		
Usability Testing	30	$50	5 days	$1,500		
Competitive Analysis	20	$50	2.5 days	$ 1,000		
Copywriting	60	$50	7.5 days	$ 3,000		
QA/Testing	15	$40	1.5 days	$ 600		
				$17,900	50%	$26,850.00

< 3.11 >

Estimate by Task.

Rates shown here are generic and are representative neither of varying levels of expertise nor of all markets.

< P H A S E 1 : D E F I N I N G T H E P R O J E C T >

Tracking Time

If you take away only one thing from this book, let it be this: TRACK YOUR HOURS. (We hope you get more out of the book than that, though.) In general, organizations that track their hours, and therefore always know where their budget stands and how it is being utilized, are profitable. Those that don't track their hours either aren't profitable or are lucky. It's as simple as that.

Establish the method by which you and your team are going to track hours... and then actually, truly, diligently track those hours. It is the only way to know whether you are making $5/hr or $50/hr. Time tracking is critical for both design firms and in-house departments, though it is more important for many design firms because they bill hourly.

Make sure your team submits accurate hours on a weekly basis (this keeps them accountable) and keep a running check of total team hours used against your budget and allocation of hours [3.12]. Staying on top of project time spent is crucial to maintaining budget and scope requirements. Any time used that was not budgeted for either is eaten by the web development company or, if authorized, scoped, and tracked properly, is billed to the client as an additional charge. The time to tell your client that you are going over budget — especially if it is due to Scope Creep — is as early as possible.

Use whatever tracking system works. Here is a suggestion: Timeslice [3.13] allows you to log time both in big chunks and in little, just-answering-

3.12 >

Each week, generate a short report for hours budgeted, hours used, and hours left. Track hours weekly to maintain scope and time estimates. Be accountable. This report means nothing if people are not forthcoming with how over, on, or under budget they really are.

3/24/00	Time Budgeted	Time Used	Time left	Comments
Design	248	207.5	**43.5**	
Production	325	18.5	**306.5**	
Admin	128	36.5	**91.5**	

3.13 >

Timeslice (www.asdsoft.com) allows for time tracking at a click, and makes sorting easy.

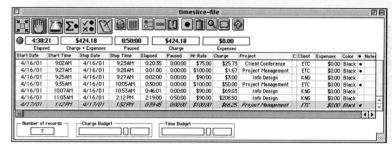

email increments (not accounting for answering email is notorious for driving Scope Creep), and it can sort multiple clients, projects, and tasks. Paper-based timesheets are good, too, but they're not very accurate if you have several clients and/or several tasks. Whichever method you choose, be diligent. Your project depends on it.

<CHAPTER 3>

Additional Charge (AC) Form
(Change Order or Track Changes Document)

Project Title:
Project ID:
Date:

Client Name:
Client Email:
Client Phone:

[company]
contact:

This item is a: 1. Client-requested change
2. Additional item request
3. Outside original budget/scope
4. Other _____

Description of change or addition:

Description of Services	Estimated Hours	Cost
		$
		$
		$
	Total	$

I am in agreement with the additional charge, description, timeline, and details outlined above. Please sign the document below and fax back to [xxx-xxx-xxxx].

_____   _____
Client Signature   Date

_____
Client Name (printed)

< 3.14

Use this sample Additional Charge (AC) Form as a basis for your own.

Client-Initiated Changes

Scope Creep is subtle. Blatant requests for project changes are not. If the client asks for an additional feature or section that is not within the original definition of the project, smile and respond confidently, "No problem, I'll get back to you with a separate schedule and budget by the end of the day." You'll be surprised at how effective this approach is at controlling Scope Creep. Clients will react by retracting the request or agreeing to the scope change.

An Additional Charge (AC) Form is a handy way to document increases in scope [3.14]. Even if you decide to not charge for a change, you can still issue an AC, mark the change as "gratis," and have a record of the change. ACs work as amendments to the approved budget.

The form seen here is available for
<<< download at www.web-redesign.com

<PHASE 1: DEFINING THE PROJECT>   <TIPS>

CREATING SCHEDULES

Projects need a schedule, and people respond to deadlines. Whether in a check-off list, calendar view, text in an email, or a weekly breakdown, there are many different ways to communicate timeline and sequence. In addition, a project schedule should emphasize immediacy of needs. Distribution of a schedule is the proverbial lighting of a fire under everybody's seat. It is a wake-up call with an obvious message: "We are starting now. Here is what is due and when." Strive for clear communication.

We recommend approaching the scheduling task in two ways. First create an overview schedule that shows methodology chronologically, and then build a detailed date-by-date format that itemizes deliverables and approval reviews according to due dates. One follows and evolves out of the other; each communicates the message from a different perspective. Get both schedules approved by the client. Leave nothing up to interpretation.

> Missed deadlines have a domino effect. Many clients do not understand that when they are late with feedback, it retards the flow of the schedule and therefore the final delivery date. Some client education may be necessary and, if done in a goal-oriented manner, will probably be appreciated.

No one should ever have to dig for a deadline. This information should always be available, front and center, and perhaps even emailed or posted to the staging area as a weekly reminder. Schedules should communicate a sense of urgency and should keep both your team and your client on track.

Overview Schedule

The overview schedule is just that, an overview. Easily referenced and descriptive, it's an excellent forum to present a big picture view — the whole project, complete with methodology and breakdown of major milestones and deliverables. This schedule, which can be quickly built, is appropriate both for the proposal stage and kick-off meeting and throughout the project as a point of reference.

Begin by separating the project into weeks or months as well as into phases and steps. We suggest using the core phases put forth in this book. See [3.15] for a generic example.

See [3.15] for a generic example.

Show Methodology

When you build the overview schedule, include methodology steps (that is, these five phases) alongside due dates. Doing so provides an excellent visual overview of the process as a whole as it relates to the project's timeline.

< CHAPTER 3 >

Date	Deliverables/Notes	Deliverables
Weeks 1 to 2 07/30 to 08/10	**Define:** Overall budget and schedule approved. Technical needs addressed and clarified. Scope of project and deliverables defined. Project plan created and approved. User testing and maintenance needs addressed and clarified. Creative brief composed (based on client survey) outlining vision and perception. Conduct competitive analysis; begin initial audience profiling. Client signs off on all materials.	CLIENT SURVEY(S): DISTRIBUTE TO CLIENT PROJECT PLAN *30% payment due to begin work CREATIVE BRIEF COMPETITIVE ANALYSIS
Weeks 3 to 4 08/13 to 08/24	**Structure:** Site structure defined; navigation and page flow developed. Sitemap completed and approved by client. User profiles created and user tasks defined. Create content-delivery plan. Content acquisition and editing/writing started. Wireframing of primary and secondary pages begins. Establish navigation, page flow, content organization, and layout and user paths. Conduct paper prototype testing.	SITEMAP USER PROFILES CONTENT DELIVERY PLAN WIREFRAMES USER PATHS
Weeks 5 to 6 08/27 to 09/07	**Design | Protosite:** Present first round of page design/layout. Design of "look and feel" approved; begin art production. User interface (UI) design begins. Necessary materials are digitized for online use. HTML protosite (nondesign oriented) developed following approved page flow and UI design. Content is collected, modified, and finalized. Production of design template begins.	ROUND 1 CREATIVE: PRESENTED ONLINE FOR REVIEW PROTOSITE: INFORMAL USABILITY TESTING *30% payment upon approval of creative
Weeks 7 to 9 09/10 to 09/28	**Production:** Production begins using protosite as outline and structure. HTML production and programming begins, incorporating content and design. Continue production, testing, and build out of site. Confirm all specified browser and platform compatibility. Begin internal QA. Beta version of site is "live" for client sign-off and internal testing and QA begins. Site moved to end server for testing/QA/cross-platform testing.	BETA SITE: PRESENTED ONLINE: MTG 09/24
Week 10 10/01 to 10/05	**Launch:** Public launch. Announcement. Postlaunch: hand off assets and templates, set up maintenance training, and conduct postmortem meeting.	FINAL SITE: PRESENTED ONLINE: MTG 10/02 *Final balance due

< **3.15**

A sample 10-week overview schedule shows methodology and a summary of tasks and deliverables. (This example is in a simple table format created in Microsoft Word. Use whatever format best communicates to your client and your team).

Detailed Schedule with Deliverables

Action items — deliverables being submitted or milestones that need to be met — push both team members and the client forward. A detailed schedule with deliverables becomes a concise day-by-day list of action items. It communicates pacing to everyone involved, and pacing is critical to keeping the project on track.

The detailed schedule with deliverables grows out of the overview schedule. Keep your overview for reference (and, of course, update it if suddenly the scope balloons from 8 weeks to 13), but itemize and delineate on the detailed schedule [3.16]. Keep schedules current as the project moves forward and changes, and make sure schedules are easily accessible in your staging area. Communication is the key to avoiding schedule lags.

For smaller projects, the schedule overview and the detailed schedule with deliverables can be combined, or the overview can be used alongside a detailed task list.

< P H A S E   1 :   D E F I N I N G   T H E   P R O J E C T >

Date	Deliverables/Detailed Summary	Notes
Week 1	**Define	Discovery**	
Mon 07/30	CLIENT SURVEY(S): ANSWERS DUE BACK FROM CLIENT	*Client Survey submitted to client 07/14
Thurs 08/02	PROJECT PLAN: OVERVIEW BUDGET/SCHEDULE/ DELIVERABLES DEFINED AND SUBMITTED TO CLIENT FOR REVIEW	*30% payment due to begin work
Fri 08/03	**Creative brief: Submit to client for approval.** USER TESTING PLAN: SUBMIT TO CLIENT FOR APPROVAL. FEEDBACK DUE EOD; SIGNOFF DUE ASAP. COMPETITIVE ANALYSIS: FINALIZE COMPETITIVE SET, DETERMINE APPROACH, USABILITY PLAN, AND TEAM	*Begin informal usability testing on site; begin informal competitive analysis
Week 2	**Define	Discovery** (continued)	
Tues 08/07	KICK-OFF MEETING: ALL TEAM MEMBERS PRESENT, REVIEW PROJECT PLAN, CREATIVE BRIEF, USER TESTING PLAN, AND OVERALL SCHEDULE	*Weekly status meeting: need client to review all materials
Fri 08/10	COMPETITIVE ANALYSIS: INFORMAL REPORT DUE INTERNALLY (REPORT USED TO INFORM DESIGN TEAM, NOT A FORMAL DELIVERABLE)	
Week 3	**Structure	Content**	
Tues 08/14	SITEMAP: SITE STRUCTURE AND ORGANIZATION PRESENTED CONTENT DELIVERY PLAN: ALL CONTENT/ASSETS LISTED	*Weekly status meeting (present sitemap and content)
Thurs 08/16	SITEMAP: CLIENT APPROVAL/MODIFICATIONS DUE EOD	
Fri 08/17	USER PROFILES: TARGET AUDIENCE DEFINED	
Week 4	**Structure	Content** (continued)	
Tues 08/21	WIREFRAMES (ROUND 1)	*Weekly status meeting (present wireframes)
Thurs 08/23	USER PATHS	
Fri 08/24	WIREFRAMES (ROUND 2)	

Date	Deliverables/Detailed Summary	Notes
Week 5	**Design	Protosite**	
Tues 08/28	ROUND 1 CREATIVE: PRESENTED ONLINE FOR REVIEW	*Weekly status meeting (present creative)
Wed 08/29	ROUND 1 CREATIVE: CLIENT FEEDBACK DUE EOD	
Thurs 08/30		
Fri 08/31	ROUND 2 CREATIVE: PRESENTED EOD (CLIENT TO REVIEW ON MONDAY, CAN WORK OVER WEEKEND IF NECESSARY)	*Weekend work if necessary
Week 6	**Design	Protosite** (continued)	
Tues 09/04		*Weekly status meeting
Thurs 09/06	DESIGN TEMPLATES: HOME PAGE TO PRODUCTION FOR BUILD-OUT AND TESTING/OPTIMIZATION	
Fri 08/07	PROTOSITE: INFORMAL USABILITY TESTING	
Week 7 09/10 to 09/14	**Production**	*30% payment upon approval of creative
Week 8 09/17 to 09/21	Continue production, testing, and build-out of site. Confirm all specified browser and platform compatibility. Begin internal QA.	
Week 9 09/24 to 09/28	**QA** Beta version of site is "live" for client sign-off and internal testing and QA begins. Site moved to end server for testing/Quality Assurance/Cross-platform testing.	BETA SITE: PRESENTED ONLINE: MTG 09/24
Week 10 10/01 to 10/05	**Launch	Public Launch** Announcement Post-launch: Hand off assets and templates, set up maintenance training, and conduct post mortem meeting.	FINAL SITE: PRESENTED ONLINE: MTG 10/02 *Final balance due

3.16 >

A detailed 10-week schedule with deliverables breaks the project down into weeks and days. (Set up in table format using Microsoft Word, specific deadlines and deliverables are clearly identified.)

<TIPS>   <CHAPTER 3>

Use Different Styles

The visual methods shown in this section are merely suggestions. People respond to different types of stimuli, and therefore different formats may benefit your projects. Some prefer a listing of key dates, and some prefer an overview schedule showing each day in calendar style [3.17]. Use whatever style is necessary to communicate to your client and to your team.

3.17 >

Macromedia Dreamweaver has a fabulous calendar extension that will help you build a detailed, day-by-day schedule. Bonus: It will already be in HTML, so it can easily be brought into your staging area. To obtain the extension, point your browser to http://exchange.macromedia.com and search for "calendar."

ASSIGNING YOUR PROJECT TEAM

You've heard the adage: You're only as good as your weakest link. With a web development team, the same holds true. To minimize potential breakdowns in your well-crafted and streamlined plan, look for people with proven track records, even if it takes additional funds to hire more experienced people. If you have newbies involved, balance them with expertise. Then, by clearly establishing individual roles and responsibilities — for both client and team — you can safeguard against tasks falling through the cracks.

On the client side, establish one contact who has final sign-off on behalf of all client decision-makers. Here's the situation: You send the client a deliverable to be approved, and it sits for three days while four people try to find the time to look at it. This happens all the time. Trust us, you will not want to redesign for an unorganized committee. If there is more than one client-side decision-maker, they must submit a single decision. If client structure or circumstances force you, the project manager, to get several approvals for each step, build more time into your schedule for it. Multiple sign-offs always mean delays.

With regard to the project team, remember that a single person can fill more than one role (for example, Mike will be acting as both visual designer and information designer), so think in terms of roles

<PHASE 1: DEFINING THE PROJECT> <EXPERT TOPIC>

JIM HEID ON ROLES AND SPECIALIZATION

As a medium, the web has become complex enough that specialization is really a necessity. It's getting harder and harder to be a generalist. Maybe you're an information architecture specialist, or a Dynamic HTML or JavaScript guru, or a Flash maven, or a streaming media specialist. The various technologies that go into a modern website are constantly evolving, and it's hard enough to just keep up with one area.

I think today's web professional needs to have a basic familiarity with the whole enchilada in order to be able to deal with clients and various specialists in each area. But you should also have one area that you focus on. My experience mirrors this: I know enough about the whole web design world to find the *real* experts in each area, and at the same time, I concentrate on keeping abreast of my particular specialty, streaming media.

It's important to know something about everything and a lot about one thing. If you work as part of a large team, having a broad knowledge will enable you to communicate with specialists on your team. If you're part of a smaller team — say, two to four people — I think it's important for each member of the team to develop a specialty that, in one way or another, enriches the capabilities of the entire team. But each specialist also needs to be enough of a generalist to be able to communicate with his or her colleagues.

Like many people in this business, Jim Heid wears a lot of hats. In addition to being a well-respected technology journalist, Jim is conference chair for several of Thunder Lizard Productions' events, including the Web Design series and Macromedia Web World. His third hat — "I've got hats like Imelda's got shoes!" — is streaming media consultant. He is located at www.jimheid.com *and is based out of Albion, California (pop. 398).*

< CHAPTER 3 >

(visual designer and information designer), not necessarily individuals (Mike). And due in part to the increasing numbers of people using WYSIWYG editing software and other HTML-easy programs, this "wearing of many hats" is happening more and more (see the Expert Topic by Jim Heid). Maybe the art director is also leading the HTML site production. Sometimes the project manager is also the usability lead. Be realistic. If you are acting as project manager and art director, chances are you will not have time to also be the information designer and the copywriter unless you stretch out your schedule to accommodate. Hire or delegate as necessary.

This chart shows a description of the *roles* of a project, not necessarily all the *people* that must be involved.

PROJECT ROLES

Project Manager

Also called site producer or account manager, the project manager organizes a web project from start to finish and is the primary contact for the client as well as the central point of communication for the team. Project managers are responsible for determining and defining the site's actual needs and for educating the client as to how much technology and development time is required to meet the stated goals within the specified budget and/or timeframe.

The project manager keeps the project on track, troubleshoots, and communicates with all team members and the client in every phase of the Core Process. Project management is the glue that holds it all together.

Information Designer

With an eye for design, structure, *and* usability, the information designer translates content and business goals into functional and visual schematics. This person develops the site map and structures the way content navigation is laid out on a page — all of this in a non-design-oriented manner. The information designer defines site navigation, functionality, and user interaction.

Information design is sometimes a shared role with either visual design or production. (For more information on information design, see Phase 2: Developing Site Structure.)

QA Lead

Sometimes known as the Exterminator, the quality assurance (QA) lead checks for bugs starting right after production, and in some cases, testing after launch. Responsibilities include building a test plan and checking browser compliance, HTML, and content placement. (For more information on QA testing, see Phase 4: Production and QA.)

Usability Lead

The usability lead gathers firsthand information about how users actually use a site and analyzes what works and what doesn't. The usability lead works with the information designer on navigation and user paths and then tests the redesigned site for usability issues at the HTML Protosite phase, alongside QA, and at launch. (For more information on usability testing, see Chapter 8.)

PROJECT ROLES

Production Lead/Production Designer

The production lead heads a team of HTML production designers to facilitate HTML production and testing, while keeping an
eye on scope and schedule at all times.

On smaller projects, the production lead often is also the
HTML production designer. The individual fulfilling this role
should be fluid in HTML and art optimization standards, including use of tables, frames, and cross-browser issues. The
production designer can also be expected to have a fluid
understanding of ASP, Perl, Java, CGI scripting, and so on.
Responsibilities include building the HTML Protosite and implementing final HTML layouts, as well as combining design
specifics and art integration into the site. (For more information on production, see Phase 4.)

Art Director/Visual Designer

The art director/visual designer creates stunning, effective
graphics while working within the limitations of the capabilities of the target audience. A fluency in industry-standard programs (Fireworks, Flash, Dreamweaver, Photoshop, GoLive)
should be a given. As with any other team position, the art
director/visual designer should know how to follow a schedule, must check in regularly with the project manager, and
should be adept in the art of client communication.

If there are several visual designers, the art director is responsible for leading the others in shaping the creative vision. (For
more information on visual design, see Phase 3: Visual Design
and Testing.)

Copywriter/Content Manager

One of the most important (and often overlooked) roles in effective web development is that of copywriter. The copywriter
should have experience with web-specific needs, including
style and tone.

In some situations, the copywriter is also the content manager
— in charge of tracking all assets (that is, photos, media,
copy) and ensuring that they are delivered to production in
accord with the content delivery plan. For content-heavy sites,
it is not uncommon for there to be several copywriters and a
full-time content manager.

We suggest that the copywriter(s) and the content manager
be hired by, and work directly for, the client, with their output
being defined as a deliverable. (For more information on content, see Phase 2.)

Programmer/Backend Engineer

Depending on the technical needs of the project, varying
levels of technical expertise are necessary to make a site
work. From basic JavaScript to more complex programming —
CGI, ASP, Java, ATG, and Perl — a careful analysis of the project from the onset is important in determining your backend
needs. The backend engineer runs a parallel workflow behind
the front-end site development.

This individual can also act as point person or liaison between
backend and front-end, especially critical during production.
Please remember that backend workflow is separate from this
Core Process.

< CHAPTER 3 >

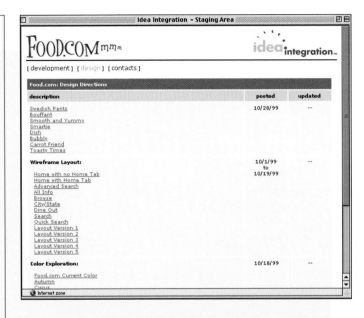

The food.com staging area shows one way to set up a client staging site. Three primary sections divide the posted deliverables into contacts, design, and development.

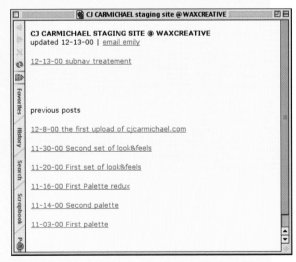

The cjcarmichael.com staging site is even simpler. It is a much smaller project with a much smaller team, so a single page of links suffices.

SETTING UP STAGING AREAS

The staging area acts as a hub of communication. Divide it into two sections: a client staging site and a team development area. Although email is very effective for transmission of information, for work in progress, and as a point of administrative reference (email links, schedules, and so on), create these staging areas.

Reserve a spot on your own server for the project's staging area. Password protect it if you can, but if you don't have that option, at least make sure the staging URL is hidden from random visitors. Once the staging URL is set up, document and distribute it to both team and client. The kick-off meeting is a great opportunity to do this.

The team development area serves as a place for the team to work. It is not for client viewing. It becomes very handy for projects with team members working remotely and needing FTP access and is ideal for developing an HTML alpha site. Once work is ready to show the client — visual design directions, the Protosite, and the beta site — it is moved to the client staging area for client access.

Every company has its own way of staging work. Whether you call it a "client site" or a "project site," a staging area should be kept simple, easy to maintain, and current. Everyone on your team should understand the setup of the file directory and how updates are listed. Consistency and organization will reflect your professionalism.

< P H A S E   1 :   D E F I N I N G   T H E   P R O J E C T >   < T I P S >

We recommend easy navigation for the client staging area ([3.18] and [3.19]). Keep it all text; images are unnecessary. From your main page, provide links to three areas: design, HTML, and admin (schedules, creative brief, contacts). On every page within the staging site, this navigation should appear along with a link to the staging home and to a contact page where email addresses are hotlinked. Make sure to put items up in chronological order and date everything. When various phases are completed, archive large sections into a separate area. Someone will invariably want to look at a previous version.

Once you set up the staging area, make sure the client bookmarks it and is reminded via email when the site is updated.

PLANNING FOR USER TESTING

One of the leading reasons for redesigning a site is the need to make it more usable. Sites *must* cater to the user. If your customers can't use your site, they won't come back. Bottom line: If your site isn't usable, your redesign will fail.

In this book, we mention usability testing frequently, always touting it as a truly effective method by which to test your site. But there are also other valid methods of gathering feedback and information (see the chart on the following page). Throughout the development process, learning about your audience — and making sure that your navigation, information design, and visual designs are working as you intended — can only raise the chances of the site being a success.

Developing a User Testing Plan

Decide here, while still building your project plan, how and where within the workflow you want to test your redesign project against your user. You may want to conduct usability testing upfront on the existing site to see what specifically is in need of fixing. Perhaps you want to use an online survey to gather audience information to aid in the Discovery process. Maybe you want to conduct focus group testing as early as the structuring phase to gather outside opinions. The following overview descriptions of different testing will help you decide on methodology. Once reviewed, decide where you want to integrate it into your workflow and then communicate that on your schedules.

What Are Online Surveys?

Email and online surveys are a valuable way to gather feedback from large groups to reach statistically significant conclusions. This type of information gathering is best for general questions with yes/no answers and should not be used to amass feedback on specifics. Online surveying is one method for finding out about your audience's online habits, tastes, and needs as well as, perhaps most importantly, what about the current site does the respondent feel needs redesigning.

Surveys can be frustrating in that the response rate is generally low. On a mass emailing to a targeted group of users, you may only get a 10% to 15% return. However, if you send out 500 surveys, even 50 responses are a lot with which to work.

What Is Focus Group Testing?

Focus group testing is used to gather opinions from and get into discussions with a representative cross-section of your audience. An advantage of focus groups is that you can test early in the process. Visual look and feel, content organization and presentation, and navigation — all these (and more) can be tested in focus group settings. Focus group testing seeks general and objective opinions. You may ask: "What do you think about this content organization?" or "What about this navigation? Is it logical?" or "What do you think about this advertising placement?" You may present several initial design directions and inquire which is preferred and why. Opinions from an objective group give great insight as to whether you are on target with your assumptions. But remember, they are still only opinions.

What Is Usability Testing?

Usability is literally the "ease of use" or understanding it takes to make something work. Website usability is the understanding of how an individual user navigates, finds information, and interacts with a website. Unlike online surveys or focus groups, usability testing is a one-on-one process in a watch-and-learn approach — one person (the tester) observing another person (the user) as he or she actually uses the site and complete tasks. Usability is goal-oriented; the user should have a series of specific tasks to perform when using the site, but not step-by-step instructions. Leading your user will skew your results.

Usability testing shows what users actually do, not what they think they might do. This is invaluable. If testing is done during the actual development process, results can be incorporated, direction shifted, and major problems avoided. We go into far more detail on usability testing in Chapter 8.

METHODS OF GATHERING USER FEEDBACK AND INFORMATION		
Online/Email Surveys	**Focus Groups**	**Usability Testing**
50 to 1,000 participants, representative of target audience. No direct interaction. Statistically significant feedback.	8 to 20 participants. Valuable initial feedback and opinions. Facilitator-to-group interaction.	4 to 8 participants. Task/action oriented. Actual results based on observation, one-on-one interaction.
What they are generally thinking.	**What they think they might do.**	**What users actually do.**

< P H A S E   1 :   D E F I N I N G   T H E   P R O J E C T >

KICKING OFF THE PROJECT

Have a kick-off meeting. Consider it the opening ceremonies of your redesign project. You have been doing a lot of legwork and have gathered the athletes (your team) and the sponsors (your clients). Now bring everyone face to face into one stadium (a conference room will do) to announce the guidelines and rules (site goals) to everybody involved. You have just done a great deal of advance planning. A kick-off meeting is a wonderful opportunity to open up the project to include everybody — both client and team key decision-makers — and officially start.

Be ready for this meeting; bring the project plan (which includes at least the following: project overview, both schedules, the creative brief, user profiles, audience technical capabilities, a team roster, and the user testing plan), and have a meeting agenda. In fact, have agendas for all meetings, whether you stick to them or not. Include these points into your kick-off meeting agenda, and modify it to fit your project.

- **Introduction of the project plan.** Introduce the project, client, and team; show Discovery items; go over Details and Assumptions; make sure everybody understands the project scope; distribute contact lists to both sides; go over roles and responsibilities of both the client and team; establish means of communication.

- **Overall site goals.** Distribute the creative brief and go over it in detail.

- **Content.** Who will provide content? How will the content schedule be worked out?

- **Schedule and timing.** Discuss the project calendar; make clear the relational importance of feedback and content delivery to the final launch date; establish and adjust the project calendar according to individual schedule conflicts; discuss Scope Creep issues.

- **Next steps.** Briefly describe what happens next and who will be in contact with whom, specifically for the immediate next steps: organizing the content and structuring the site.

The kick-off meeting is where expectations are aligned and scope is established. Fill everybody in on the boundaries of scope. State that the next steps for the client include determining content, while the team will begin to structure the site.

< C H A P T E R   3 >

PHASE 1 SUMMARY

The kick-off meeting signifies the end of the first phase of our Core Process. Your project has been organized, approved, scheduled, budgeted, staffed, and kicked-off. Defining the scope of a redesign project, as we have shown in this chapter, involves a great deal of legwork and a huge amount of planning. After reading through this, the longest chapter in this book, you may be questioning the effort. Why spend the time? Why poll the client so extensively? Why not simply take the information the client provides to the team and work with that?

Data. The more data you have at the outset, the better you will set the stage for your redesign project. The Client Survey alone contains more than 30 questions. The Expanded Tech Check worksheet, the Maintenance Survey, and all the tools presented in this chapter are designed to help you gather the information you need for your redesign project.

A project that is clearly defined establishes several points of reference, including the tone and the overall goals for the redesign. By making these known to all team members as well as to the client, you have ensured that everyone is working with the same assumptions and terminology; everyone sees the same finish line. Also high in importance, you have defined your users and their needs. You know all about their online habits and their technical capabilities. At each step in every phase that follows — Structure, Visual Design and Testing, Production and QA, Launch and Beyond — the entire team must work at redesigning *for the user*. But if you don't understand your audience... Enough said. Only after defining the project can you begin hands-on site development.

Structuring the site, the second phase of the Core Process, begins right on the heels of the kick-off meeting. Armed with defined goals and specified direction, you will begin to design the site's information and address site content.

PHASE 1 CHECK-OFF LIST

Discovery

☐ Distribute/collect/analyze the Client Survey

☐ Distribute/collect/address the Maintenance Survey

☐ Collect existing marketing and research materials from the client

☐ Identify audience demographics

☐ Create user profile(s)

☐ Identify the audience's technical capabilities

☐ Identify backend programming needs (if any exist, employ additional workflow)

☐ Analyze your industry (see also Chapter 9)

Clarification

☐ Determine overall goals

☐ Prepare a creative brief

Planning

☐ Set your budget

☐ Establish a means of time tracking

☐ Create schedules

☐ Assign your project team

☐ Set up a client staging site

☐ Set up an internal team development area

☐ Plan for user testing (see also Chapter 8)

☐ Assemble your project plan

☐ Have a kick-off meeting

☐ Get client signatures on all documents

< C A S E   S T U D Y >

Internap

Client: Internap Network Services Corporation
URL: www.internap.com
Design Team: Phinney Bischoff Design House, Seattle

Interactive Director: Karl Bischoff
Director of Brand Strategy: Dave Miller
Senior Designer: Cody Rasmussen
Technical Director: Neil Robertson

Internap Network Services Corporation, a leading provider of fast, reliable internet connectivity services, has created a platform that doesn't just route data — it does it intelligently.

< P R E V I O U S >   < C U R R E N T >

INTERNAP.COM [OLD] wasn't communicating its brand. Internap had reasonably good brand-name recognition among "core" technology decision makers (CTOs and senior network engineers), but was challenged to grow its brand awareness "upstream" in organizations.

INTERNAP.COM [REDESIGNED] includes upgrades to its visual design interface and overhauls to its branding, adding a tag line and imagery that playfully reinforce clever ways of thinking. The site presents Internap as the "intelligent" service provider. (2000)

Result: Better accessibility for a wider audience.

> Designing for the user compels creativity to rise to
a new level of problem solving that requires both
practical and innovative thinking.

Phase 3: Visual Design and Testing

<CHAPTER 5>

Phase 3: Visual Design and Testing

Today's web is inarguably about accessibility and the user. Designing for the web means creating something that looks two-dimensional like a printed piece but upon deeper involvement reveals interactivity and layering of information. This makes web design a lot like product design, a discipline in which you design something that actually gets used (for example, a better snowboard binding, a more usable corkscrew, or a revolutionary self-sifting litter box). Your website *is* a product; it gets used.

Not so very long ago, a basic design-world scenario looked like this: one individual — maybe two — conceptualized, designed, and constructed a layout through mechanical and finished printed piece. Then came the web. We are now working in structured teams, dealing with high-level interactivity and needing to be more user-centric than ever before — and on schedules to which few print jobs ever had to adhere. And because web design necessarily rests on a technical element, designers cannot simply whip out concepts without considering how the design is inescapably wedded to the technology. Then consider that a huge majority of people working on websites have no design background — many are technical or marketing folks who have been thrown into a design role. Today's design talent is feeling pressure; most trained web designers either are still adjusting from the print world or are coming straight out of school, all the while dealing with a volatile market. Now is a time of merging disciplines and uncertainty.

WHAT THIS CHAPTER COVERS		
CREATING	**CONFIRMING**	**HANDING OFF**
> Starting the Creative Process	> Confirming Flow and Functionality	> Creating Graphic Templates
> Defining Smart Design	> The HTML Protosite	> Creating a Design Style Guide
> Reviewing Site Goals	> Testing Functionality	
> Developing Concepts		
> Designing for the User		
> Presenting Designs and Gathering Feedback		

<PHASE 3: VISUAL DESIGN AND TESTING>   <TIPS>

Finding a balance between the limitations and restrictions of the web and the driving need to express brilliant creativity is more challenging than ever. Although current technical constraints may significantly change in the future (how soon is anybody's guess), reality now includes some fairly rigid frameworking that must be considered at all steps of web development — especially, perhaps even most importantly, during visual design creation.

This phase is a two-track, parallel process: As the visual designers experiment creatively with looks and feels and ideas for the interface, the functionality that these concepts employ must get tested by the production designers. Visual design is self-explanatory, but testing? At every stage, assumptions need to be tested so that subsequent steps can be confidently taken. Finding out that your design won't work after you have sign-off and approval from the client is problematic. And what about the content and the navigation? It worked on paper, but does it flow in an HTML environment? For this, we recommend building a Protosite, also called an HTML click-thru.

Visual design and Protosite development are individual processes; they don't develop interdependently. Rather, each naturally follows the structuring phase. Visual design takes the established information design and puts a graphic interface to it. The Protosite confirms, among other things, content organization: Is there too much content? Too little? Does it read well? Are there holes?

In a perfect world, the visual designers wait until the information design is established and content is determined and delivered before starting to create. In this same perfect world, the laundry folds itself, takeout is delivered in 10 minutes instead of an hour and a half, and clients pay invoices upon receipt. In real-world redesign projects, timelines rarely allow for waiting until site structuring is complete before visual design begins. The real world is rarely that linear and is never on that relaxed a schedule.

By this point in the process, clients are dying to see something. Some overlapping between the structure phase and the visual design phase almost always happens, and that's okay. But even though the visual design team can indeed start sketching, brainstorming, and homing in on a palette, it shouldn't start actual layout until the information design is established.

Because this book cannot address two things at once, we first address the visual and then the functional aspect of this phase. But the truth is, they develop simultaneously.

Keep Your Designers Happy

Yes, it costs money to upgrade hardware and software, but consider that creativity does not flow from the disgruntled, the overworked, or the under-resourced. Keep your team motivated. Make sure you have a fast system and the latest versions of software. Pay for licenses so that designers don't have to log off the network to launch an application (besides, you'll be legal this way). Provide good workstations. If you care, invest. It will return to you three-fold.

Mac vs. PC

Ninety percent of all websites are designed on Macs, but ninety percent of all sites are viewed on PCs. A PC workstation for your designers will allow them to look at the site they are redesigning the way much of the targeted audience will look at it. Get a PC, set the monitor resolution to your project's target audience (yes, that will make the designers groan), and then make sure your designers actually review work-in-progress on it.

< C H A P T E R 5 >

STARTING THE CREATIVE PROCESS

Here is what the client has been patiently (or not-so-patiently) waiting for: a glimpse at the redesigned site. But before that happens, the design team needs to do some serious solution-oriented brainstorming on both creative and technical levels (and sometimes the greatest creative solution is a technical innovation). Creativity doesn't just get churned out, it needs to be kneaded and coaxed and slept on. Don't expect to redesign your visual interface in one take and don't let your client think that this is possible.

Defining Smart Design

Visual web design must be more than just a pretty interface; it must also follow overall site objectives while being functional. Here is where the information design and advance planning takes shape, finds a face, and begins to communicate. The visual design phase is often called "the fun part." Here is where designers work their magic. Here is also where falling off track can hemorrhage your budget. Hold that tendency at bay. Practice Smart Design.

It is important when designing any site — new or redesigned — to understand the concept of Smart Design. Smart Design serves the user's environment and capabilities. Smart Design is functional and fast loading. Smart Design is focused on the user's experience rather than the ambitions of the designer, the desire to use Flash, the positioning of the company's advertiser, or even the personal quirks of the CEO of the client's company itself. If it detracts from the user, it is not Smart Design — even if it is cool.

How do you practice Smart Design? Simple. Think like the user. Browse, click, and download like the user. Incorporate your information design rather than fight it. And check in with production frequently — think of your HTML production designer as your babysitter: "Can I do this?" "Is this permissible?" "Will I get in trouble if I do it this way?" Even if your designs are beautiful, hip, *and* perfectly aligned with the needs of the audience, if they are neither producible nor easily downloaded, they are not smart. Through testing and discussion, production can guide as to what is feasible. Production can help design become smart.

Smart Design is fluid. It works.

Reviewing Site Goals

As the visual designers get ready to begin the visual design phase, pull out the creative brief and use it as a springboard for the creative process. What was established for the tone? Corporate and solid and clean? Cutting edge and funky and bizarre? Elegant and smooth? Something else entirely? The creative brief also lists the client's redesign objectives, including visual goals such as a more professional look and feel, trendier graphics, more live area for content but less scrolling, and so on. During creative brainstorming, the design team should see and

<PHASE 3: VISUAL DESIGN AND TESTING>

identify the visual problems of the existing site, review the redesign goals, view competitive sites, and discuss the proposed solutions.

The creative process does not develop in a vacuum. While brainstorming on colors and fonts and feels, the visual designers should also muse about technical and structural solutions (for example, use of DHTML, Flash, JavaScript, and so on). Before doing this, review the target audience's technical capabilities. And remember, don't use tech solutions just because they are current. You must make sure they facilitate the redesign goals and are appropriate for the audience.

Developing Concepts

The development of the look and feel can start by gathering colors and putting rough ideas on paper or screen without concern for the content and labels that the information design will provide [5.1]. While waiting for the information design, the visual design team can refer to the creative brief for guidance. Once the sitemap and wireframes are in, however, designing can truly begin. Refer to the creative brief for tone and feel, to the sitemap for structure, and to the wireframes for navigational elements. Pull together everything to date and begin to "paint" around it.

5.1 >

An early-stage proposed palette for New Riders' redesigned site. As the design team progressed, the palette was fine-tuned. Several palettes were presented. In this case, a modified version of these colors was chosen.

NEWRIDERS : COLOR SCHEME 1 : GEOGRAPHIC

PALETTE

HTML COLORS

Color	BLUES	2	3
WEB:	003366	99CCCC	CCFFFF

Color	GREENS	2	3
WEB:	669966	66CC99	CCFFCC

Color	EARTH TONES	2	3
WEB:	999966	CCCC66	FFFFCC

Color	BLACKS	2	3
WEB:	000000	999999	CCCCCC

Color	ACCENTS	2	3
WEB:	000000		

< C H A P T E R 5 >

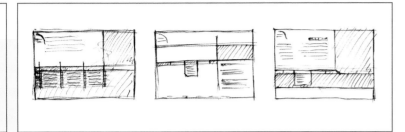

< **5.2**

Initial sketches or thumbnails on paper allow for easy brainstorming on several solutions. By starting on paper, the designers are able to quickly outline grid patterns and layout directions.

There are two camps as to how to start designing. Traditionalists like to put pencil or pen to paper; others render straight into the computer and create a series of drafts ([**5.2**] and [**5.3**]). Either way, it is the beginning of concept development, and regardless of technique, at this point in the Core Process, visual designers get to start experimenting with colors and layouts. They get to produce design after design. Visual designers should brainstorm until there are two or three solid design directions to flesh out further.

During this initial brainstorming, don't forget that download time, functionality, and user browser variables must be addressed. Make sure you run your designs by your HTML production designer, who will assist in determining the feasibility of translating those designs into workable web pages for the targeted audience. The design directions may be really cool but might not come close to working efficiently (or at all) in HTML. A great example of what your production designer might catch is font usage. Since PCs render HTML fonts 2 to 3 points larger than Macs do, and Internet Explorer renders

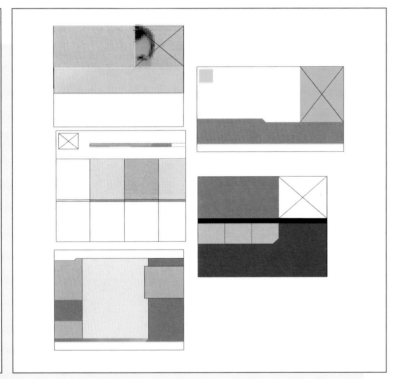

< **5.3**

Initial design directions started in Freehand, Illustrator, or Photoshop.

As project manager, make sure the visual designers don't spend hours refining and tweaking the directions for client review until the information design is set.

< P H A S E   3 :   V I S U A L   D E S I G N   A N D   T E S T I N G >   < T I P S >

larger than Netscape. It's just the way the world is. Our recommendation for the optimum HTML font size is 2. Any bigger and it looks clunky (except on Netscape on a Mac). Designers often create layouts that are dependent on a specific HTML type size. But doing this will create huge production issues. Web design that depends on font sizes is never Smart Design. Designing graphic text might seem to be the answer, but keep these points in mind: a) download time, b) users may have their graphics turned off or may be on hand-held devices, and c) disabled people often don't receive graphical information due to accessibility limitations (read more on this topic in Phase 4: Production and QA).

Involve production. It is embarrassing and it undermines your credibility to present a design that the client loves but that must be retracted as unfeasible.

Designing for the User

When the design team is finished brainstorming, the art director or designer should pursue the three to five directions agreed on by the team and concentrate on fleshing out the information from the wireframes, including navigation, global elements, content, and so on. Make sure to determine when and where to place visual/graphic cues (for example, buttons and icons) to help guide the user through the site.

As the visual design develops, the team should take the time to truly visualize the site from the audience's viewpoint. For instance, if the target audience is largely using T1 lines at the office, take into account the download time of your design. Perhaps you can get away with more images and less text. Is your audience largely at home on 56K modems? Consider more pages with less on each. More often, however, bandwidth limitations necessitate compromises. Make sure the visual designers redesign *for* the targeted audience, not *at* them.

Keeping designers focused on the user and on the redesign goals is a challenge. Problems arise when designers get excited and want to design the coolest thing possible. This is perfectly fine as long as this excitement does not overshadow the importance of the user, the production feasibility, or the client's wishes. Of course, it is entirely possible that the goals of the project are to make it as hip and as design-centric as possible. Maybe the goal *is* to be totally cutting edge. Maybe the audience for your site *is* entirely comprised of power users on T1 lines. If so, let your designers go absolutely wild. But anything less than super-high concept and... well, we've already said it.

Gamma Gamma

Colors, even web-safe colors, look slightly different on Macs vs. PCs. Some say brighter on Macs; other camps claim truer and bluer on PCs. The argument will never die. Just know that they are slightly different, even if you set your Mac gamma to match a PC. Upload your proposed palette onto your server and view it on both platforms before showing it to the client. You may change your mind.

Web-Safe No More?

As far as the web-safe color cube is concerned, yes, people are indeed beginning to design outside of the strict 216. It will become more and more possible as time goes on (and as browsers update to new versions) to work in thousands and millions of colors. But for now, if you decide to brave it, test, test, test. It is our experience that most of the time, designing outside the cube is still problematic. When placing optimized graphics over a web-safe hex color (as in a cell or a background), there is still a line, especially cross-browser.

123

< CHAPTER 5 >

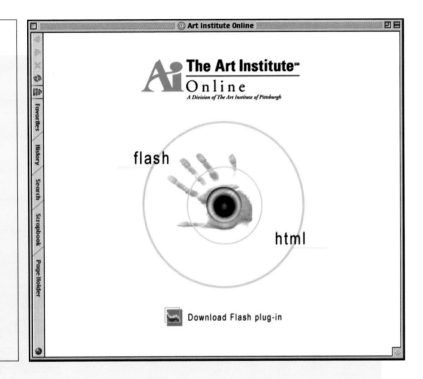

flash

html

Download Flash plug-in

< 5.4 >

For accessibility purposes, create a low-bandwidth version of your website. Give users the option whether to go to the Flash site, or to stick with the HTML version. It is done all the time.

Flash Considerations

Flash is everywhere, and it seems that every client thinks they need to have it. The keyword here is "thinks." Don't use Flash just because you can — we call that "Gratuitous Flash," and it's rampant. Flash is fabulous, but have a reason for it — a reason that serves the user. And if you are going to use it, make sure your audience can access it.

With a 96% penetration rate for the latest plug-in, most browsers are indeed ready to view Flash animations on the web. But even though the Flash technology has enabled the creation of slick animation, sound and graphics at a relatively low-file size, most Flash sites are still too heavy to fully enjoy without a high-bandwidth connection. Design for your audience. What is their connectivity? They could be in for a long (in web-time) loading period, and most users don't like to wait. If you are building a Flash site, consider giving your audience options [5.4].

Connectivity isn't the only concern. Other Flash issues include incompatibilities with text-to-speech translators (for visually impaired or non-graphics enabled browsers), and the fact that pages cannot be bookmarked. Consider also maintenance. The web designer may be a Flash master, but what of the maintenance team? It is considerably harder to update Flash than straight HTML. Plus, Flash tends to thwart search engines. Currently, Flash content cannot be indexed. META information can be included but not easily accessed. (For more information on search engines, see Phase 5: Launch and Beyond.)

Solutions?

1. Provide an HTML alternative site for lower bandwidth and text readers.

2. Provide ALT text alternatives for smaller animation pieces and graphic text.

Macromedia has addressed many of these issues (search for flash+accessibility at www.macromedia.com); however it is still important to know what you are working with when creating content for a mass audience on the web.

<PHASE 3: VISUAL DESIGN AND TESTING>

<EXPERT TOPIC>

Talk to the customer. You should be doing this at every step of the design process, but a good example of when this is particularly important is while designing comps. You create a lot of comps, but to whom do you show them? The client? The client isn't going use the site and spend money that gets desired business results. You should be showing comps to the customer. The last thing you want is for the client to say, "We like this," and leave it at that. In the old days, you would get client approval, and then if the client didn't get the desired business results, you could say, "But you liked it." Don't be your own worst enemy. As designers, we have to stop thinking about what we (designers and clients) like and focus on asking the customers what they like.

Listening to the customer doesn't mean you are no longer listening to your own creativity. Just don't get your ego involved. Short-cut all the stuff that makes you think you are a genius and just hand it over to the customers and let them be the geniuses. Keep it simple. Designers get all excited about the new rollovers they are going to do, but they just end up putting lots of effort into doing cool things that just don't get customer feedback. Take your site down to as simple as you can get it and then add things back only as you *and the customers* agree it's a good thing.

Don't compete with the content. Never use

DAVID SIEGEL ON VISUAL DESIGN AND THE ALL-IMPORTANT CUSTOMER

a pattern in a background. Put *nothing* in the background. Backgrounds have to be a flat color. Flat doesn't mean it can't be layered, but you shouldn't be trying to re-create angles and bevels and chrome. Technically, there is no reason for them. No 3D. We are already using 2.5D wherever we have index tabs, but 3D is ridiculous for the medium. The web is not fly-through, and 3D is just noise to compete with the signal, the content. And the content is why people — customers, site users — go to a site.

Definitely break some rules. Start designing sites outside of the venerated color cube. It's what we've always wanted, but we got so conditioned to 256 color spaces that it became a religion. But now you can't order a computer without it having 8 megs of video RAM — twice as much as you need to see millions of colors. Get rid of the color cube.

Try new things. Remember that browsers were not designed with visual presentation in mind. Browsers were designed with physics papers in mind. With visual presentation, some things that are seemingly entrenched can indeed be played with. For instance: hotlinks. Blue underline links are just the way the web

has been, and when tested, it's true: That's what people expect. But if you force underlining off and make hot links red, it's not going to test that badly. Personally, I think you can find things like that, ways to change and push limits without alienating the customer.

Good designers ought to be able to work in any medium. This medium is about the people who use the web — they are the customers. Design and redesign for them, not for awards or to be cool. The business results will follow.

David Siegel is one of the world's foremost authorities on internet strategy. His book, Futurize Your Enterprise *(John Wiley & Sons, 1999), has been on the Business Week bestseller list and has a large following of enthusiastic supporters. His 1996 book,* Creating Killer Web Sites *(Hayden), is Amazon.com's longest running #1 bestseller and has been translated into more than 15 languages. In 1995, he started Studio Verso, a high-end web-design and strategy consulting firm that was sold to KPMG in 1999. David has been featured in such magazines as* The Harvard Business Review, Fast Company, *and* The Industry Standard.

< C H A P T E R   5 >

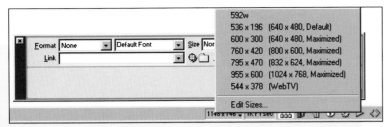

< 5.5

Dreamweaver has a handy reference bar at the lower-right of the toolbar; it allows you to quickly check your true screen size when creating comps or pages.

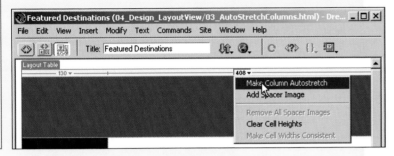

< 5.6

Dreamweaver has an easy solution to the creation of dynamic browser resizing (liquid pages). If you use the Make Column Autostretch option, the HTML table is then set up to automatically flow text to the width of the browser.

The Truth About Screen Sizes

Viewable screen sizes vary — they are all totally dependent on the user's own environment. The current, as-of-publication, most popular setting is 800×600. This setting, where most redesigns probably aim, is really only 760×420 viewable. It's true. Where do the extra pixels go? The browser takes them.

If you are working in Dreamweaver, look at the bottom right of the page window to the drop-down options listed [5.5]. There are several window sizes. Select any of them. It will say, for instance, "760×420 (800×600 maximized)." These settings will help keep your designers realistic. Not everyone has a 21-inch monitor.

Designers like to work at 1024×768 because, almost exclusively, they all use high-resolution screens. But designers must look at their work-in-progress on different monitors. On an average-size monitor or with different resolutions settings (always determined by the user), you may discover that both the right and bottom get cut off. To combat this problem, consider designing the browser window to be stretchable, dynamically resizable, scalable, liquid — all terms to describe pages that expand to the width of the browser. We like the term "liquid" because the page and the text *flow* with the browser, whatever the size. Dreamweaver 4.0 has an easy-to-employ feature for this exact purpose [5.6].

< P H A S E   3 :   V I S U A L   D E S I G N   A N D   T E S T I N G >

< T I P S >

Presenting Designs and Gathering Feedback

Before presenting first-round visual directions to the client, the designs should have already gone through several steps internally. Keep two important things in mind: First, presenting too many choices too early in the process slows things down; you're promoting client indecision. Three design directions is good. Second, do not present any design you hate just because you need another design. Chances are, you will end up producing that direction.

Post the designs to the client staging area and invite review ([5.7] through [5.10]). With some clients, you will get your feedback in one swift take; with others it will trickle in. In this second scenario, the client articulates a few minor points, and you refine the design accordingly, recheck with production to ensure continued feasibility, represent to the client, and then the client has a few more minor points. Clients can keep you in a frustrating circle of endless tweaking if you let them. Project management should endeavor to educate the client as to what constitutes helpful feedback. Two or three rounds of design are appropriate. Anything after that may need to be renegotiated and additional budget added — dependent, of course, on factors such as level of talent vs. expectations, rounds of changes, indecision, etc.

At the end of this first stage of Phase 3, you will have an appropriately smart visual design that fits your client and its audience. The pace just picks up from here. With the design direction finalized (and approved by the client — don't forget to get it signed), you can confidently take the next step toward HTML production.

Client Control

Sometimes clients suffer short-term memory loss. Perhaps the creative brief stated "classic, elegant," and that's exactly what you're presenting, but the client says it's not cutting edge. What? "Cutting edge" wasn't in your creative brief. What happened? The client wasn't able to articulate their wants until they saw actual designs. Suddenly, none of your brainstorming applies to this new direction, the tone is now wrong, and your schedule feels much tighter.

Sometimes clients love the first thing you present, sometimes they are unpleasant. Regardless, they will often have a hard time articulating their feedback. This is simply part of the creative process — budget for it. But there is also the possibility that your designers may be slow to hit upon a winning design [md] a few additional rounds of design may be required to fulfill the vision stated in the creative brief. You cannot blame (and therefore charge) the client for a slow design process.

You can, however, hold the client responsible for changes in direction, the addition of more pages, or changes in navigation. Gently remind the client about the creative brief. Often clients "forget" what they've said about tone and perception, and you budgeted based on knowing certain givens *before* commencing visual design. It is absolutely acceptable (and common) for clients to change their minds after seeing visual directions, but if you need to significantly backtrack, the scope of the project has changed.

User Feedback

Take advantage of any and all user-testing opportunities. Right around the presentation of the second round of visual comps, somewhere between initial client feedback and final tweaking, lies a perfect point at which to gather user feedback. Although it isn't appropriate at this point in the Core Process to run usability testing, conducting a focus group will offer you some very valuable answers. Does your navigation get misunderstood or misinterpreted? Is your labeling sensible? Is the site organized in a comprehensive manner? Is the interface appealing? Should you move forward and execute your designs or backtrack and redo?

< CHAPTER 5 >

Challenge

New Riders' old home page [5.7] is cluttered with content that takes up valuable space that could be better used to convey the New Riders personality and brand. This site needed a new structure and organization to highlight the company's products (books) in a more dynamic fashion. Key words: elegant, edgy, sleek, high end.

<BEFORE>

APPROACH 1>

< 5.7

The old site is cluttered and static.

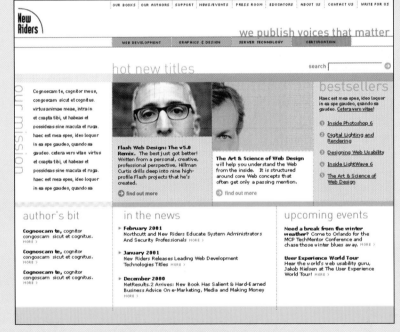

< 5.8 > *This initial design direction is hip and friendly in a modular grid system. This approach allows for several features to appear at the top of the home page.*

< PHASE 3: VISUAL DESIGN AND TESTING>

Approach

Focus the home page on communicating the New Riders personality and vision through the use of strong imagery and a clear welcome or mission statement. Limit content to "teasers" or lead-in to different areas of the site. This approach also serves the first goal in clarifying navigation, as excessive content does not detract from the user paths.

APPROACH 2>

APPROACH 3>

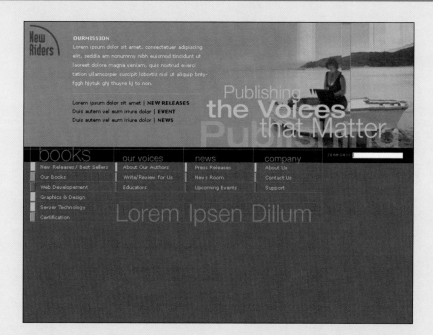

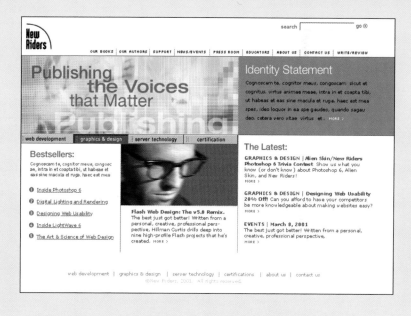

< 5.9 > This initial design direction shows a subdued/elegant look and feel. This approach highlights the mood and feeling of the company, with a simple linking system to the main areas of content.

< 5.10 > This initial design direction shows a corporate/current look as well as a strong company branding and identity treatment. It also allows for book features to appear prominently on the home page.

Users Don't Read, They Skim

Information-heavy sites must pass the squint test. As a designer, push your chair back, squint (or take off your glasses), and skim. There, now you are "inspecting" the site just like a majority of users. Can you identify where to click? Quickly and easily? No? Make it more obvious. (Note: More obvious does not necessarily mean bigger and bolder and clunkier.)

Take the squint test one step further. Grab someone totally uninvolved with your site (like your UPS delivery person, someone from personnel, or your mate who's come to meet you for lunch), sit the person in front of your layout, and give him or her all of 10 seconds to find what you want him or her to find. Can the person do so? No? Make it more obvious.

VISUAL DESIGN CHECKLIST: PRE-REVIEW (BEFORE SHOWING CLIENT)

Before you present your designs to your client, make sure you have checked the following:

1. Does the tone of the design to be submitted match the tone stated in the creative brief?

   ☐ Yes   ☐ No

2. Do the functionalities of the design to be submitted fall within the range of the targeted audience?

   ☐ Yes   ☐ No

3. Have you checked the proposed design with your production designer? Is your presentation feasible from a production standpoint? Is it sliceable?

   ☐ Yes   ☐ No

4. Are the colors web-safe? (As a rule, stay web-safe as much as possible. Yes, there are times you can deviate from this, but you must do additional testing.)

   ☐ Yes   ☐ No

5. Have you made certain that the design to be submitted is *not* dependent on a specific HTML font size? (Remember, you have relatively *no* control over HTML font sizes unless you are using CSS or DHTML, and even then your control is not total.)

   ☐ Yes   ☐ No

6. Have you checked the proposed design on both a PC and a Mac?

   ☐ Yes   ☐ No

7. Have you checked the proposed design on an 800×600 browser to make sure no key items (navigation, company name, and so on) are cut off?

   ☐ Yes   ☐ No

If you answered No to any of these questions, you should take a step backward, rethink, and modify the design(s) before submitting them to the client.

LYNDA WEINMAN ON DESIGNERS AS PROBLEM SOLVERS

A designer is a problem solver. By nature, developing a website is a series of problems in need of solutions. Usability, navigability, download speed, and so on are components of the problem. If a designer doesn't pay attention to what problems to solve, he or she will have failed. How good the site looks after those issues are resolved is the measure of how creatively the problems were handled. Visual design should support the functionality and goals of the site, not detract from or overwhelm those issues.

Designer ego is a potential problem to be solved. Easy solution: Park your ego at the door. Just because you're trying to show off your animation skills or you like a certain font or color isn't a reason to put these things into a site design. Design should be deliberate to meet the goals of the site, not to meet your personal design goals. It's great when the two can meet, but the goals of the site need to come first.

When redesigning a site, a design team needs to be armed with some important information. Data should be collected by testers to find out where current end users would like to see improvement, as well as what is currently working very well for them. The design team should keep these points in the forefront of the creative process. Of course, any redesign

begins with clearly defined goals. From these, a hierarchy of importance should be established that is carried through with the design.

To that end, team members have to feel what it's like to be in the end users' shoes. Try this exercise to help them do so: Have all the members of your team list the top five things they would look for on a similar kind of site. Instruct them to find five competitive sites, rate them, and write about their strengths/weaknesses. Have them come up with reasons behind the strengths and solutions for the weakness.

When the project is a redesign, there is an insistent lure to employ the latest and greatest technology because it is often perceived as a catchall "fix" for ailing sites. Beware of using technology for the sole purpose of using technology. There should always be a purpose behind every decision. For example, the goal should not be to use Flash, but what can Flash provide that can't be achieved any other way and/or that is necessary to the success of the site?

For any designer, maintaining a solution-oriented, problem-solving approach to the actual design and comping process is possible as long as you make sure that you know the goals of the site, that these goals are measurable (for example, are click-thrus or actual sales more important), and that you approach reaching the goals from the end user's perspective (that is, you want to sell something, but they want to buy something). Keep your eye on the target — make sure your goals are clear and stick to them.

Lynda Weinman is co-founder of lynda.com, a company that specializes in educating creative professionals in web design and graphics. Lynda is the author of numerous books, CD-ROM training disks, and curricula. She owns a training center that provides hands-on classes. Recently, her company created several events that drew attendance from thousands of web developers from all over the world. Visit www.lynda.com *to learn more.*

<CHAPTER 5>

CONFIRMING FLOW AND FUNCTIONALITY

There is no need to wait until the design is finalized, optimized, and coded in order to test light functionality, content, or navigation. Modify whatever isn't quite working while the visual design is still coming together; you won't necessarily have time to adjust the look and feel during production. We recommend two avenues of testing. Set the production designers to work on testing DHTML, pull-down menus, pop-up screens, multiframes sets, basically anything that needs to be worked out cross-platform. We also recommend building a Protosite.

The HTML Protosite

An extension of the wireframes from Phase 2: Developing a Site Structure, a Protosite is used to confirm the flow of the pages, the navigation, and the content. The Protosite usually does not include functionality, although sometimes light scripting is involved. Usually the Protosite is just a simple wireframe (non-design oriented — a few colors are fine to separate navigation) made clickable through HTML [5.11].

> If the site is incorporating backend engineering, a technical Protosite is built by engineers to demonstrate functionality and to confirm requirements, though this is a situation that is outside the range and scope of the Core Process.

The Protosite, also called an HTML click-thru, is a skeletal representation of the site that allows you to go through the content, navigation, and light functionality (or a mock-up of desired functionality) to establish whether or not your informational model makes sense. By this point in the Core Process, you have a clear idea of what information goes on each page. When your production designers build the Protosite — at least all of the main and secondary pages — this information should be included. Specifically, you are looking to determine whether your site is shaping up as planned.

One of the key strengths of the Protosite is exposing content and information-flow design issues as well as navigational issues. When using place-holder content, it can be difficult to put things in their proper perspective. For instance, perhaps you have a main page called "Office Locations" with four secondary pages, one for each of the four offices. Only by plugging in content do you realize that there is nothing (in terms of content) on the actual "Office Location" page — all the content is on the specific location pages instead. This is a great thing for the client (and the team) to discover before production actually begins.

Have both your team *and* the client test the Protosite. Populate your click-thru with whatever content has already come in. Letting the client see content on a page, even if it is not in its final layout position, can only stimulate and upgrade the client's own internal proofing and evaluation. If clients can see it, they can more easily find holes in the content, discern whether a page is too text-heavy, or decide that the content just doesn't make sense in the spot for which it was specified. Your client may be surprised at the scrolling necessary on some pages and the bareness on others and may decide to rearrange the content placement. Now is a better time than after launch for that kind of decision-making.

How Necessary is a Protosite?

Confirming assumptions before significant dollars are invested in design and production is always valuable. Testing should be part of every workflow at as many stages as possible.

Sometimes a Protosite gets completely scrapped after functionality is tested and navigation confirmed. But sometimes, production takes the HTML Protosite and builds the actual redesigned site on top of it (it's nice when you can keep what you build). Either way, it is still a form of preproduction, even if you scrap it and build the actual redesign from scratch (an occurrence that is not uncommon).

The Protosite step can be skipped if you are very confident in your content, navigation, and visual design. If your resources are tight, testing functionality can indeed be folded into production, and confirming your information design can indeed be adequately done with wireframes. But "adequate" isn't great, and if you struggled over your navigation and organization, or if you require other-than-basic

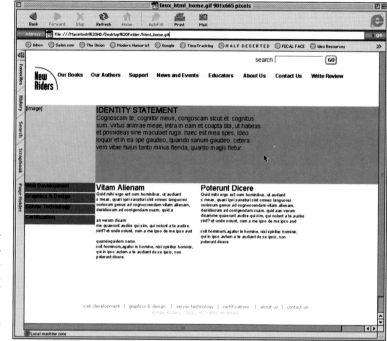

5.11 >

A sample page for New Riders' Protosite. This click-thru contains navigation, headers, and placeholder content (only some actual content had been received), all in basic HTML — no graphics.

< CHAPTER 5 >

coding, you may want the peace of mind that comes from a Protosite at this juncture.

Testing Functionality

Testing functionality of individual features prior to actual HTML production is a smart move. Browser compatibility, connection speed, platform, and plug-ins are functionality issues that are historically problematic and that need to be checked against both your audience's capabilities and production feasibility. An innovative idea for a pull-down menu using DHTML might seem like an excellent solution during brainstorming, but if in reality it is neither cross-browser compliant nor Mac-viewable, then you are losing a significant percentage of your audience, and the solution is not acceptable.

In addition, by testing assumptions now, you are able to determine whether there are changes to project scope with which to contend. Having to build two versions of the site — one for Internet Explorer and one for Netscape, or one for high-bandwidth capable audiences and one for low-bandwidth — would be a significant change.

Any of the following scenarios should be tested:

- **Complex frame sets (not recommended unless absolutely necessary)**

- **Functional rollover menus in DHTML or JavaScript**

- **Pop-up windows, especially if size- or placement-specific**

- **Style sheets or any browser-specific treatment**

- **Pull-down menus (especially ones that load pages automatically)**

- **Simple shopping cart features**

- **Anything needing light scripting or Server-Side Includes (SSI)**

Testing your functional assumptions during the visual design phase allows you to fix problems before the design is finalized, a point at which they can still be dealt with in a streamlined manner. Testing also helps prepare the production staff for the task ahead. Working out technical issues in advance saves a lot of time in the end.

CREATING GRAPHIC TEMPLATES

Here is where the established look and feel needs to be translated and applied across multiple pages. Download size and feasibility of optimization already should have been addressed as the design was being created. But now that a direction has been decided on, applying and establishing standards across your site is a must as graphic templates get built for the various types of pages. With several people working on this step, the potential for breakdown of standards is significant.

First, let's establish the difference between a look and feel and a graphic template. In the first step of this phase, you presented your client with design directions. You established a look and feel. This is

<PHASE 3: VISUAL DESIGN AND TESTING>

different than a final design. The look and feel is just an approved direction; it still has to be refined (there will almost certainly be details to work out) and then reapproved. A graphic template takes the final, approved look and feel and preps it for optimization and HTML production. It is called a template because it will be used for both the HTML page it is directly designed to be and any similar pages. It is a master graphic file that will soon get handed over to production for slicing and optimization during the next phase of the Core Process. Creating a graphic template is refining a look and feel to achieve a layered file ready for production.

The first parts of the graphic template to be designed are your globals. Refine your navigation bar with on/off/over states. Do you have a text footer? Add it now. If any interesting JavaScripts are planned for your nav buttons (for example, pull-down menus or disjointed rollovers or plug-ins that are global), you already should have consulted with production during the look-and-feel stage about coding feasibility and how they want to receive the to-be-coded design. Now is the time to build the graphic layers that will support all this functionality. If your redesign is incorporating dynamically generated content, now is the time to create a separate layer that specifies where content will appear in your templates.

Asset Control

Keep track of all images — which image came from which stock house. Even when putting together comps, make a note of image origin because you never know which design direction will make the final cut. When presenting concepts to clients, it should be made very clear that the image they are falling in love with could cost them $800 each year for site usage plus additional costs if they want to use it for printing and marketing. Let clients know their options (that other stock images exist), and perhaps they can use a slightly less riveting image that is copyright-free for an under-$100 one-time fee. Educate clients early... before opinions lock in. Everyone will save much time and trouble if they understand how usage rights work before the design is approved.

Be sure to get information on all photos and illustrations on your site. Turn this information over to the client. The Details and Assumptions of your project plan should clearly state that outside costs for photography are not part of the estimate. Also state that obtaining usage rights is the client's responsibility, especially if the client is planning to further use any of the site images (for example, for marketing brochures, mailers, and so on). Today's online stock photography sites (for example, www. tonystone.com, www.photodisc.com, www.comstock. com) have increased functionality to create a streamlined usage acquisition process.

< CHAPTER 5 >

< 5.12

The home page (top) and a secondary page (bottom) in progress. Each is its own layered file, complete with naming and text carefully called out. The clearly labeled layers indicate rollover states and functionality. Make sure to include a reference layer that contains the entire file flattened. Production designers will need it.

Keep in mind that you will probably have several graphic templates to create, each with at least one or more similar pages created from this master. Small redesign projects may be able to get away with only a few graphic templates, but large sites can easily have a dozen or more. (www.webvan.com had more than 40 templates!) For sites with many graphic templates, consider building a spreadsheet that lists them all so you don't overlook any — a template completion plan. It is likely that you will have a graphic template for your home page, another for your main pages, a third for your secondary pages, and so on. Don't forget about error pages, pop-up windows, or redirects following form submissions or transaction completions. Your visual designers may not be able to actually design them all. Take care to note standards in the Style Guide (discussed later in this chapter) so that the production designers can improvise if necessary.

Files should go to production as layered Photoshop or Fireworks files that call out all functionality (including on/off/over states) and that contain placeholders or dummy text for content [5.12]. Make sure your graphic templates include all the information production will need to successfully turn the file into an HTML page. An accompanying printout is often helpful for these callouts. (Note that wireframes don't call out specific layouts; they just indicate what is on the page.)

Fonts can be a big issue when creating graphic templates for handoff. Visual designers usually work

<PHASE 3: VISUAL DESIGN AND TESTING>

on Macs, but production workstations tend to be on PCs. Plus, production designers rarely have the same font libraries that visual designers use. As a result, production designers may not be able to work with unrendered, editable text. Consider purchasing the fonts included in the final design for the production team, or at least make sure the production designers have access to a Mac. Regardless, make certain that the visual designers retain a copy of the file in its pristine, unrendered, unflattened (layers intact) state in the likely event that changes have to be made (and there may be additions down the road as the site grows). Incomplete graphic templates — whether due to fonts or lack of called-out information — will slow down production. Carefully checking over these files before handing them off to production is advised.

CREATING A DESIGN STYLE GUIDE

Every page on your redesigned site is different, and yet each contains global elements. Maintaining consistency should be a priority. Make sure you establish your rollovers for all states, linking colors, fonts, headers, and HTML size text. Your production designers shouldn't have to ask too many questions.

A Style Guide is a key element for post-launch maintenance, but it is also extremely helpful for reference as the pages are being built out in production. Created in two parts by both the design team and the production team (one part per team), a Style

---

What Graphic Templates Should Include and Clearly Indicate

- Text in rendered and unrendered states. (These can be separate files.)

- All individual layers intact (not flattened) for revisions.

- All individual layers clearly labeled. ("Layer 7" helps nobody; "Main Nav" communicates layer content.)

- Each state — on/off/rollover — on separate, clearly identified layers.

- Flash/animation placeholders (use a single-frame, still image).

- Points where special technologies and complex functionalities integrate.

- An accompanying GIF or flattened Photoshop or Fireworks file that shows how the page should look once rebuilt in HTML. This reference document is a critical part of any template.

< CHAPTER 5 >

Guide can be in-depth or very simple — it depends on how much standardization and direction you want to give for the lifecycle of your redesign and, of course, on budget and resources. The more detailed the Style Guide is, the better insured the site is against the almost certain eventuality of design breakdown during maintenance (see Phase 5: Launch and Beyond for more on maintenance). Clients often take over the maintenance of their own sites, and usually they are not designers. Help them.

We recommend that you include a core set of components in your Style Guide, as shown in the accompanying chart. How you lay out the Style Guide is entirely up to you. We recommend that it be both visual and informative [5.13]. The design Style Guide is only the first half of this document. After production is completed, as part of the handoff to maintenance, the HTML production designers will complete the Style Guide with detailed production information.

< **5.13**

*This basic design Style Guide
is presented in HTML.*

Establishing Standards

Standardized treatments for global elements and graphics — rollover states, HTML hex colors, font choice sizes, headers, background functionality — all need to be established so they can be applied across all pages. In addition to defining graphic treatments for globals, however, address any specific design issues that weren't defined and approved in the look and feel. These include items that appear on one page but not another, a random form, a pop-up screen, or an error message. Plus, there might be additional graphics that weren't designed into the final look and feel. And of course, changes will come in with final content. Without standards for all elements, everyone will generate his or her own way of handling not-yet-standardized issues.

These treatments are not necessarily signed-off on by the client; rather the client approves the pages that incorporate the established standards. This system of standards is established and approved by the design team to ensure that consistency is maintained throughout the design phase and graphic template creation. Encourage communication between members of your design team so that standardized issues only need to be decided once; create a new standard and then move on. HTML production designers should not have to get too creative.

< P H A S E 3 : V I S U A L D E S I G N A N D T E S T I N G >

RECOMMENDED STYLE GUIDE COMPONENTS

SPECIFICATIONS

Page dimensions	Specify target window size, viewable and maximized. Specify whether liquid pages or fixed width.
Headers	Include navigation and subnavigation callouts such as styles for active vs. inactive states, dimensions, logo and/or tag-line inclusion, banner specifications (if applicable), text sizes and styles for graphic vs. HTML headers, and so on.
Colors	Specify hex numbering for the background, main palette, and accents. Clearly indicate which colors get applied to navigation headers, what color for text when background color changes (if it does), what color for buttons, bullets, arrows, stars, and other graphic accents. Be sure to specify all body text/content and links.
HTML text	Describe all text treatments, including color and/or specific HTML font (by name) or size, and include usage for linking.

GRAPHIC TREATMENT

Graphic type	Identify all graphic type styles. Name the graphical fonts and the HTML fonts. Log point sizes, colors, and any special kerning or leading.
Photo/image treatment	Specify any Photoshop or Fireworks actions (for example, edge or border treatments such as feathering or keylines, or special filters). Also be sure to specify how the photos appear on the HTML page. Are there any standard gutters or spacers? Any other images that always accompany photos?
Embellishments	Describe the treatments for buttons, lines, arrows, and other dingbats. Where and how can they be used? Specify the rules. Otherwise, they will get used in ways the designers never intended.

PHASE 3 CHECK-OFF LIST

Creating

- ☐ Review site goals
- ☐ Develop concepts
- ☐ Present designs
- ☐ Gather feedback

Confirming

- ☐ Create the Protosite
- ☐ Confirm navigation and content
- ☐ Test functionality

Handing Off

- ☐ Create graphic templates
- ☐ Create a design Style Guide
- ☐ Establish standards

PHASE 3 SUMMARY

Visual design is indeed the fun part of the Core Process — watching a design take shape is always exciting. During this phase, the designers create the visual design and graphic user interface: the first thing the world sees when visiting the redesigned site, the first experience the user has with the client's brand. Thanks to all your preparatory planning from Phases 1 and 2, this "face" of the redesigned site accurately represents the desired tone, the stated goals, and the established structure of the site in a visual format that is ready to be sliced and optimized. As important as the creative product, you have tested functionality in anticipation of the production phase, and you have confirmed your information design assumptions through the Protosite click-thru. On all levels, the design is ready for production.

But why the rigid process? This is the creative phase; why not simply coach the design team a bit so that they practice Smart Design and then let them do their thing? Here's why: Although visual web design is unquestionably about creativity, it is also about problem solving. It is about effectively communicating information through an appealing and appropriate design that is meaningful to the audience, and that also works within technical and budgetary constraints — and doing it all on time.

Staying streamlined is important to the bottom line, and visual design is the spot in the Core Process where both scope and budget can expand out of control. A hundred things can go wrong: Your client may never be happy, the designs aren't producible, the content isn't working, the visual designers aren't paying attention to the audience specs, the visual designers create the perfect look and feel but they go 80 hours over budget, and so on. By sticking with the Core Process and being diligent about tracking and logging hours, the project has a good shot of staying on target.

The next phase is production, the nuts and bolts of the project. If visual design has been done right, the next phase, while hard work, will flow very smoothly.

< CASE STUDY >

DiverseWorks

Client: DiverseWorks Art Space
URL: www.diverseworks.org
Design Team: Idea Integration, Houston
Creative Director: Jeff McLaughlin

Art Director: Joel Harris
Sitebuilders: Gregory Taylor, David Shepherd, Katherine Matthews

DiverseWorks is one of the leading contemporary art centers in the United States. Known for its ground-breaking art education programs and distinguished by its financial stability, DiverseWorks serves as an open venue for artists, a training ground for future arts administrators, and a model for art centers across the country.

< PREVIOUS >   < CURRENT >

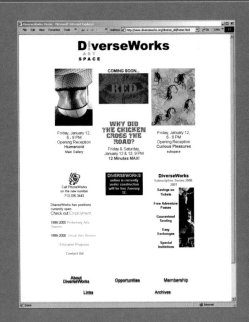

DIVERSEWORKS.ORG [OLD] was rich in information, but pages were content heavy and cumbersome to navigate. It neither communicated the artistic nature of its community nor allowed easy volunteer signup or member registration.

DIVERSEWORKS.ORG [REDESIGNED] shows a distinct contemporary style, updating DiverseWorks' image as a contemporary art and performance gallery. The redesign also improves navigation, simplifying it into five main links with DHTML menus. Easy-to-use forms were constructed for new member signup and volunteer work, a must for any nonprofit. (2000)

Result: Increased member and volunteer signup and greater credibility through the improved design.

HTML process, either through pure hand-coding using BBEdit or Allaire's Homesite or the like, or by using a WYSIWYG editor such as Adobe GoLive, Macromedia Dreamweaver, or Microsoft Front-Page. Here's the burning question: What is the level of that understanding?

Reassess your HTML production team's capabilities now that you know the true extent of the design and technical requirements, and if you are not qualified to make the assessment, find someone who is. Coordinating web production takes both ability and experience. Depending on your team's level of expertise, you will need to determine the true level of complexity that the site production can handle. For example, if you are creating a 20- to 40-page brochure site with light JavaScript, you can probably get away with using a WYSIWYG editor. If the site is more complex — intricate tables and/or frames usage, additional scripting and/or DHTML implementation — you will need to have the knowledge to troubleshoot problems along the way, which usually means utilizing people with a fluid understanding of HTML. This tends to call for people who can code pages by hand or who at least can read and understand the code well enough to tweak HTML and troubleshoot during the production process.

And before any coding truly begins, a final just-before-production-starts review of audience needs (browsers, screen size, connection speed), technology (plug-ins, scripting, backend needs), and redesign goals (download size, user experience goals) can only help. You will have to address complex questions about servers, directory structure, and the HTML production specifics that may have been left until this phase. The Client Spec Sheet will help.

Your goal? No misinterpretation of user capabilities or project goals. No backtracking. Code each HTML page only once.

ESTABLISHING GUIDELINES

Establishing clear guidelines for HTML production during the initiation of a web redesign project helps to answer questions and avoid costly backtracking. The Client Spec Sheet sets parameters for audience capabilities and technical standards for the site. This is a worksheet. It is long and detailed and technical. The client may simply say, "I don't know. You're the expert; you tell me." Some discussion is likely necessary. For instance, the project manager or lead production designer might have to explain what effect choosing to support 3.x browsers might have on being able to support certain functionality, or what effect selecting Flash might have on wanting to support dial-up modem connections, and so on.

The Client Spec Sheet is available for download from www.web-redesign.com. Due to its length, we

< EXPERT TOPIC >
< CHAPTER 6 >

CHAD KASSIRER ON KNOWING YOUR CLIENT BEFORE YOU CODE

Clear communication with the client is the key to a successful web project. Before beginning the production process, it is important to have agreed on and signed off on two things: a composite of the target audience and the client's expectations concerning the site production details. To assist with this process, I rely on a Client Spec Sheet to document these items. Ideally, this document is administered shortly after the project has been kicked off. This way, there is one central document that can serve as a guideline for everyone contributing to the building process. Not only does this assist in all phases of the process from information architecture to design to production, it also establishes some necessary parameters for the site's requirements and identifies possible limitations early on.

It is every web designer's, programmer's, and production engineer's goal to create a website that looks and works the same for every user. However, with the numerous possible combinations of platforms, browsers, connection speeds, and monitor resolutions, this is nearly impossible to accomplish. To decide the best way to design and build the website, you need to identify the target audience. Once this is established, you can tailor the site to best suit this audience's needs before being concerned about other users. This is not to say that no one other than your target audience is important, but the client's priorities need to be established. These priorities will impact decisions made during the production process. A more realistic goal is to make the site as close to perfect as possible for the target audience while still being functional for everyone else.

By initiating a conversation at the start of the project, a dialog is created between production and the client. During this conversation, the client's expectations and preferences can be discussed before deciding the direction the client wishes to take and documenting this on the Client Spec Sheet. The production lead, as the integrator of design and engineering, uses this document as a reference for making decisions during the design and production phases. When used properly, the Client Spec Sheet is extremely useful and saves time and money by eliminating ambiguities, which cause unnecessary delays and frustration.

I recommend using the Client Spec Sheet early in the process. It documents and clarifies to everyone what the initial goals of the project are, even if changes are made during the process. In case the requirements or expectations of the client change, the Client Spec Sheet also serves as a contract to refer to when additional costs are required or disputed. By using the Client Spec Sheet as a reference to help guide your decisions throughout the project, you can build a site with the client in mind.

As director of production for web development shops Red Eye Digital Media and Idea Integration/San Francisco, Chad Kassirer (www.whatdesign.com) has played a key role in the production process for many award-winning websites such as Adobe's Splatter-punk, One World Journey's Georgia Revealed, and SFMOMA's Making Sense of Modern Art. Chad has never appeared at any web conferences or written any books, but he knows people who have.

could not show it in its entirety in this book, so we show only the first two parts: Target Specifications, and Functionality and Features (see worksheet on next page). All told, it is five parts long, as follows:

Part 1: **Target Specifications**

Part 2: **Functionality and Features**

Part 3: **Design and Layout**

Part 4: **File Structure and Directory Preferences**

Part 5: **Server and Hosting Information**

As tedious as filling out this worksheet may be, the information needs to be addressed and answered before any HTML production can begin, and that includes conferring with the visual designers at the onset of Phase 3: Visual Design and Testing. Encourage client feedback within a short timeframe. This information should be back to the team and analyzed before the visual designers start developing concepts and definitely before the production designers start building the Protosite.

The team's lead HTML production designer should be the team contact; the project manager may or may not be as technically savvy. Have the client — or the client's key tech lead — answer all questions as thoroughly as possible, adding additional comments as necessary. Encourage the client

to write "N/A" next to nonrelevant items and to identify areas in which advice, suggestions, or clarification is needed. Filling it out should be taken seriously; the results from this analyzed worksheet serve as a set-in-stone guide for production.

The worksheet on the following pages will help you articulate and identify the technical parameters of your site redesign, including specific questions regarding target audience connectivity capabilities, browser versions, functionality, and actual file structure. When you are finished, please return all compiled information back to the project manager on the web development team.

Scope Expectations Meet Scope Reality

An estimate of 100 hours can easily turn into 300 hours if the complexity of the site has been underestimated. In Phase 1: Defining the Project, you estimated the project's budget based on the projected scope. Did you plan on 50 pages and now there are 120, or are you still on target? Assess. Has your scope grown, either through Scope Creep or as a result of client-requested changes and/or additions? If so, you will need to either increase the budget or downsize the allocation of hours... or take a loss. Regardless, if you haven't yet addressed potential budget changes with your client, do it now — *before* you start coding. And make sure you have included resources for QA along with the time necessary for fixes.

HTML Expertise

Although this chapter concerns HTML, it is not about how to code, the ins and outs of HTML, coding theory, nor advanced scripting implementation. We focus on the redesign workflow process and how it relates to the actual site production — keeping your project moving smoothly, staying on schedule and on budget. For guides to actual hands-on coding, seek alternative resources such as *HTML Artistry: More Than Code* (New Riders, 1998) by Ardith Ibanez and Natalie Zee or *Creative HTML Design.2* (New Riders, 2001) by Lynda Weinman.

< CHAPTER 6 >

TARGET SPECIFICATIONS | PART 1

Establishing clear audience specifications enables production to have a targeted goal. It is often difficult, if not impossible, to maintain consistency of experience from one browser or platform to the next. It is important for the HTML production team to understand not only the target end user but also who can be left behind.

	Existing Site Specs (Check One Below)		Priority/Target (Check One Below)		Others to Support (Specify One or More)	
Resolution	☐ 378×544 (web tv)	☐ 1024×768	☐ 378×544 (web tv)	☐ 1024×768	☐ 378×544 (web tv)	☐ 1024×768
	☐ 64×480	☐ Other (explain)	☐ 64×480	☐ Other (explain)	☐ 64×480	☐ Other (explain)
	☐ 800×600		☐ 800×600		☐ 800×600	
Browsers	☐ Netscape	☐ AOL	☐ Netscape	☐ AOL	☐ Netscape	☐ AOL
	☐ Internet Explorer	☐ Other (explain)	☐ Internet Explorer	☐ Other (explain)	☐ Internet Explorer	☐ Other (explain)
Browser Versions	☐ 3.x	☐ 6.x	☐ 3.x	☐ 6.x	☐ 3.x	☐ 6.x
	☐ 4.x	☐ Other (explain)	☐ 4.x	☐ Other (explain)	☐ 4.x	☐ Other (explain)
	☐ 5.x		☐ 5.x		☐ 5.x	
Platforms	☐ Macintosh	☐ Other (explain)	☐ Macintosh	☐ Other (explain)	☐ Macintosh	☐ Other (explain)
	☐ Windows		☐ Windows		☐ Windows	
Connection Speed	☐ Wireless/handheld	☐ DSL/cable	☐ Wireless/handheld	☐ DSL/cable	☐ Wireless/handheld	☐ DSL/cable
	☐ 28.8/33.6 dial-up	☐ T1/T3	☐ 28.8/33.6 dial-up	☐ T1/T3	☐ 28.8/33.6 dial-up	☐ T1/T3
	☐ 56.6k dial-up		☐ 56.6k dial-up		☐ 56.6k dial-up	
Page Download Size (typical page)	☐ 30K and under	☐ 80K (graphic heavy, animation)	☐ 30K and under	☐ 80K (graphic heavy, animation)	☐ 30K and under	☐ 80K (graphic heavy, animation)
	☐ 30 to 80K (typical page)	☐ 100K+ (not recommended unless a high-bandwidth site)	☐ 30 to 80K (typical page)	☐ 100K+ (not recommended unless a high-bandwidth site)	☐ 30 to 80K (typical page)	☐ 100K+ (not recommended unless a high-bandwidth site)

<<< This worksheet is available in full (all five parts) for download at www.web-redesign.com >>>

< P H A S E   4 :   P R O D U C T I O N   A N D   Q A >

FUNCTIONALITY AND FEATURES | PART 2

The addition of specific technologies that allow greater functionality can greatly enhance your site. These same features can exclude a percentage of your audience, however, and can cause production scope to increase, usually due to unforeseen technical errors and troubleshooting. Please identify which features you already have on your site and how they are currently being used. Please also indicate which features you are looking to add and how you foresee them being used.

	Preferences/Status (Current and New Site)		Issues	Comments and Usage Details (How It Is or Will Be Used)
Frames	☐ Used on current site ☐ Yes (use on new site)	☐ Will not be using ☐ Not sure (list comments)	Causes difficulty printing and navigating and may require additional scripting and quality-assurance testing. Causes difficulty for search engines. With a multiframe setup, could incur extra programming and QA costs.	
Forms	☐ Used on current site ☐ Yes (use on new site)	☐ Will not be using ☐ Not sure (list comments)	Requires additional programming and integration. Specific and detailed information is necessary to determine complexity.	
JavaScript	☐ Used on current site ☐ Yes (use on new site)	☐ Will not be using ☐ Not sure (list comments)	Does not require a plug-in, but is not supported by all 3.x browsers. Adds noticeable download time.	
Pop-Up Windows	☐ Used on current site ☐ Yes (use on new site)	☐ Will not be using ☐ Not sure (list comments)	May require use of JavaScript; may not be supported by 3.x browsers. Inconsistent size and placement depending on platform and browser.	
Cascading Style Sheets (CSS)	☐ Used on current site ☐ Yes (use on new site)	☐ Will not be using ☐ Not sure (list comments)	Does not require a plug-in. Allows for global updating of fonts, colors, and styles. Supported by most 4.x browsers and above.	
Dynamic HTML (DHTML)	☐ Used on current site ☐ Yes (use on new site)	☐ Will not be using ☐ Not sure (list comments)	Does not require a plug-in. Used to create special features such as dynamic menus. Supported by most 4.x browsers and above. May require additional testing, programming, and QA.	
Flash	☐ Used on current site ☐ Yes (use on new site)	☐ Will not be using ☐ Not sure (list comments)	Requires a plug-in. Sometimes causes accessibility/download issues; may require two versions of a site to be built (HTML only and Flash) or use of a browser sniffer.	
Media (Video/Audio)	☐ Used on current site ☐ Yes (use on new site)	☐ Will not be using ☐ Not sure (list comments)	Requires plug-ins. May involve download and processing time. If using any type of media, please list as much detail as possible, including type of media, format, and desired output.	

<<<   This worksheet is available in full (all five parts) for download at www.web-redesign.com   >>>

149

< C H A P T E R 6 >

Do a project-wide time check. You should have been tracking your hours on a weekly basis, so this should be a relatively easy assessment. How much of your allocated time and resources have you used up? Are you on budget? Has the scope increased? Do you have the time left in your budget to comfortably complete the site? Knowing how many resources and hours are necessary to complete a project's production and QA is regularly one of the gray areas in project estimating. The hard truth? Most things that appear to be simple are not and will take much longer than you estimate. Coding an HTML page or template can take a few hours or a few days — it is one of the factors contributing to Scope Creep that is extremely difficult to gauge until actual production begins.

Readdress Audience Capabilities

Focus on your user. You are producing the site based on the capabilities of your target audience, and you cannot translate the visual design into HTML unless you know your parameters: target operating systems, browsers, monitors, and connection speeds. Use the results from the Client Spec Sheet as a guide.

Check Content Status

Content should be in — all of it. But chances are it won't be. You must be on top of content status. Your Content Delivery Plan was clear: Content must be in before production can commence in earnest. Alert your client that the time has come, that a content freeze is imminent.

Announce to the client early in the process, as early as with the initial proposal that accompanied the budget, that if/when content is late, production will be held up and cost overruns will commence. Billing for overruns is never painless, but it will be far more viable if you warn the client of consequences ahead of time.

SCOPE: ARE YOU ON TARGET?	
Sitemap	How big is the site? How many pages? Is it what you planned for?
Visual Complexity	Is the slicing a nightmare or fairly straightforward?
Light Scripting Needs	DHTML, JavaScript rollovers, forms, pop-up windows, frames, pull-down menus, and so on. What did you plan for when you initially budgeted/scheduled? What are you now slated to include? Do the two match up?
Backend Engineering	Are the engineers on budget/schedule? Have the requirements been adequately defined, and do they still match the scope/cost expectations?

< P H A S E   4 :   P R O D U C T I O N   A N D   Q A >

Considering Accessibility

Imagine your only web access is through a browser that does not support images. Pick any site — if the navigational aids and buttons don't have descriptive ALT tags, you won't be able to differentiate between graphics.

Recent government backing and new Accessibility with Disabilities Act (ADA) standards are behind an ongoing push to support full-access web sites. This new set of standards, led by the World Wide Web Consortium (www.w3c.org), aims to connect all people to the web regardless of disability, including the handicap of older browsers or outdated technology. Understanding accessibility needs before you start coding — especially if your site is bound to comply to accessibility standards — will avert damage control later (for example, coding ALT tags into 100 pages instead of having done it once at the outset on the HTML template).

Here are two free tools that can help you test your site for accessibility after it's up: Bobby and Macromedia's Section 508 Accessibility Suite.

Bobby (www.cast.org/bobby) is an online tool that rates your web page immediately. Enter an URL, and Bobby identifies the areas that are not accessibility compliant and will let you know if your images have proper ALT tags. It's fast and impressive; the results may surprise you ([6.1] and [6.2]).

The Section 508 Accessibility Suite for Dreamweaver 4 and Dreamweaver UltraDev 4, created by UsableNet [6.3], enables web sites to be checked for accessibility in the same way that a document is spell-checked. The extension, available for free on the Macromedia Exchange (www.usablenet.com/macromedia/index.htm), helps ensure that web content meets Section 508 and Level 1 W3C/WAI guidelines. Reports can be run on one page, a complete site, selected sections, or any folder.

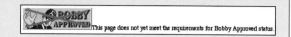

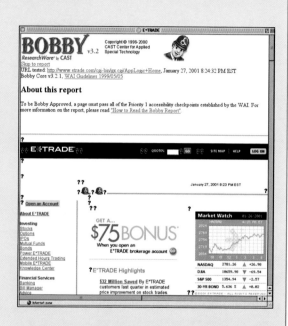

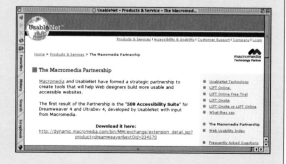

< **6.1**

A Bobby Approved icon appears when a site meets all requirements for disability standards. When a site does not meet the standards, Bobby clearly does not approve and lists the site's errors as well as suggestions for improvement.

< **6.2**

This screenshot shows the results of running an URL through Bobby. The question marks show areas that either are noncompliant to ADA standards for accessibility or could be improved upon.

< **6.3**

Usable.net and Macromedia team up to help check for accessibility.

< CHAPTER 6 >

Check Design Status

Have the graphic templates been finalized, approved, and turned over to production yet? If not, light a fire under the chairs of your visual designers. They are holding up production. Have a delivery schedule set up so that graphic files can be handed off in a phased process: the home page and a representative subpage first, and then let production figure out the HTML templates before the remaining pages are delivered.

During Phase 3, the visual design team met with production to ensure that the designer's vision could be feasibly carried out through Flash, DHTML, JavaScript, and/or straight HTML. By the first delivery of graphic templates from the visual designers to production, certain issues such as projected K-size download and potential optimization hiccups should be resolved.

Slippage and Consequences

Content will be late; this is predictable. Anticipate it. But what do you do when that magic date has passed, the content officially becomes late, and your production is compromised? After a few gentle reminders via phone and/or email, send a firm yet diplomatic email restating due dates, details, and the costs associated for each day the content is further delayed. What follows is an excerpt of a letter that addressed slippage as it was happening, and spelled out the consequences.

"… for clarification, we have determined some associated costs for the addition of the animated product demo and also for additional production work if our content delivery deadlines slip further.

"We realize you have tight budget constraints and do not wish to incur extra charges unless absolutely necessary. As explained earlier, we have allocated resources for a particular timeframe in order to produce and complete your project, and this time window is quickly evaporating… "

Furthermore, financial consequences were clearly outlined: For each day until the final content was delivered in full, a rate was applied for "holding" resources. The effect was dramatic. The first part of the content was delivered by the end of the week, and the rest of the project ran smoothly through launch. Should you find yourself seeing deadlines slip by, consider incorporating this slippage and consequences terminology into your workflow.

< P H A S E   4 :   P R O D U C T I O N   A N D   Q A >

Confirm the Backend Integration Plan

Is your redesign a static site or a dynamic site? If static, and you are not involved with a backend engineering team, this section does not apply to you. If the site is dynamic, however, plan on having a meeting before production actually starts, a front-end and backend status update. Restate all technical specifications to all team members, review the technical requirements, confirm the integration plan, and clarify responsibilities.

SETTING FILE STRUCTURE

Often confused with site architecture (Phase 2: Developing Site Structure) by newbies and clients with just enough knowledge to make them dangerous, file structure is, in fact, simple — but important — housekeeping. Starting out organized will help you stay organized, so make it a priority. (This is especially true for projects with multiple team members.) Although there is no best way to organize a site's file structure, different strategies support different goals ([6.4] and [6.5]).

The Client Spec Sheet asks about redesign specifics regarding existing HTML page-naming conventions and the existing file structure. Does the client want to leave things as they are, and if so, why? Whichever method is eventually decided on, it should be aligned with redesign and maintenance goals (such as how the site plans to add and archive post-launch content).

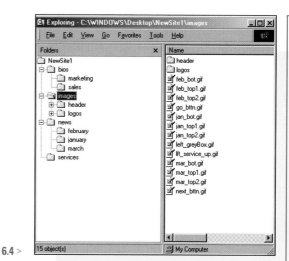

6.4 >

6.5 >

Two structures, different strategies. [6.4] has images listed at the root level, and [6.5] lists images within the current month folder. When to use which strategy is totally dependent upon preference.

<TIPS>   <CHAPTER 6>

Three File Structure Questions

1. How is the folder structure currently set up, and is there a client-desired reason for this method?

2. Does the folder structure follow the content structure in organization of the content?

3. Will the images be at the root level or separated into individual folders?

Redesigning offers an opportunity to start over clean. Chances are, the HTML structure of the old site is a mess: files duplicated, images scattered among folders, old versions of files still up on the server... Establish a logical, maintainable file structure for the redesign site. The goal? To start out as clean, organized, and scalable as possible.

File Structure and Scalability

How much growth (increased traffic, added content, new products) is anticipated in the 12 months following launch? Are you planning to add additional sections? How do you see them growing? By date? By topic?

When determining the file structure, know that it depends largely on how the client envisions the redesigned site growing and evolving. The plan you adopt for your file structure must be aligned with the anticipated maintenance, including logical archival of outdated content. Create subdirectories that will make sense to the maintenance team after launch and include file directory instructions as they pertain to archived or added pages in the Style Guide. Disorganization and clutter is a regular post-launch occurrence in situations in which maintenance has been handed over to a new team. An organized file structure that anticipates growth and regular updating can help counter the almost-inevitable degradation of site organization. For setting the file structure, a few pieces of information that are essentially based on client preference should be known. For instance, will the redesign repurpose existing files and the existing file structure, or will it start from scratch? How often will updates be made? Daily? Quarterly? The Client Spec Sheet asks for this information.

The big question here is this: Does the client care? Possibly, but not likely. Does the client even understand? Maybe, but probably not. But whether dictated by the client or established by your team, the file structure should respond to and fit with the answers of the preceding questions. The goal? Be scalable. Stay organized.

QUICK REFERENCE: STATIC VS. DYNAMIC	
Static Site: Front-End Only	Pages are prebuilt in their entirety and are viewed when referenced by a browser, usually using the .html or .htm extension.
Dynamic Site: Front-End and Backend Teams	Pages are created "on the fly," usually by pulling content-specific information from various places such as from a database. The site usually contains standard HTML pages as well. Additional code (ASP, JAVA, PERL) can be added to the HTML pages to allow for dynamic content population.

< PHASE 4: PRODUCTION AND QA >

SLICING AND OPTIMIZATION

After reviewing your information (the **Prepping** part of this phase) and making sure your redesign project is on track, you are ready to start HTML production in earnest and begin **Building**. At this point in production, the graphic templates **[6.6]** are processed (sliced and optimized) into HTML elements (graphics) so that they can be put back together (spliced and coded).

Prior to production, during the design phase, before any visual design directions are finalized and approved, they must get checked by the production team to ensure that the files are, in fact, sliceable and optimizable under target-audience download requirements. Visual designers need to work closely with the HTML production team to determine the best way to slice the graphic templates so that the HTML tables — the rudimentary basis for HTML layout — can be constructed.

<
BUILDING
> Slicing and Optimization
> Creating HTML Templates and Pages
> Implementing Light Scripting
> Populating Pages
> Integrating Backend Development (If Applicable)

> Expert optimization should be a high priority. For an excellent how-to resource, we recommend Lynda Weinman's *Designing Web Graphics.3* (New Riders, 1999).

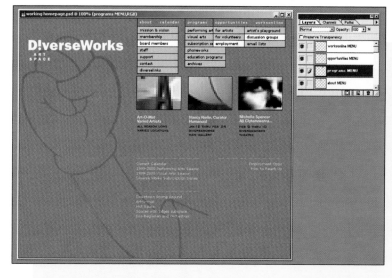

6.6 >

The graphic template for www.diverseworks.org *is delivered to production from design as a layered Photoshop or Fireworks file. This file contains all the elements of the page, including all rollover states, each in their own layers. Shown here are the pull-down menu bar graphics shown in their "on" state.*

< CHAPTER 6 >

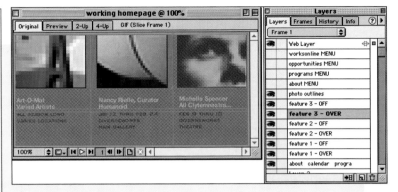

< **6.7**

Graphic templates are divided into sections and sliced in either Fireworks or Photoshop. Clearly identified layers indicate on/off/over states or DHTML callouts.

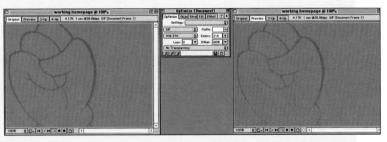

< **6.8**

Before and after shots of a background image being optimized in Fireworks. The file size is reduced to 16K by reducing colors in GIF format.

After the Photoshop/Fireworks files are actually handed off in a state that is producible, production does the actual slicing [6.7] and optimization [6.8] of the pieces. Note that sometimes, when budget and resources dictate, one designer may fulfill both visual design and production roles.

CREATING HTML TEMPLATES AND PAGES

If building a website is akin to building a house, you are currently at the point at which you have your graphics and content (your building materials) and your file directory (your house frame). Now you can build your HTML templates and the contentless pages that get saved from them (drywalling your rooms). As the templates are being created, you will want to incorporate light scripting (wiring, plumbing, and other functionality). After that step, you will be able to populate your pages (furnish your house) as you get close to launch (your housewarming party).

The first HTML template sets the standard for globals such as navigation; table structure; HTML font usage; ALT, COMMENT, and TITLE tag treatments; and so on. Take the optimized graphics that were sliced from the graphic template, add any other elements that need to be included (including any light scripting that should be incorporated; light scripting is discussed next in this chapter), and build in HTML. Test the initial HTML file(s) on various

< P H A S E   4 :   P R O D U C T I O N   A N D   Q A >

browsers and platforms. Make sure the graphic template translates and the HTML tables don't break [6.9]. This file will be your base. If it is faulty and you don't fix it here, its errors will propagate in every page saved from it. Note that this testing is not considered QA per se; it is simply standard procedure for the production designer to check for errors.

Save from this initial template to create a page — the first of many. This new page (no longer a template) becomes a designated page within the site and is ready to be populated with content, whether static or dynamic. These pages now can be linked and tested.

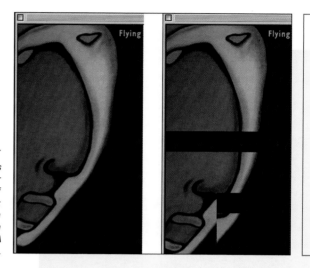

6.9 >

Large graphic elements often get sliced into pieces for easier download. Beware of tables breaking. Shown here: www.flyingsparkfurniture.com with a workable table (on the left) and during pre-QA troubleshooting.

A Few Definitions for the Uninitiated

graphic template   *n.* A layered, digital file (usually Photoshop or Fireworks) containing unrendered, editable text, built by a visual designer, that clearly indicates all information necessary for producing the design in HTML. Once a graphic template is sliced, optimized, and coded, it becomes an HTML page.

HTML template (also called **HTML shell**)   *n.* An HTML page containing no page-specific content, built by the production designer by splicing together all the elements that were sliced and optimized from the graphic template. Visually matches the graphic template. (Utilized by production to create further files using the Save As command.)

optimize   *v.* 1. To compress an image or code into as small a file size as possible to minimize download time. Usually saved in GIF or JPG format. 2. To webify, to make web ready.

slice   *v.* To separate a graphic template (or a portion of a template) into two or more images (usually either GIF or JPG). *n.* A sectioned-off area of the Photoshop or Fireworks file designated to be a single image (usually either GIF or JPG).

splice   *v.* To reassemble GIF and/or JPG images in a seamless manner using HTML so that the file, when viewed on a browser, looks like the original graphic template.

Version Control

Make sure it is very clear to anyone with access to the active HTML files when a file is being worked on. This is, obviously, meant to prevent two or more team members from working on a file at the same time. Such miscommunication usually results in wasted time, overwritten files, and lost work. If you have two or more people working on the HTML, having an established method of version control in place facilitates efficiency. Dreamweaver 4 includes a handy feature that allows people to check in and check out files. Third-party programs such as SourceSafe, Perforce, and WebDAV might be appropriate for your workflow as well.

As you build the HTML templates on which your pages will be based, the production designers should take care to adhere to visual standards established during the design phase and written into the Style Guide (see the end of Phase 3). In anticipation of the QA testing you will need to conduct later in this phase (the **Testing** part of this phase), keep checking your work against all browsers and on both the Macs you might be working on and the PCs most of your audience will use.

Including Includes

Is one of the reasons your site is being redesigned that it became cumbersome to upkeep? Sometimes a simple maintenance need like updating a copyright footer turns into such a mammoth job (as it would be on a site with hundreds of pages) that the updating task often goes undone. When building, you sometimes find yourself repeating things: bits of code, headers and footers, and so on across the entire site or at least on a majority of pages. Using the common example previously mentioned of a copyright footer, how do you change the year on every page? You can do one of the following:

1. Hand open each page (time consuming) and edit each. Reupload each page.

2. Do a global search-and-replace using an HTML editor. (This assumes that there are no variations and that your original text is all the same.) Reupload each page.

3. Build an include. Reupload a single page.

An include (noun, not verb) is a chunk of text coded and stored separately but applied globally so it can be edited in one place. A JavaScript include is a repeating functionality. Rather than plugging the repeating code into every page, simply reference an external file that is saved on the server separately from the HTML page. No complicated nested frames necessary. An include is an src property (source indicator), which is not so different from an IMG tag (image indicator). It is even almost dynamic in this way, except that includes don't require a backend database. Note that using includes somewhat slows loading. Assess your priorities: Does ease of updating outweigh the quarter-second of loading? Probably yes, but it's worth the evaluation. Regardless, including an include streamlines future production and is a great feature for redesign projects for which upkeep was a challenge on the old site.

< P H A S E 4 : P R O D U C T I O N A N D Q A >   < T I P S >

IMPLEMENTING LIGHT SCRIPTING

Rollovers, forms, pull-down menus, pop-up windows, image swaps, frames... all are the result of light scripting. By "light," we mean essentially do-it-yourself or basic JavaScript that requires very little understanding of complex programming. Light scripting should not be confused with anything like JAVA, ASP, or CGI. Rather, it is standard functionality that appears in site after site, such as rollovers [6.10]. It is code that can be "lifted," or shared, and slightly modified to fit to your site's needs.

As software improves, implementing light scripting and special features (such as media requiring plug-ins) gets easier and easier. This should come as

no surprise. If you used Fireworks to slice out and optimize your graphics templates, you were able to attach simple behaviors such as MouseOvers and SwapImages as you optimized and exported. If you exported an HTML file of the graphics template, much of your light scripting is already done.

Include all light scripting at this point in your workflow. Add browser sniffers and redirects. Drop in QuickTime or Flash files. Test all added functionality against specified browsers and against your audience's capabilities. Test, test, test. Look for errors. Yes, there is still QA coming up, but don't wait until then to catch bugs.

Smaller Is Better

Yes, you are responsible for maintaining the K-size for the file. This includes more than just the K-size of the graphics involved; make sure to take note of HTML K-size (source code) and any outside programming. You have a target, and now you have a "finished" piece. Too big? Go back and reoptimize. See if you can shave off a few bytes here and there. Make some decisions. Adjust.

Resources abound for code sharing. "Lift" JavaScript from any of these sites: www.javascript.com, www.builder.com, developer.netscape.com, www.scriptworld.com.

6.10 >

On the home page of www.diverseworks.org, the rollover is a dithered close-up shot of artwork that rolls over to become sharp. ON and OFF states for the rollover are specified in the layers palette of the graphic template.

159

< E X P E R T   T O P I C >   < C H A P T E R   6 >

JEFFREY ZELDMAN ON WEB STANDARDS

Write once, publish everywhere. That's the goal.

To achieve it, the Web Standards Project (www.webstandards.org) has called on browser makers to support a core group of standards. These standards have several names (CSS, HTML 4, XML, and so on), but they all support a very basic idea: the separation of style from content.

What does this mean? It means your design lives in one place (for instance, in a Cascading Style Sheet [CSS]), and your content lives elsewhere (for instance, in HTML or XHTML documents, or in a database of XML-formatted text entries).

Why would web designers want this? Why would we want to separate our design from our data? For one thing, if the template for an entire site (or a section of a site) lives in a single CSS document, redesigns are a piece of cake. Need to change your background image, color scheme, margin widths, text size, fonts, and/or

leading? Edit one CSS document, and an entire site (or section) instantly changes to reflect the new design. Try doing that with traditional "HTML-as-design-tool" markup. You can't. Even with sophisticated HTML editors, you're looking at hours or days of monkeywork, not to mention additional hours of browser-specific testing and debugging.

For another thing, if you can separate your design from your data, then people using non-traditional browsers will no longer be barred from your site. Whether they're on web-enabled cell phones, Palm Pilots, nongraphical browsers like Lynx, or special browsers to accommodate a physical disability, they will now enjoy full access to the site's content. With the separation of style from content, you don't have to create alternate versions of entire sites to support these folks (an expensive and time-consuming process in its own right); you simply add a rule or two to your style sheet.

With full support for web standards that facilitate the true separation of style from content, our jobs will get easier, mindless and repetitive tasks will be greatly lessened, and larger audiences will be able to access our sites with fewer problems. Instead of wasting our time and our clients' money on alternate

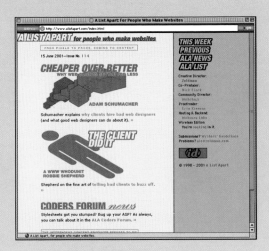

<PHASE 4: PRODUCTION AND QA>   <EXPERT TOPIC>

versions and cumbersome hacks and work-arounds, we can spend it on richer content, enhanced design, and additional functionality.

I creative-direct A List Apart, a weekly on-line magazine for people who make websites (www.alistapart.com). Because I control the site — it's not something I handed off to a client and forgot about — and because I update the content each week, I am also constantly upgrading the site's design and user flow in small and large ways. It's an ordeal because my style and content are tragically

yoked together in a manner that is practically unsustainable. I use CSS to control typography, but because of current browser limitations (especially in 4.0 browsers), I still abuse HTML tables to control the layout. So any design change, even the smallest, takes hours.

When I finally get that page where I want it, can I automatically upgrade the rest of the site to work like that page works? No, because each page is a nest of painfully interdependent, hand-coded table cells. It's too complex for global search-and-replace. And I have no production budget (the site is independent and noncommercial). So there's an archeological effect as you delve back into older issues: The design is always subtly worse than the issue you've just read. A redesign downward, as it were. That may be interesting as a historical curiosity, but site-wide, consistent branding and user flow go right out the window.

Within the next 18 months, if standards compliance improves across all browsers and users upgrade, I'll redo the layout entirely in CSS, which will enable future redesigns to take minutes instead of hours — giving me more time to spend developing site features and cultivating guest authors. I'm currently trying to make changes like that, but with 10 percent of

our readers using Netscape 4 and another 25 percent sporting IE4, I can't really move.

I've described a simple, content-based site. Imagine bigger and more interactive sites, liberated by standards like XML, CSS, and the DOM. Imagine one team redesigning while another implements new functions without either team worrying that they're canceling each other's work. It's going to be amazing, but we're not there yet.

Jeffrey Zeldman, (www.zeldman.com), *the author of* Taking Your Talent to the Web *(New Riders, 2001), is also the publisher and creative director of A List Apart, a weekly magazine "For People Who Make Websites"; co-founder and current group leader of The Web Standards Project, a grassroots coalition fighting for standards on the web; and founder of Happy Cog, the New York City web agency least likely to go public. In his free time, Zeldman, a popular speaker at web conferences, writes columns for Adobe Web Center, PDN-Pix Magazine, and Creativity.*

<TIPS>   <CHAPTER 6>

Cascading Style Sheets and DHTML

DHTML is JavaScript combined with Cascading Style Sheets (CSS) to manipulate HTML. It allows for multiple levels of HTML that can be put into layers and independently controlled. When using CSS, you define a set of attributes, apply a name, and then reference that name. If you want to change every header to a different color, CSS makes the task much quicker. Unfortunately, 3.0 browsers don't support CSS, and some 4.0s have difficulty with it, too. For the time being, if you want to use CSS, you need to do twice the work because you will usually need to create two side-by-side sites or suffer degradation of design as users view your site on browsers that don't support CSS.

Hand Coding vs. WYSIWYG (What You See Is What You Get)

They say hand coding is a lost art… or is it? Many projects require the knowledge and flexibility that comes with an advanced level of HTML expertise. For many of these projects, the HTML production designers create code one tag at a time — called "hand coding" — using programs such as BBEdit or a hybrid such as Homesite. Hand coding almost always results in "cleaner" code than WYSIWYG editors generate. And as HTML purists tend to be adamant about the crispness of their code, many coders avoid WYSIWYG editors not only because they tend to add extra and sometimes cumbersome proprietary code, but also because WYSIWYGs often don't allow tweaking to as fine a level as can be achieved by hand.

With recent versions, WYSIWYG editors have enabled individuals who are not HTML savvy (designers and non-technical team members) to create HTML pages with drag-and-drop ease. Adobe GoLive and Macromedia Dreamweaver, the two industry-standard WYSIWYG editors, are each making huge strides to offer more than just an easy-to-use interface. One of the biggest advantages of WYSIWYG editors is saving time. Hand coding can be a tedious and lengthy process.

Even though WYSIWYGs have their downsides — most notably the extra source code — these applications are excellent for getting started in web design and are definitely appropriate for a large percentage of projects. But learn the HTML, too. You will be better able to tackle any development challenge.

POPULATING PAGES

Your content is due. Chances are, some content is in, some is late, and some is still being changed. But with your HTML templates completed and your pages built out, if you don't have content to work with at this point, your production designers will be idling... on the clock.

Anticipate this moment. Before the deadline actually comes, email the person who is responsible for content delivery and let that person know that the content-submission deadline is imminent. Make it clear that as of a certain date, content will be frozen, period. Frozen means no longer changeable. Final. If you do not do this, content will continue to trickle in, and content that comes in after the freeze constitutes Scope Creep; you can charge for it (see the "Slippage and Consequences" sidebar earlier in this chapter). Be aware that content will still come in even after you officially freeze it. Trickle happens. Build a cushion into your freeze date if you can.

Once you begin to populate your pages, make sure the content goes into the correct places. But who can remember (or intuitively know) where content goes? Someone, probably the project manager, has been receiving the content from the client. With this person as development-side content coordinator, use the Content Delivery Plan as a checklist, rely on the naming conventions of the web-ready files that were delivered, or develop another method of ensuring proper content placement. Whatever the plan, communicate the content-tracking plan to all production designers involved in populating the pages. Make certain nothing gets missed or placed in the wrong spot.

As you place the content, pay attention to both the layout and the HTML text style standards set by the visual designers. Be on the lookout for content that was not anticipated and therefore has no standard. Contact the visual designers and ask them to define the standard right away. Likewise, if you come across headers that need to be graphic images, make sure to alert the visual designers. Sometimes there is a template for the headers. If so, production can simply create what is needed without involving the visual designers.

Invisible Content

Populating your pages involves *all* content, including the frequently forgotten, production-specific "invisible content" — ALT, META, and TITLE tags. Some invisible content, like ALT tags on graphic globals such as navigational elements, should be added at the HTML template creation stage so that it only needs to be done once. Others, like TITLES, should be included when pages are built from those templates. Invisible content is regularly left until the very end or is flat out forgotten. Keep it in your workflow.

Content Buckets

Dynamic sites often have designated areas, or "content buckets," where dynamically generated content (for example, "Today's Top News" or a database-built shopping list) gets placed. This is usually an HTML placeholder built into your page that will get filled by dynamic content. Content buckets need separate consideration because they are points of integration between backend and front-end.

If your site is not dynamically driven but you have an area where content regularly changes, make certain you specify clearly in your HTML Style Guide how to properly update that area.

< CHAPTER 6 >

Meta Generator

Title: Featured Destinations

Refresh after: [ ] seconds. Refresh URL: [ ]

Referal URL: [ ] ☐ Generator ☐ Pragma

Description: (less than 256 words) Featured Travel Destinations from Compass Travel - Highlight this month is California Surf Safari starting at $869.

Keywords (,): Travel, Surfing, Vacations

Language: [ ] Copyright: 2000

Author: [ ] Reply e-mail: sales@compass.com

Document Class: [ ] Classification: [ ]

Document Rights: [ ] Document Type: [ ]

Rating: [ ] Distribution: [ ]

Robot Searching: All Revisit Every: [ ] days.

Document State: Static Cache Control: [ ]

© 2000. Aitor Asencor. Digital Media. · email: webmaster@dmedia.net . Version: 1.2

OK Cancel Help

< **6.11**

Dreamweaver 4's Meta Generator screen helps make the creation and implementation of META tags streamlined and part of the workflow.

Make sure the invisible content is ready to go before the coding process begins. Few things are more frustrating than starting to work with a page or section and then having to go back and back again to fill in blanks. Know what the blanks are and how to fill them *before* you begin. Dreamweaver 4 has a handy form that asks you questions up front before you start each page. Copy this form [6.11] for your client to fill out as part of content delivery.

The client may not have every last item or image ALT tagged, and that is okay. But ALT tags can go a long way to add clarity, further define a word, or work with light functionality [6.12]. Regardless, as long as a naming convention or style is established, the production designers can move forward.

INTEGRATING BACKEND DEVELOPMENT

Communication between the backend development team and the front-end design and production teams has always been important, but at this point in the web development process, it becomes absolutely crucial. Suffering a lack of consistent communication is an exceptionally easy trap for any project to fall into, especially because some backend engineering can take months while the front-end is usually measured in weeks.

< P H A S E 4 : P R O D U C T I O N A N D Q A >

The logical place in the workflow for backend and front-end to integrate is during or right after all of the HTML pages are complete. At the beginning of the production phase, however, gather all front-end production and backend engineers, and work out a plan for integration and communication. What is the best way to create the HTML templates so that they can be handed off to the backend team for dynamic content population and programming? How much programming should be done in the HTML stage? How much experience with programming do the HTML production designers have? Which team will be responsible for inserting the actual backend code into the HTML pages? What is the timeline for integration? Who will be doing what to the templates from each team? A typical meeting will require the project managers or leads from both teams to meet. Key members from the development team should also be present, including the information designer and the art director. The technical specifications document and the Client Spec Sheet should be pulled out and reviewed by everyone.

6.12 >

ALT tags can further define a particular link, eliminate guessing, and/or help the user make a decision to click or not to click. Here, www.zeldman.com's simple text link uses the ALT tag to quirkily identify what clicking will open: a pop-up window of Tipi the cat.

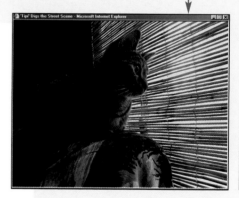

In the works: a standards-compliant redesign of **A List Apart** (no, it won't work in Netscape 4; it's a *standards-compliant* redesign) and the resurrection of the ALA mailing list. No, they're not ready yet.

Cat photo? **Why not**. 6 am Sunday morning, 'Tipi' digs the NYC street scene many stories below.

'Tipi' digs the street scene. Will open in a popup window.

3 February, 2001
[2 pm]
"There is a moment in each of these transactions where an information architecture reveals itself. When IA is narrowly defined as the internal organization of Web sites, or as usability, or as an

< C H A P T E R 6 >

UNDERSTANDING QUALITY ASSURANCE TESTING

You've built your site; now make sure it works. Quality assurance (QA) is one of the most often skipped steps (besides usability testing) in the development process. Not surprisingly, we highly recommend *against* skimping on QA. Broadway productions wouldn't go live without a full dress rehearsal with sound and lighting in place; you shouldn't launch a site without a comprehensive run-through, either.

We recommend shooting for a QA budget of approximately 10 percent of your total time and resources. You need this time to track and fix mistakes such as spelling errors, orphaned and rogue links,

misplaced content, and so on [6.13]. But the even bigger job is bug tracking and fixing: broken tables, functional errors, browser crashes, everything that is not up to specifications. You then need the time to fix those bugs and then to crosscheck once again before the site goes live. And, if you have access to the client server, you will want to QA immediately post-launch as well.

However, in many projects, there is seldom time left in the budget for QA testing. More often than not, the testing and acceptance of production are slammed right up against launch. All too often, production deadlines have been pushed (usually due to late-arriving content and technical snafus), and the time allotment for QA is compromised. The extent

The QA Lead

In Phase 1, we outlined various roles and responsibilities, one of which was that of the QA lead. Depending on the size of the project or the extent of your development team, you may not have the luxury of having a dedicated individual assigned to overseeing and managing quality assurance. If this is the case, chances are the project manager will have to fill this role. For project managers new to this role, we recommend a crash course in QA — some expertise in the testing and launch of any product is

far more valuable than "winging it." For an excellent overview of QA principles and philosophy, go to www.philosophe.com.

If you are managing this task, make sure to keep client expectations in line. Educate your client as to the value of comprehensive QA and to the extent and the cost that QA can take. Make sure the client understands that "comprehensive" calls for more than one day and more than just a few thousand dollars.

to which you will actually be able to conduct QA will depend largely on three things: 1) how close you are to your launch date — usually a result of how well you were able to adhere to your schedule, 2) acceptance criteria, or how perfect the site needs to be prior to launch, and 3) how flexible, if at all, the launch date is.

This critical testing process can take place informally with just a few team members, or it can be a larger undertaking, done either in-house or by hiring an outside company or team. The real-world tendency is to approach this process haphazardly, but be forewarned: Without a cohesive QA plan, you are taking a big chance. And chance is never a good step to stand on, not when there is a budget at risk. Have a plan.

CREATING A QA PLAN

You have known since the beginning of your redesign project that you would need to QA your site and that you would need a plan for it. Chances are, however, the extent of your QA plan is a budgetary/scheduling line that looks something like this: QA = 12 hours. Or 5 hours. Or 20+ hours. That budgetary line depends on the scope of your project, client expectations, and the expertise of your team. Reassess your QA plan. Keep in mind that complicated frame sets, intricate HTML templates, light scripting, and links all need to be QA tested. There

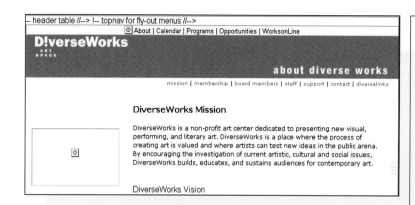

6.13 >

A typical, simple bug: The image isn't loading (top). A quick directory check and reupload of the image solved the problem (bottom). An example of a bigger bug would be a DHTML pull-down menu that crashes certain browsers (this is harder to get screenshots of).

<CHAPTER 6>

Quality assurance testing can employ several procedures, most of which typically are used both in software development and for testing websites and web applications. In all testing situations, the extent of testing varies widely depending on technical complexity and the detail of the test plan.

BASIC/STANDARD TESTING PROCEDURES	
Smoke Testing	Testing without a formal test plan, smoke testing is also called "ad hoc" or "guerilla testing." Often, due to time and resources, this is the only type of testing conducted prior to launch.
Alpha Testing	Also referred to as "internal testing," alpha testing is the initial testing of a site after the production and functionality are in place but prior to public display.
Usability Testing	An analysis of a user interacting with the site's interface through task-oriented actions, usability testing determines a site's ease of use through observation. (For more on this topic, see Chapter 8: Testing for Usability.)
User Acceptance	Usually performed through a number of specific tests, user acceptance is dependent on scope, budget, and expertise. User acceptance verifies customer requirements (platform, browser, operating system, connection speed, and so on).
Content Check	The content check confirms content placement (not just copy — check also for image utilization and positioning), spelling, and syntax.
Beta Testing	A final check to confirm that all is functioning as intended prior to the actual launch of a site, beta testing is generally performed on the client staging site or in a subdirectory on the live server.
ADVANCED/FORMAL TESTING PROCEDURES	
Load Testing	Also called "stress testing," load testing utilizes software programs that simulate multiple users hitting the site simultaneously to determine a server's breaking point. (Costs vary widely; research is necessary to determine needs.)
Functional Testing	Also known as "black box" testing, functional testing confirms actual functionality against the specification document. Specific setup involves the person testing the functionality having knowledge of the intended outcome, but not the programming details.
Unit Tests	A test of individual components on a web page to make sure they function as specified, unit tests are verifications conducted before the code is submitted for integration of intended versus actual functionality and response.
Regression Testing	Also known by the simple name "retesting," regression testing confirms that all tracked bugs have been fixed, that the old code is still working as intended, and that no new problems were created due to said fixes. Note: The level of regression testing and confirmation varies widely.
Security Testing	A check that confirms that database and transactional information is secure from unauthorized users or hackers; a security test usually involves inside understanding the server setup.

< P H A S E 4 : P R O D U C T I O N A N D Q A >   < T I P S >

are essentially three levels of QA: light/informal, semiformal, and formal. Make the decision as to the level of QA your project requires.

A core plan for running quality assurance shows resources, time allotted, the extent of QA expectations, who is involved, criteria for acceptance, and what the development team and the client are each responsible for prior to site launch. Running QA should involve, at the very least, two complete run-throughs: first to generate a comprehensive bug list and second to go back over that bug list and make certain that the cited bugs have been fixed. For informal QA, this basic plan should suffice. For semiformal and formal plans, this core plan is expanded on accordingly.

Every test plan or testing situation will contain different criteria for acceptance. Each site will need to check functionality against requirements and across browsers, platforms, and operating systems, from simple pop-up windows and submission of forms to complex login procedures and e-commerce ordering systems. As the web continues to evolve from basic HTML to a functional, application-driven environment, more and more attention needs to be allocated to ensuring integration success.

QA & Servers

Prior to a site going live, the production team should test on both the staging/development server and then again when the site is moved over to the actual server environment where eventually it will be live. When the site is moved over, the testing environment needs to be exactly the same as the live environment. This means that the folders, file structure, and server-side scripts must be correctly in place; otherwise, many of the scripts and CGI elements may not work properly.

The Problem With Frames

If your site contains frames, expect QA to take at least twice as long. Nested frames? Even longer. As a rule, the more frames you have, the more QA is needed. Moreover, frames thwart search engines (see Phase 5: Launch and Beyond). Frames, while appropriate and good for some situations (for example, portfolios, maintaining several levels of navigation, and so on), are so problematic that most often they are simply not worth it. We recommend no frames unless absolutely necessary.

Test Usability During QA

QA testing and usability testing are similar in approach and scope but different in expertise and goal. At times, however, the two overlap, especially when technical errors and complications (checked for during QA) affect a user's ability to move successfully through a site (checked for through usability testing). In fact, usability testing can sometimes be considered a type of QA.

While you are QA testing your site for errors, technical glitches, and cross-browser compatibility, we strongly suggest you also conduct one-on-one usability testing (also called "verification testing" at this stage). Why? To ensure that your site works from the user's point of view.

Naming and labeling must be clear. Navigation must be intuitive and easy to follow. Your site might be clean and free from bugs, but if it isn't easy to use, the chances are it won't get used and will fail.

Conversely, the redesign might be easy to use (congratulations!), but if you have broken links and spelling errors, users won't get very far. Moreover, they will have a poor impression of the site and the company. Make a bug-free and user-friendly site your prelaunch goal. We recommend *both* QA and usability testing prior to launch. For more on usability testing, see Chapter 8.

< T I P S >   < C H A P T E R 6 >

Include the Client

For informal testing, clients should also participate in the QA process in the same fashion as the team members: checking the site and submitting a sheaf of printouts with errors clearly indicated as well as browser and platform types noted. For any level of testing, the client should proof the content. Only the client will be able to truly know if content is in the wrong place or is incorrect. The client should be treated as (and should hopefully act as) a partner and not a finger pointer.

Informal testing is very basic and is doable by the development team. Formal usually entails hiring an outside, trained team. Semiformal is, logically, in between the two. Most sites with a development budget under $30,000 can usually get away with informal testing. Sites with complex functionality and an application layer normally include formal or at least semiformal testing in their workflow.

Light/Informal QA

For informal QA processes, the QA lead or the project manager coordinates and tracks all planned tests and assigns team members to sections of the site, individual browsers, browser versions, and platforms. The assigned team member then goes through the site and compiles and lists all bugs for the HTML production team to fix. An easy way of doing this involves printing out pages that have errors and clearly indicating each error on the printout. Note that these printouts are only complete and

A Core QA Plan

- Summary of overall goals for QA including methodology, schedule, and resource allocation.

- List of specific browsers, platforms, and operating systems being tested.

- List of desired connection speeds being tested.

- List of any specific paths or functions that need to be tested.

- A plan for bug tracking (using a web-based program or Excel spreadsheet or printouts).

- A plan for confirming that fixes have been made prior to launch.

- Any stated assumptions (known risks) to protect the team if all fixes cannot be caught prior to launch. These should be listed in the Details and Assumptions section (in Phase 1) of the project plan or contract and be signed off on prior to the final site being delivered or launched.

- A plan for fixing bugs that cannot be resolved prior to launch. Who is to handle them, how will any additional costs be identified, and so on.

< PHASE 4 : PRODUCTION AND QA >
< TIPS >

helpful if the browser and platform is noted on the printout that notes the bug. Without knowing the browser and platform, it is difficult to re-create the error and therefore fix it.

The project manager also tracks the "bug list," which, in informal testing, is really no more than a stack of printouts with bugs noted. A big red checkmark through the noted bug indicates that it has been addressed, and an accompanying initial indicating "Fixed" or "Deferred" with a date helps track the fixes.

Usually, for small- to medium-size sites (under $30,000 budgets) with very little technical complexity, this informal process is a perfectly adequate method. Informal testing is also referred to as "ad

hoc" or "guerilla testing" in that it has no formal test plan or approach. Testers are just "banging" on the site, looking for bugs to slay.

Semiformal QA

If your project requires more than "guerilla testing," yet your budget will not accommodate formal testing with an outside company, the perfect middle ground is semiformal testing. Stepping up from informal to semiformal testing involves more time, expertise, and planning — and if possible, the addition of a trained QA lead and a test bed setup. A semiformal test plan should contain a one- to two-page overview that highlights the scope, timing, and goals of the QA testing process.

Test Beds

The bank of computers (set up in the testing area) that reflects the target browsers, platforms, and connection speeds of the audience is often called a "test bed." It is difficult to list every combination of browser and platform; at least use the main ones [6.14]. Even testing a smaller, representative group will result in catching many errors on the site. Test beds are common for semiformal and formal QA. Often for informal testing, the various browsers and platforms are not in the same location.

6.14 >
A chart like this one will help track all of the platform/browser configurations of the target audience. It can reflect the test bed setup. This sample audience does not include users on 3.0 browsers or UNIX platforms.

	NET 6.x	NET 4.x	NET 3.x	IE 5.0	IE 4.0	IE 3.0	AOL 4.0	AOL 3.0
MAC OS9	X	X		X	X		X	
WIN 2000	X	X		X	X		X	
WIN NT	X	X		X	X		X	
UNIX								

<TIPS>   <CHAPTER 6>

Bug Tracking Tools

Although you cannot substitute automated software systems for actual QA testing with humans, there are many available tools that can aid in the process. For complete HTML validator testing, links, spelling, load time, and more, try www.netmechanic.com. Fees range from $35 to $200 for testing up to 400 HTML pages.

Other online tools? They are plentiful. Try www.scrubtheweb.com to help check your META information. www.w3.org/People/Raggett/tidy will help you clean up your HTML. For an excellent bug-tracking tool, visit www.alumni.caltech.edu/~dank/gnats.html. Want to learn more about bugs? Go to www.mozilla.org/bugs. Mozilla itself is handy for QA as well.

Formal QA

Planning for formal QA testing requires experience, time, budget, and most of all, attention to detail — minute detail. The biggest difference between semi-formal and formal QA is the level of test planning, the cost, the generation of documentation, and the degree of expertise.

Formal QA uses a comprehensive bug-tracking system and a fully trained QA staff (yes, staff) to test requirements and pages against specified browsers and platforms. It includes test plans, tools, use cases, a test bed, and reports. To illustrate the extensiveness of the formal testing process, consider this example of a typical formal QA plan: Identify at least 10 different paths through a site and test each path on three platforms (MAC, WIN, UNIX), with each platform hosting three browsers (IE, Netscape, AOL), with each browser having several versions (3.0 through 6.0, note that Netscape skipped 5.0) — all needing to be tested. This example now has approximately 450 different tests ($10 \times 3 \times 3 \times 5$) for the defined paths. Overwhelming? Yes. Impossible? No. Impossible in an informal setting? Yes. Recommended for large sites with a significant backend engineering and extensive functionality? Absolutely.

Bug Reporting

Reporting a bug is easy. Reporting bugs in a way that is meaningful, reproducible, detailed, and solution oriented is a challenge. Here's the old, serviceable, good-for-informal-testing way: Print the page out, note the browser/platform, circle the error, fix the bug, and then check the error as fixed (or deferred if the bug can't be fixed yet). Here's another (and maybe better) way: Use some kind of tracking device — even an Excel spreadsheet will suffice — although you can only have one person working with the file at a time. Whatever your tracking method, make certain to note the following information:

- Browser type/platform type.

- Operating system.

- Description of problem (one line).

- Detailed description.

- URL of page.

- Severity of problem.

- Can the error be reproduced?

< P H A S E   4 :   P R O D U C T I O N   A N D   Q A >

PRIORITIZING AND FIXING BUGS

Decide what needs to be fixed immediately. These are the showstoppers — the glaring errors. Continue your list and prioritize the remainder of the fixes with headings such as showstoppers, high priority, medium priority, and low priority. Understand that some bugs may be unfixable because they are end-user dependent. If you can't re-create the bug, mark it as such. They might be due to end-user browser settings [6.15]. Depending on the time left before launch and the level of perfection that is necessary at launch, plan for prelaunch fixes and post-launch fixes alike. Postlaunch fixes should happen in an iterative fashion.

After addressing bugs, test your fixes. Try to re-create the error. Some fixes may require several tries.

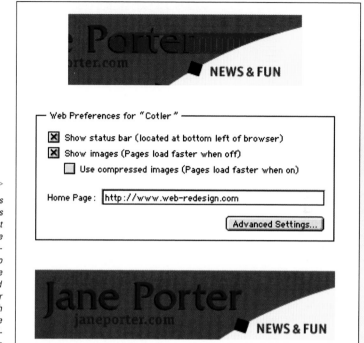

6.15 >

An image glitch (top) shows up on AOL 4.0 browsers during the QA process, but randomly — only on some laptops. End-user preferences setting were to blame: Unchecking "Use compressed images" and then dumping the browser cache remedied the glitch and displayed the image correctly (bottom). End-user-caused bugs are largely out of QA control.

QA BUDGET COMPARISONS BY OVERALL PROJECT BUDGET RANGE AND TECHNICAL LEVEL		
Light/Informal QA	Semiformal QA	Formal QA
For projects with budgets under $30,000, estimate the QA budget at 1% to 3% of project cost. **Technical level: light.**	For projects with budgets ranging between $30,000 and $70,000, estimate the QA budget at 5% of project cost. **Technical level: moderate.**	For projects with budgets over $70,000, estimate the QA budget at 10% to 20% of project cost. **Technical level: moderate to complex.**

NOTE: For projects at or under the $10,000 budget mark, a mere $100 worth of time and resources will not work. You do need to go through the entire site.

<TIPS>   <CHAPTER 6>

Showstoppers

There are bugs and then there are
big bugs (sort of the difference
between a harmless little earwig and
a thumb-sized Palo Verde beetle).
Big bugs are showstoppers —
errors that simply cannot go live.
These errors *have* to get fixed before
launch (for example, the home page
loads incorrectly, a pull-down menu
crashes IE, the frame sets are mis-
targeted, and so on). As you track
bugs, prioritize. What are showstoppers? What can get fixed in an iterative approach in the first week of
launch? Sometimes the launch date
is set in stone, and you do not have
the time to fix all bugs. Prioritize and
slay the showstoppers first. The rest
can wait a few days.

CONDUCTING A FINAL CHECK

Conduct a final check with all teams involved. Make
sure all systems are go. Here are the key five items
to confirm:

- **Design check.** Designers have a keen eye
  for detail; they might catch misalignments
  and incorrect graphics that a good QA team
  might never notice. HTML text might be
  placed incorrectly; a photo treatment may
  have been misapplied. Have the art director
  or designer give the site a thorough look on
  both Mac and PC to ensure quality control.

- **HTML check.** Confirm that all tables, cells,
  and graphics are lining up properly. Your
  team may not have had enough time for
  ample tweaking. After QA is in full gear and
  fixes are being implemented, let the HTML
  team check once more that the site is visually
  working on both MAC and PCs. Sometimes
  QA fixes alter/wreck code.

- **Functionality/engineering check
  (if applicable).** Confirm that all functionality is working in accordance with the technical specifications. Make sure that database
  integration is complete and that all transactions can be accomplished on the live server.

- **Content check.** Confirm that the headlines
  are reading as headlines, that body copy
  reads like body copy… you get the picture.
  Make sure that the content formatting was
  appropriately applied by the production
  team and that everything is lining up
  as expected.

- **Client approval.** Making sure the client sees
  and approves the entire site prior to launch
  might seem like an obvious check-off item.
  Surprisingly, it is often the case that,
  although the redesigned site has been signed
  off on by the marketing department the
  entire time, the CEO or advertisers who need
  to approve the site before it goes live may
  never have seen the final site. Sometimes it is
  appropriate to wait until the last possible
  moment to get the approval from the highest
  level; sometimes this delay causes chaos.

< P H A S E   4 :   P R O D U C T I O N   A N D   Q A >

PHASE 4 SUMMARY

The production phase is probably the most straight-forward phase in the Core Process. You actually produce and build the site. There is little room for improvisation. Production is a straight shot from start to finish: Query your client, compose the Client Spec Sheet, consult on feasibility with the visual designers and the information designer (Phases 2 and 3), build the Protosite and test functionality (Phase 3), receive the graphic templates from the visual designers, slice and optimize graphics, build HTML templates and integrate light scripting, build and populate individual pages, integrate complex functionality and backend applications and/or engineering, and test. Then breathe. Then build the HTML Style Guide and prep for handoff (Phase 5).

Why involve the production team throughout the entire process? Quite simply, without advance checking, testing, and confirming, the building phase can be risky. You may as well get off a ski lift and ride down any random run without checking its skill level. Think of the possible crises: finding out as you build the HTML templates that your pull-down menus block the contracted advertising space, or trying to slice and optimize a layout that simply does not translate to HTML. Either of these scenarios would involve chalking up as a loss the numerous hours spent coding. The team would have to backtrack, and if the launch date is firm, you might not have enough time.

Not to worry, however. The Core Process sets you up so that production can get pulled off with minimal hitches. Sure, you encountered bugs — every site has them. Be thrilled that production is done! Well, almost. Your site is built. It is logically organized and will be easy to maintain thanks to well-thought-through HTML. Your site is bug free. It is user friendly. It looks exactly as your visual designers intended. You are ready to take care of launch and what follows. If this were that pie we mentioned at the beginning of this chapter, it would be baked.

Now get ready to serve.

PHASE 4 CHECK-OFF LIST

Prepping

☐ Compose the Client Spec Sheet

☐ Assess project status

Building

☐ Set file structure

☐ Receive graphic templates from the visual designers

☐ Slice and optimize graphics

☐ Create HTML templates

☐ Implement light scripting

☐ Build individual pages

☐ Populate individual pages

☐ Include invisible content

☐ Integrate complex functionality and/or backend engineering

☐ Freeze production

Testing

☐ Create QA plan

☐ Conduct QA testing

☐ Prioritize and fix bugs

☐ Conduct final check

< CASE STUDY >

Janus

Client: Janus Capital Corporation
URL: www.janus.com
Design Team: Sapient
Maintenance Team: Janus in-house

Janus Capital Corporation has been a key player in the mutual fund business for 30 years. Janus primarily targets the individual investor with its aggressive investment objective. Based out of Denver, the majority of its business is conducted over the phone or online.

< PREVIOUS >   < CURRENT >

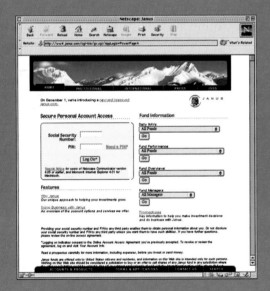

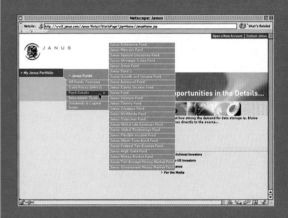

JANUS.COM [OLD] LAUNCHING NEW JANUS.COM [REDESIGNED] offered its audience a preview of the new site before it launched, allowing a buy-in from the user base prior to making the change. (2000)

JANUS.COM [OLD] shows a very task-oriented process. 24-hour self-service through the web was the goal, even with the old site.

JANUS.COM [REDESIGNED] employed social research findings to understand how investors behave. More intuitive navigation allows for a truly efficient customer experience. The visual iconography was changed to position Janus's brand more effectively.

Result: Greater productivity and lower costs. In January 2001, 62 percent of investors contacted Janus through Janus.com as compared to 32 percent in January 1999.

Launching your site is a major milestone —

celebratory, even. But it is only a step; a website

is an evolving production.

Phase 5: Launch and Beyond

< C H A P T E R 7 >

Phase 5: Launch and Beyond

In today's web development world, this moment — launch — should not be an end; it is a transition into an entirely different workflow: maintenance. Who will maintain the site and what are their qualifications and capabilities? Who will be responsible for the creation of post-launch content? And don't forget about evaluation — you still need to determine the measurable success of your site. Did the site meet the original goals of the creative brief? Are users finding it usable? Are users finding it at all?

Here, in the fifth and final phase of the Core Process, the distinction between internal and exter-

nal teams becomes even sharper than before — and therefore, so does the difference in the usage of the word "client." In the beginning of this book, we explained how we use the word "client" to apply across the board. In the instance in which a company contracts a web development or design firm to produce its site, the "client" is the company that does the contracting. We also use the word "client" to denote the decision-makers in a company in which the web/design department is in-house. In either case, the client is whoever signs off on budgets, schedules, and designs. Intepret the word "client" as it best suits your particular situation.

The workflow involved in this phase covers what you need to know as you smoothly transition your redesign project out of the hands of the web development team and into the care of the maintenance team. Even if these teams are made up of the same people, the roles are very different.

Specifically, this chapter is about launching your site and what you need to think about before, during, and after your site goes live. Phase 5 includes loose ends that need tying up, some suggestions on

WHAT THIS CHAPTER COVERS		
DELIVERY	**LAUNCH**	**MAINTENANCE**
› Handing Off	› Going Live	› Maintaining the Site
› Completing the Production Style Guide	› Prepping an Announcement Plan	› Assessing Maintenance Team Capability
› Creating the Handoff Packet	› Registering with Search Engines	› Internal vs. External Maintenance Teams
› Tracking Documentation	› Launching the Site	› Developing a Maintenance Plan
› Conducting a Postmortem Meeting		› Measuring Success
› Scheduling Maintenance Training		› Confirming Site Security

< P H A S E 5 : L A U N C H A N D B E Y O N D >

how to announce your site and register with search engines, and also some tips on how to assess and measure the site's success and usability. Whether your project is small or large, refer to this chapter to help make sure important things don't slip through the cracks during the final hours.

HANDING OFF

As any designer will tell you, a project is only done when someone says it's done. It always feels like more fine-tuning is possible. As a result, it is difficult to actually "freeze" development. Somewhere, however, it needs to stop. Establish a point in time when the design, production, and development of the redesign project has reached a full cycle — if for nothing else than to send the final invoice. Understand that there may never be a perfect moment to do this; ongoing errors and issues will continue to crop up. Websites, by their very nature, are never "finished" the way a printed piece is finished. The client and development team should mutually decide in advance what defines the point of transition between a site-in-development and a site-in-maintenance. Clearly defining responsibilities and transition points, as well as handing off a packet of materials, helps make the gray area between development and maintenance much more black and white.

Most projects have one team responsible for the building and launch of a site and another team set to take care of the site's ongoing maintenance. Even

for internal teams, the individuals who created the site are often not the ones maintaining it. But regardless of who is transitioning the project to whom, now is the time when several items need to be wrapped up so that the maintenance team can do its job.

Completing the Production Style Guide

After the site is launched, the production designers have a moment to breathe and recoup. Now, before too much time passes, have them add production information to the Style Guide that was started by the visual designers in Phase 3: Visual Design and Testing.

Production complexity will vary from site to site. Heavily nested tables, complex frame sets, includes, and style sheets — not to mention content management systems and other backend functionality — all add to potential confusion as a second team takes over. Make the Style Guide comprehensive because it will be used as a reference guide for the maintenance team when adding or modifying HTML pages or graphics.

Include any and all information necessary to update and maintain the site. Be clear and concise and be available should the maintenance team have questions. Establish — and get it in writing — a predetermined timeframe for back-and-forth questions and tech help. A few weeks of emails flying back and forth should be expected. A few questions within a few months after that are also acceptable.

<TIPS>   <CHAPTER 7>

Who Broke It?

Who is responsible for fixing problems that arise in the first few days/weeks following handoff? Here's a real story: A web development team handed off a fully QAed site. Upon going live, a programming error appeared. The client's in-house team claimed no responsibility. The development team countered that, due to firewall issues, the feature could only have been tested on the client's server, to which they didn't have access. But because there was no predetermined statement of responsibility, the development team had to spend more than 30 nonbillable hours troubleshooting.

In any web project, there is bound to be some back and forth, but if handoff is approached in a proactive manner, issues can be resolved without pointing fingers. Lesson learned: Decide billable factors in advance and get it in writing.

RECOMMENDED PRODUCTION STYLE GUIDE COMPONENTS

DEFINITION OF GRAPHIC ELEMENTS

Sample code for all graphical elements	For all visual design elements (page dimensions, headers, colors, type, photo treatments, embellishments — reviewed in Phase 3's Style Guide), include a sample of the accompanying HTML code (the code for a particular bullet, the code for photo insertion, and so on).

NAMING CONVENTIONS

For TITLE tags	Specify how the names of each page appear in the browser bar. Will there always be the company name? How will subsections be shown?
For images	Are you using any prefixes and/or suffixes to identify images (e.g., hd_contact.gif or nav_services.gif)? Are you using underscores and/or mixed case (e.g., nav_contact_on.gif or navContactOn.gif)? Where are images kept (e.g., images used in multiple sections are kept in /images/global/, whereas section-specific images are kept in /images/section/; or they could be divided by type such as /images/header/ and /images/nav/)?
For Cascading Style Sheets	What are the CSS names for each FONT set? The font may be Arial Regular 8-point gray, but if you are using CSS, you create a style and name it. List those names and the treatments for naming the styles.
For files/folders	Are you using prefixes and/or suffixes to identify files? The same considerations as for images (above) also apply here.

FORMATTING OF CODE

Tab	When to tab? When to break lines?
Comment tags	When and how to use? Include sample code.
Case sensitivity	Uppercase versus lowercase (for example, tags are UPPERCASE; attributes are lowercase).
Absolute vs. relative links	Define when to use which and where (if applicable).
Includes	Define when, where, and how to use (if applicable).
JavaScript	Define code conventions for ease of manipulations (how to create additional rollovers, how to change link references, and so on). Graphic and code examples of these elements may need to be included.
Definition of templates (if used)	Describe how the template is broken down into parts and how to properly populate it. This section should include code and graphical elements examples.

< P H A S E 5 : L A U N C H A N D B E Y O N D >

RECOMMENDED PRODUCTION STYLE GUIDE COMPONENTS

STRUCTURE/ORGANIZATION

Site structure	Identify where everything is being physically kept in the directory. Identify where new files (as a result of maintenance) will be kept.

PAGE LAYOUT

Page layout	Add code illustrating the basic outline of the page layout, including **\<body\>** tag info and margin attributes.
Type/fonts	Add code illustrating the CSS being used; for example, **a.red:link { font-family: verdana, arial, helvetica,sans-serif; font-size: 10px; color: #CC3300; } .body { font-family: verdana, arial, helvetica, sans-serif; font-size: 10px; color: #666666; }**.
Sizes/colors	Add code illustrating the fonts being used with their sizes and colors; for example, **\<font face= "verdana" size=2 color="#c9c9c9"\>**.
Navigation	Include sample code illustrating the navigation if explanation is necessary. If JavaScript functions pertaining to navigational elements warrant, describe with a brief walk-through of code.
Menus	Show sample code illustrating the menus (if applicable). Include explanation of any JavaScript functions pertaining to menu elements with a brief walk-through of code.
Forms	Walk-through of code for form elements (if applicable). What information is being passed, where is it being sent, how is it processed, where is it stored, how can information be reviewed, and so on?
Additional elements	Banner ads, placements, and sizes. Integration with third-party vendors. User tracking: How is the info collected, where is it stored, and so on. Additional JavaScript, PERL, ASP components that need explanation. META tag information.

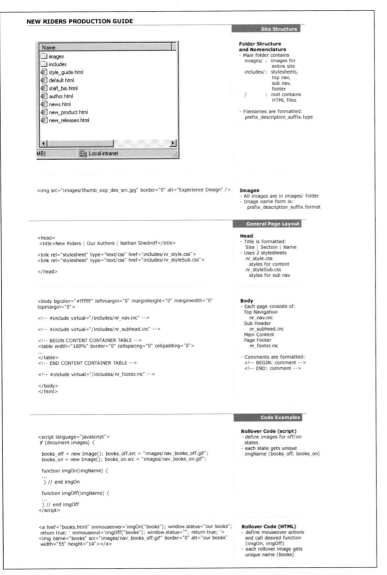

< CHAPTER 7 >

But three to six months down the road, if the maintenance team still needs regular assistance from the original web development team, then that constitutes billable services. Long in advance of handoff, set up a firm understanding that post-launch technical assistance and maintenance needs will be billable as of X number of days after handoff. Whether 30 days or 45, 60, or 90, the point is to preset the duration. State this in writing and have the client sign off on it. (The best place for this documentation is in the Details and Assumptions section.)

The production portion of the Style Guide should include code information for HTML tags, attributes, and definitions of graphic elements. Please refer to the comprehensive set of components to include in your Production Style Guide. The level of detail is project dependent. The layout of the Production Style Guide should compliment the layout of the Design Style Guide. We recommend that it be both visual and informative [7.1]. Portions of your project may be very straightforward and not need code called out. Conversely, your project may require additional items (for instance, a frame map). If your frames require a significant understanding of logic, include a detailed chart of what frame targets which files [7.2].

Creating the Handoff Packet

Consider the handoff packet to be like a baton in a relay race — you are passing on what is needed to

< 7.1

A portion of the Production Style Guide for newriders.com.

< P H A S E 5 : L A U N C H A N D B E Y O N D >

keep running. The handoff packet is the collection of all the assets, materials, and documentation of the project. It contains all source files, images, templates, and specs necessary for another team or individual to understand the site after the initial launch.

Gather all files relevant to the site's production. Communicate clearly between team members when determining which files — both design and HTML — are worth archiving. You probably have many intermediary files, perhaps called layout_01, layout_02, layout_06, final, final_2, final-final, and so on. Cull aggressively. Clean up files you want to keep and name and archive everything clearly.

Materials will vary from project to project, but a complete packet should be burned to CD-ROM and should contain at least the following:

- **All Photoshop/Fireworks files (in layers, text *not* rendered)**

- **Fonts (or information on where to purchase fonts)**

- **All photos/illustrations (including copyright information — don't forget about usage rights!)**

- **HTML pages and templates**

- **Style Guide (design and production) in HTML**

- **Technical specifications**

- **The root folder of the site and other relevant files**

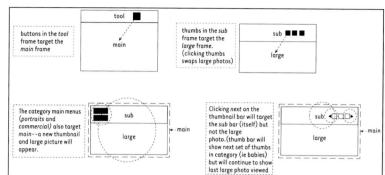

7.2 >

For a frame map, identify which links target which frames. Make it very clear.

<TIPS>

<CHAPTER 7>

Plan for Usability Testing

Conducting usability tests on the live site is the first chance to see how real users interact with the site. One of the best comparison methods for obtaining measurable results is to conduct usability testing on the existing/outgoing site — and then compare results to the newly launched redesigned site. If any areas are still hard to use, incorporate appropriate modifications into the maintenance plan and retest for usability after a subsequent update of the site.

This handoff packet should be approved by the project manager, lead production designer, and art director. Once the packet is handed off, the transition has happened. At this point, the site is the maintenance team's responsibility.

Because no one knows a site as well as those who built it, training and direction will almost always have to accompany the handoff materials. When planning maintenance training, set up a predetermined number of hours for the task; otherwise, it may turn into a never-ending process. Be timely with handoff materials; maintenance starts right away.

Tracking Documentation

Although you don't need to print out every last email, the relevant ones — especially anything that demonstrated client approval — should be gathered for internal archival. Also gather anything else (AC forms *with* signatures, memos, project plans, contracts, and so on) that discusses scope changes. In the possible case of dispute over invoice, these documents go a long way toward clearing up miscommunication. Furthermore, when it comes time to bid on a new redesign project, you can refer to actual costs versus guesswork.

Sort through all documents — some hard copies, some electronic — and cull. Archive everything relevant by whatever method your company uses to handle archival: a binder, folders, or CD-ROM. As always, the more organized you are throughout a project, the less work will be required to wrap it up.

What Archived Documentation Should Include

- Budget approvals: initial budget and weekly budget reports (signed and dated whenever possible)

- Additional charges (ACs) — signed!

- Emails (especially those with any approved changes or requests from the client)

- The original proposal

- The project scope or project plan

- Submitted documents: reports or studies generated during the project, including the creative brief, competitive analysis (if conducted), usability testing reports, and so on

- Printouts, records, or sketches of information from the design and visual design phases

- A hard copy of the Style Guide

< PHASE 5: LAUNCH AND BEYOND >

Conducting a Postmortem Meeting

The postmortem meeting is an excellent chance to reflect on the project as a whole and revisit lessons learned. A total recap of the project's development, this meeting should be attended by all key members. If you are on an external team, this meeting is usually conducted without the client present. If you have an internal team, then the client is often part of the team.

Every project is a learning experience. Some projects go well; others are challenging. Begin the postmortem meeting with a broad overview of the project from start to finish, and then isolate areas where there were innovative breakthroughs, issues, communication gaps, and/or places to improve on methodology. Maintain a positive approach and avoid blame or finger pointing. Don't turn the meeting into a gripe session (you still need to work with these people); rather, identify the spots in production where the flow was impeded. What caused slow-downs? What ran smoothly, and how can that successful workflow be duplicated in the future?

Scheduling Maintenance Training

With most sites in maintenance, the unfortunate tendency is for the layout, graphic treatment, and information design to slowly break down and lose cohesion. With the original designers no longer choosing photos, laying out pages, and signing off on new content placement, the maintenance team begins to impart its own sense of design and organi-zation, especially when incorporating new content. Avoid this eventuality. Set maintainable standards. Even if the maintenance team has a background in design and layout, and even if its members are creative individuals with design ideas of their own, the integrity of the site depends on maintaining the look and feel *that has been established*. It is heartbreaking to watch the redesigned site slowly fall apart, often through no fault of the maintenance team. Usually, it is because they have not been adequately prepared for the task.

Communicate clearly by explaining the Style Guide, the graphic and HTML standards, and the technical goals of the site. Consider it preventative medicine for your redesigned site.

GOING LIVE

With the site poised to move to the live server, all testing should be complete, and production *must* be frozen. Because there are probably still bugs to be slain, have a solid plan in place for post-launch fixes. But with the QA process essentially finished, the site is ready for public viewing. Congratulations! Just as moving to a new location provides the impetus to send moving announcements, a new site launch offers the opportunity to announce a new, redesigned site at the same, familiar URL.

Plan your announcement strategy long in advance of the launch date. Know how you intend to advertise and promote the site once it goes live and know

185

<TIPS>
<CHAPTER 7>

Soft Launch

Imagine a schedule that has breathing room. Imagine the luxury to launch on the live server and test there without the timing constraints of outside factors such as a big advertising campaign or the release of an annual report. A soft launch is a nonpressured posting of the site to the live server. Sometimes a soft launch also means the site is not yet complete, as in "We are soft launching on October 1 with 85% of content in place. We plan to fill in the remaining content by December 1 and advertise the redesign then." A hard launch is simply a situation with a hard deadline — a "drop-dead" date that is usually accompanied by outside timing restraints. Always plan for a soft launch. If the client can't accommodate, make the risks abundantly clear: If there are bugs associated with the live server (this includes firewall issues), they may not be found before going live.

who will be involved. Is the external web development team involved? Is the internal team handling it all? Has an advertising firm been brought into the mix? What about timing? Often there is an immovable date — called a "drop-dead" date — for the launch. This can be dependent on a variety of outside factors, any of which might announce the redesigned site. These might include an upcoming tradeshow or company presentation, the release of an annual report, or anything else happening with a firm date. If outside factors are fueling the launch schedule, make sure to know who is in charge (for example, the marketing department or an outside advertising agency) so the person can be contacted should schedules slip or content radically change.

Your Current Audience and Its Comfort Zone

Part of easing your current audience into accepting your redesign is to let these people know about it in advance. Create a page to introduce the redesign and clearly identify the new features and navigation. Link it directly from the home page. Make your current audience part of your newly launched redesign. Consider the following list as a guide:

- **Redesigned.** Tell your audience that you've redesigned your site. Let people know that this will only help you do a better job for them.

- **New Features.** List your new content features. Did you add new media? Add more FAQ items? If you are launching your redesign in iterative sublaunches, list what is coming soon.

- **New Navigation.** Tell your audience what you've done. Here is an example: "We've restructured our site and provided more page-to-page links to make it easier than ever to get around and to get the information you look for regularly. We've broken up long pages that required lots of scrolling and added 'bread crumbs' at the tops of pages so you always know what part of the site you are in."

- **Feedback.** Make it easy to get feedback. Try the following text: "Like the redesigned site? Have any suggestions? Find any broken links or glitches? Email us. We'd love to hear from you."

< PHASE 5: LAUNCH AND BEYOND >

SITE ANNOUNCEMENT PLAN TIPS			
Before Launch	**During Launch**	**After Launch**	**Off Site (Should Be Planned Far in Advance)**
• A month or so prior to launch, announce the impending launch of the new website on your existing site [7.3]. • A few weeks prior to launch, preview the redesigned site from your home page [7.4].	• If customers will notice that your site is down while you are uploading, put up a temporary page announcing that the redesigned site is launching "right now" [7.5]. • Some companies launch sections in phases and announce certain times when the site will be down for maintenance while the sections are being updated.	• Send an announcement inviting customers to see the "new and improved site." • Have an area on the new site explaining what changed, why it changed, and how the improvements will help the customer experience. • Take screenshots for promotional use.	• Determine how you can promote your site on other sites with a similar audience profile using banner ads and links. Set up advertising agreements prior to launch so that after launch, and after an advertising delay, banners and links can run. • Determine what offline printed materials can announce the relaunch: monthly newsletters, brochures, a new mailer, and so on. Have the plan in place so that after launch, and after an advertising delay, printed materials can run. • Confirm traditional offline marketing methods. Depending on advertising budget and the marketing effort supported by the client, this campaign could be local, regional, or national in print and media. Get everything in place so that after launch, and after an advertising delay, advertising can run.

< **7.3** >

Smug.com ran this humorous splash-page announcement for months prior to launching its redesign. The options smug.com offered were entry into the existing site or an email link that offered notification of when the redesign would be launched.

< **7.4** >

Allow users to become familiar with the changes. (Remember that people generally dislike change, even if it is for the better.) Before launching their redesign in late 2000, Janus Funds (www.janus.com) had a pop-up window offering the option of previewing the new site or closing the window.

< **7.5** >

Artist Booking International (www.artistbooking.com) pushed a soft launch that allowed for QA on the live server before going truly live to users. This page, announcing that the redesign was uploading right then, sat on the URL for the duration.

<TIPS>   <CHAPTER 7>

Preparing an Announcement Plan

Depending on your audience, the redesigned site can
be announced both online and offline. Use existing
methods already in place with current materials
(brochures, business cards, printed collateral, advertising) and explore new options as well. Regardless of whether or not you are working toward a soft
launch or a drop-dead launch date, make sure marketing and promotional cues are in place, but don't
let marketing drive your launch to the detriment of
the integrity of the site (if you can help it). See the
Site Announcement Plan Tips chart for some suggestions as to when and where to announce the
redesigned site.

Registering with Search Engines

According to a NetMechanic.com newsletter, 85
percent of internet users use search engines to seek
sites. Getting your site listed in reputable search engines involves more than simply sitting back and
waiting, although waiting does eventually work

There are a lot of resources on the web that help give advice
and also help submit your site more effectively. We recommend www.searchenginewatch.com, www.selfpromotion.
com, and www.workz.com — all good resources full of helpful information.

(sort of). Websites are launching daily, and competition is always increasing to be one of the top 10
matches in search engine results.

Submitting to search engines is not as easy as
"$99 will submit your site to ALL THE TOP
SEARCH ENGINES!" Beware of internet offers
that resemble used car ads. Although services like
these will indeed submit your site, and possibly
eventually lead to *some* placement in search engines,
the results may not be what you'd hoped.

In a study by www.workz.com, a survey was sent
out to 37 member site owners to gather data about
what methods they used to influence their search
engine rankings, how much time they spent on the
task per week, and their measurable results. The survey results clearly stated that the best results came
from manual submission to key search engines, with
about an hour a week allocated to modifying and
improving keywords. Successful search engine registration takes time and a customized approach.

For search engine submissions, there are basically
three approaches to follow:

1. **Submit directly to individual search engines.**
   Submitting directly is time consuming because
   each search engine has different requirements.
   However, this method is also touted as one of
   the more effective ways to submit, monitor,
   and finesse keywords, TITLE tags, and other
   elements to get better results.

< PHASE 5: LAUNCH AND BEYOND >   < TIPS >

2. **Submit using a paid search engine submission company.** There are services (some good, some not so good, some a waste of time) that seem valuable in that they claim to be familiar with the industry and have automated systems set up to allow registration and submission to occur quickly and easily. Submitit.com charges a minimum of $59 for two URLs. Registerit.com is a free service with submission of up to 12 search engines for free. Although these services can save you time, opinions on the results remain mixed.

3. **Use software to monitor and submit.** Software tools exist that help check HTML pages and uploads, as well as submitting to search engines automatically, all in hopes of keeping your site in the top 10. Web Position Gold (www.webposition.com) has been favorably reviewed and is relatively inexpensive.

Title Tags

So much more than just the name at the top of the browser bar, TITLE tags are often misused and underused. They are one of the most important factors involved in generating effective search engine results. When creating the title, assume that this is all a potential user will see in a search engine result list. Titles are also used for bookmarks; having a descriptive title makes the bookmark easy to use and identify.

Preserving Bookmarks and Search Engine Links

As you retire the current site, consider that a significant percentage of your existing audience — an audience that you want to keep — may have bookmarked heavily frequented pages from your old site. And what about search engine rankings? Do any of your pages rank high? You want to preserve this placement. Due to information design changes, specifically with file/directory structure and naming conventions, many of your site's URLs may now be obsolete.

Don't lose traffic due to this potential hiccup. If you have a small site, put an announcement on the pages in question and redirect users to the home page of the new, redesigned site. Many servers can be programmed to redirect to any specified HTML page if a "page not found" error occurs. The error page can be custom coded to fit your needs, including having it redirect back to the home page, provide email links for customer or technical support, or show a message that the site has been redesigned.

< C H A P T E R   7 >

Here is a tool to help you create META information, primarily keywords. Please don't confuse this tool with a "how to list your site with search engines" tool or a "how to get the best listing results" tool. Rather, this tool is a list of items to consider as you generate META information that will be relevant to search engines. Have the client use the tool to make the appropriate lists and then return it to the project manager. Then submit it to the HTML production team for integration.

Download a blank META data creation tool from www.web-redesign.com >>>

META DATA CREATION TOOL

1 Basic Company Information provides for <TITLE>

Company name	List company name, parent company name, and any derivatives, including misspellings or abbreviations.
Company description	Write a brief description about the company (20 to 30 words), which will be coded in the <META NAME ="description"> and will appear in search engine results.
Key principals/ management team	List names and misspellings of all key individuals in the company (include maiden names if a principal recently married).
Index/home page title	Create a TITLE tag for your home page that is clear, descriptive, and concise. This content usually appears as the linkable text when your site is returned as a search criteria match.
Location	Relevant cities, states, regions, or areas.

2 Industry/Service Information provides for <META NAME="keyword" CONTENT="xxx">

Key industry terms or buzzwords	List all key industry terms that describe your business, services, and offerings.
Products or services offered	List any and all key products or services offered; list specific product names if relevant.

3 User-Oriented Information provides for <META NAME="description" CONTENT= "xxx">

Sample searches	How might your target audience search for your site? Come up with several sample search queries for different results: industry-, job-, investor-, product-, or service-related.
Theme and content	What is the theme of your site? What kind of content do you have on your site that users might find relevant?
Subpage searches	Besides the home page, are there any other sections of your site that users might find and go to directly? If so, create <META> information for these subpages.
Key phrases	What might people trying to find you type in when they search? Think especially of people who don't know who you are. "Bed and breakfast" isn't as good as "bed and breakfast in San Francisco" or "small hotels in San Francisco." Be creative. Think like your users.

< P H A S E   5 :   L A U N C H   A N D   B E Y O N D >

COMPILED META INFORMATION

www.Purina.com

<TITLE>	Come to Purina for expert advice on caring for your cat or dog.
"description"	Let Purina enrich your life by improving the lives of your pets. See us for nutrition, health care, training, and grooming.
"keywords"	Purina, dogs, cats, pet care, pet products, pet nutrition, pet institute, dog food, cat food, Purina O.N.E., Dog Chow, Cat Chow, Kitten Chow, Fit and Trim, Meow Mix, Tidy Cats, SecondNature Dog Litter, Purina Treats, CNM, Pro Plan, cat litter, veterinarians, breeders, Ralston Purina, St. Louis, MO

www.petsmart.com

<TITLE>	PETsMART.com — The smarter way to shop for your pet.
"description"	Products, food, and supplies for cats, dogs, birds, fish, reptiles. Pet trivia and pet of the week.
"keywords"	Petsmart.com, Petsmart, Pets, pet, Pets.com, Dog, Dogs, Cat, Cats, Fish, Pet supplies, Pet supply, Horse, Veterinarian, vet, aquarium, pet store, bird feeder, pet adoption, pet food, pet rescue, adopt a pet, kitten, puppy, dog training, pet toy, distemper, bird, reptile, small animal, bird, reptile, small animal

Here are two examples of compiled META information.

> **Compare and Copy:** Search for companies that offer similar services and look at their keywords. Underhanded? Maybe, but it happens all the time.

ERIC WARD ON MAKING YOUR SITE LINKWORTHY

Why do some sites seem to be linked to from all over the internet while other sites are nearly invisible? Why does a search engine rank one site above another?

The basic architecture of the web lets any document link to and be linked from any other document. It's legal, proper, expected, and the essence of what makes the web so useful. Without links, what is the web? Imagine seeking information on the web if sites had no links to other sites. Imagine Yahoo! with no links.

There are several ways in which a link can lead to another site. Banner ads are just a link from one site to another, so are text links in e-newsletters. Buttons, badges, icons, affiliate links, directory listings, search engine listings... all nothing more than links. Click them and you get sent somewhere else.

There are three main reasons why a site would have links to it. One, the site paid for them. Two, the site was designed so that search engines could easily index it. And three, the site had content that other webmasters felt was useful enough to link to.

As for search engine links, the reality is harsher. With thousands of new web pages added to the web every day, you compete against an ever-growing database of content. Given the challenge of competing against so many other sites, it's surprising how many sites make design choices that render it nearly impossible for search engines to index them at all.

To make your site more "indexable" by search engines, avoid common design elements that confuse search engines. For example, big graphical image maps do nothing to help the search engines know what your site is about. Search engines look at HTML text only. There are so many ways that sites sabotage themselves with regard to search engines that they can't be covered in a single article, but here are some general tips for removing the impeding qualities your site may have:

- **Try to have all your web pages reachable from your home page within three clicks. Most engines will only crawl three levels deep when indexing your site.**
- **Make sure every page on your site has TITLE tags and META description and keyword tags; and use ALT tags on all your images. Put some thought into these tags.**
- **If you use frames on your site, make sure you use NOFRAMES tags. If you don't, your pages will not be indexed.**
- **If you use image maps, make sure you have an HTML-based text navigation menu somewhere on the same page.**

These points merely scratch the surface, but they illustrate the complexity of the topic. One of the best moves you can make is to go to a site like Danny Sullivan's Search Engine Watch (www.searchenginewatch.com), an entire site devoted to these exact issues. A few minutes each day reading about these issues will give you both an education and some perspective.

Eric Ward created the web's first service to announce and link new websites way back in 1994 — services he still offers today. His client list is a who's who of online brands, including the original site launches for Amazon.com, Virtual Vineyards, OnSale, The Link Exchange, Microsoft, Rodney Dangerfield, Kellogg's, the AMA, the BBC, and The Weather Channel. His services won the 1995 Tenagra Award For Internet Marketing Excellence, and he was selected as one of the web's 100 most influential people by Websight *magazine. Eric also writes columns for* ClickZ *and* Advertising Age.

Launching the Site

All testing has been completed on the staging server, fixes have been made, production is frozen, and the announcement plan is in place. All systems are go. Plan to upload to the live server during nonpeak hours to allow for downtime to interfere as little as possible with the regular web traffic. Then… Launch! Have a "live" moment. Be accessible to your real audience and customer base.

An important part of launch is an immediate QA test on the live server. If you were able to schedule a soft launch, this is a nonpressured event, and testing can be conducted in a relatively leisurely timeframe (a few days, close to the first 24 hours but hopefully no overtime). If you launched on a drop-dead date, some rushing is probably in order to test on the live server. Be prepared to roll back to the old site if any showstopper bugs pop up.

Launch is a big black dot in the very gray area between development and maintenance. Client and development teams need to agree on when the site is

Prioritize Fixes

You may not be able to catch every last thing prior to launch. You should have a list of prioritized changes and fixes for post-launch maintenance. A perfect site is very hard to achieve, even with QA completed and usability testing performed. There has to be some threshold of acceptable losses. First take care of showstoppers — bugs that must be fixed prior to launch — and then launch. Fix the next most important bugs and then fix the rest. If you are an external team readying for hand-off, determine what is feasible for the maintenance team to handle. Hand off when appropriate.

Four Surefire Ways to Hide from Search Engines

1. **Fancy TITLE tags.** Avoid fancy or irrelevant TITLE tags. Some designers like to lay out titles like this: "a c m e   h o m e" so that it looks nicely designed in the browser. While this may be prettier than "ACME HOME" and simpler/sleeker than "ACME ROAD RUNNER EXTERMINATION COMPANY," it results in a search of the letter "a" — totally ineffective for someone searching for "acme" and clearly of no benefit for the Acme Company.

2. **Splash pages.** We have already recommended not having a splash page, but if you must, give it a descriptive TITLE tag and META "description" and "keyword" information. Remember, most search engines only dig three levels deep. If your first level is taken up by a splash page, you waste the opportunity to have your true third-level pages indexed.

3. **Frames.** If you want to hide the contents of your site from search engines, use frames. Enough said.

4. **Capitalization.** You'll drive yourself nuts. Search Engine Watch (www.searchenginewatch.com) stresses the fact that 85 percent or more of all searches are all lowercase. You can try and do every iteration of each keyword (Grocery Store, grocery store, Grocerystore, and so on), but we recommend keeping it simple. List it once, all in lowercase.

< CHAPTER 7 >

truly ready to go live. This may sound simple, but often there is a lot of going back and forth between fixing and refining, and finally having the okay to go live. There is also the potential problem of handing off a site to a client without first being able to test on the client's server. All kinds of issues can pop up at that point. And whose responsibility is the immediate post-launch testing? The maintenance team's or the development team's? Make sure this is clear. And if you are an external team launching on a client's server on a drop-dead date, make certain you have the access you need.

When it is finally time to go live, go live. Voilà! You are now in maintenance. Have a celebration. Get some sleep. Then get ready to track the results of your labor.

MAINTAINING THE SITE

Maintenance is the fuel that keeps a site alive. Your announcement plan may get visitors to your site once, but twice? What about regularly? In a recent study, Forrester Research Inc. interviewed 8,600 web-using households to find out why people return

A rollback is the last saved and approved version of a site. Have a rollback of the old site standing by just in case something goes horribly wrong with the launch.

to websites [7.6]. High-quality content led the poll, closely followed by ease of use, quick download time, and frequent updating. Consider that only regular updating keeps high-quality content fresh and new. This makes maintenance responsible for both the first and the fourth top reason why a visitor returns to a website.

Maintenance, however, doesn't just happen. There needs to be a plan for immediate, post-launch fixes and ongoing, long-term regular updating. A 12- to 24-month maintenance plan is a good timeline to undertake. Include in the plan ways for dealing with glitches, usability issues, and scheduled updates. Don't forget about getting user feedback and usability testing results both immediately after the site is live and a few months later. User feedback is integral to shaping the redesigned site.

Assessing Maintenance Team Capability

In most situations, the development team hands off to a maintenance team that is already in place. "Who will be maintaining the site?" the development team asks. It is not uncommon for the client to answer with pride, "Charlie in marketing knows some HTML. He's been posting our press releases for six months. We think he's doing a bang-up job. We're planning on having him take care of the new site, too."

Here is a simple, straightforward fact: The individuals responsible for updating need to have a high enough level of skill to handle the maintenance of the redesigned site. The web development team should assess the capabilities of the maintenance team against the complexity of the redesigned site. It presents an obvious problem for someone like "Charlie in marketing" to suddenly maintain a dynamically driven site or a complex multiframe nesting setup when all he has is a basic understanding of FrontPage. Either Charlie needs tens of thousands of dollars worth of training or the client should be advised to hire an expert or two and let Charlie do some of the less technical production work.

We recommend a test. Far in advance of handoff, preferably after the Client Spec Sheet is filled out and analyzed so that the production designers have an idea of the complexity of the redesign, give the maintenance team a proficiency test. Resurrect an old project, one of your more complex HTML layouts. Have the maintenance team update it. Have them fix code. See how they handle adding information that breaks tables. Suggest that they add information and archive the old. Can they follow the file structure? Can they read the HTML and understand it? Do they know Flash or DHTML (if either is applicable)? Do they understand the content management application (if applicable)? Watch them. Do they understand what they are doing, or are they guessing? Quite often web maintenance folks possess an admirable level of production knowledge and only need some training on the specifics of the site. In other situations, it becomes clear that additional maintenance personnel will be needed.

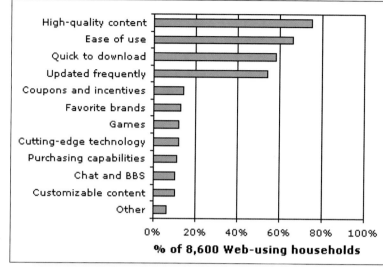

7.6 >

Forrester Research Inc. interviewed 8,600 web-using households to find out why people return to websites. Chart courtesy of system concepts (www. system-concepts.com/ articles/forrester.html).

Monitor Your Server

In case you can't monitor your server 24/7, there are services that can. Server monitoring for less than $10 per month is very reasonable when you consider that it isn't *if* your server goes down but *when*. One server notification service called Server Check Pro (through NetMechanic at www.netmechanic. com/monitor.htm) pages you or emails you when there is a problem. Its web bots check your site every 15 minutes. It's pretty cool and easy on the human resources.

Internal vs. External Maintenance Teams

For many companies, increasing expectations for daily site updates, dynamic content generation, management of e-commerce systems, and effective customer service have engendered the development of web-savvy and detail-oriented in-house maintenance teams.

Maintenance needs vary. Depending on the depth of post-launch content and the frequency of updates, the development of a maintenance team can

MAINTENANCE TEAM SCENARIOS		
Most Often...	**Sometimes...**	**With Increasing Frequency...**
Most often, the client company hires an experienced web development firm to create the redesigned site but expects its own internal team to handle all post-launch maintenance.	Some companies (usually smaller businesses) have the web development firm that designed the site maintain it, or they hire a third-party firm or outside consultant and keep that person/firm on retainer for site maintenance.	With increasing frequency, companies are developing and maintaining in-house and are recruiting experienced talent (art directors, visual designers, information designers, production designers, and engineers) for their internal teams.
Pros: • The experience and resources of the web development firm. • The cost savings of conducting the maintenance in-house.	**Pros:** • Having the same web development team develop, design, and maintain the site is obviously optimal. (It combats the natural degradation of a site over time.) • Hiring expertise for site maintenance can be cheaper than hiring staff if hours per month are low. • Lower overhead.	**Pros:** • The experience and resources of professional expertise for the web development team. • Having the same web development team develop, design, and maintain the site is obviously optimal.
Cons: • The expertise of in-house maintenance teams tends to be on a lower level than the web development team's, resulting in site degradation over time. • Higher overhead for internal maintenance.	**Cons:** • The cost of an outside web development team to maintain the site can be high. • Dealing with an outside firm can be cumbersome.	**Cons:** • Keeping the talent happy in a situation in which they only have one project to work on is difficult. Turnover can be high. • The cost of expertise on a full-time basis can be high.

< P H A S E   5 :   L A U N C H   A N D   B E Y O N D >

be as simple as hiring one HTML production designer for straightforward content updates. For more complex sites, a full team, complete with a full-time project manager, may be required. If you are working on a fairly static site with very simple daily or weekly changes (or even brochure sites with relatively few monthly or quarterly changes), an outside contractor or part-time in-house individual might be a better bet.

There are several things to consider when comparing in-house maintenance to paying an outside development company a retainer (an ongoing payment, usually on a month-to-month or, for more static sites, quarterly basis). It is almost always cheaper to hire internal resources for full-time work. If your maintenance need is only 20 hours per week, however, it doesn't make sense to hire a full-time staffer. There are pros and cons for different scenarios; it must make sense from several standpoints: facilities, management, and financial.

Developing a Maintenance Plan

In the first phase of web development (Phase 1: Defining the Project), we recommended that your client fill out the Maintenance Survey to help align and define post-launch goals. You used the information gathered to help structure the redesigned site so that it could grow with the planned maintenance.

Revisit the Maintenance Survey. What were the goals? Daily news updates? Weekly HTML advertising emails? Press releases? Product additions?

Housekeeping concerns like copyright updates, archival of articles, and so on? Now that production is complete, update the answers from the survey to include anything the client may have added during the course of development. Now is the time to plan for all these things. Be aware of what is required for maintenance and make sure the resources will cover it. A simple spreadsheet — with time on one axis (in hours/days/weeks/months) and the site sections to be updated on the other — clearly communicates what gets updated and when [7.7].

7.7 >

A simple spreadsheet provides a guide for scheduled maintenance.

SAMPLE MAINTENANCE SCHEDULE for a simple site that updates monthly					
	HOME	**PRODUCTS**	**NEWS PAGE**	**BIO/FAQ**	**OTHER**
March 01	Announce new product	Post new product info	Announce new product		Register with Yahoo
April 01			Post reviews of new product	New FAQ	
May 01			Preview new product		Register with Google
June 01	Announce new product	Post new product info	Announce new product	Update Bio to include new product info	
July 01			Post reviews of new product, Preview new product		Register with HotBot
August 01	Announce new product	Post new product info	Announce new product		
Sept 01			Post reviews of new product	New FAQ	Register with Alta Vista
etc.					

197

< CHAPTER 7 >

When Bad Links Happen to Good Maintenance Teams

Links that go nowhere, or that go to the wrong place, are a web reality. They happen even after QA has crawled all over the site. And, as maintenance pours new content into the site, the possibilities for error multiply.

There are resources on the web that help track bad links, slow pages, and errors. Two of the top ones are Web Site Garage [7.8] and Net Mechanic [7.9]. Both sites help to monitor, maintain, and promote your site. Different tools and services are offered for free, with some at a fairly low fee.

If you are working in Dreamweaver, take advantage of the Check Links Sitewide feature [7.10]. Although this will not catch good links going to the wrong place, it will find broken or orphaned links. A double-click will bring up the HTML file and highlight the errant link.

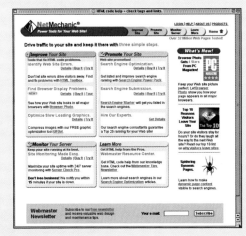

< 7.8 >

websitegarage.netscape.com (no www.).

< 7.9 >

www.netmechanic.com.

< 7.10 >

Dreamweaver's easy-to-use Check Links Sitewide feature.

<PHASE 5: LAUNCH AND BEYOND>   <TIPS>

Measuring Success

With the rapidly changing internet economy and the evolving nature of the web, it is more important than ever to track your site's success after launching. An overall goal of a site redesign is not just to change it but to improve on specific business objectives. These goals, stated in the creative brief, might include increased usage/traffic, increased online sales, fewer customer calls, greater visibility, and so on. Understanding these goals both qualitatively and quantitatively is integral to determining the best methods of measuring the success of the redesigned site.

Often a site's value is measured by traffic, with success measured in hits. Sales, especially directly from the website, are another success indicator. But because advertising is also one of the sources of revenue for companies, it has become increasingly important to *understand* site traffic and page hits as well as the demographics of your user base. This understanding helps not only to provide advertisers with specific data so they can meet their own revenue goals, but also to help companies understand which parts of their sites are getting used the most, which features are working, and — just as important — which aren't.

Many companies spend a lot of money and time analyzing server logs that monitor who is coming to their site (and from where), how long they stay at the site, what major paths they take, and where they usually end a session. This is great information if relevant data can truly be gleaned from pages and

Gather User Feedback

One of the best ways to gauge a site's success upon launch is through user feedback. Gather comments, complaints, and accolades on your site's redesign quickly and easily. Have a prominent link — a feedback button — on each page. Ask users to comment specifically on the redesign's new features. Quantitative data can be tricky to obtain. Some sites have advanced features for gathering customer feedback. OpinionLab's (www. opinionlab.com) product, OnlineOpinion, provides a page-specific rating system that allows sites to capture instant feedback [7.11]. A key factor here is that the user does not need to do more than click.

< 7.11 >

OnlineOpinion is used by adobe.com, netscape.com, dell.com, and others.

Real Story of Real Success

It is important to the success of a site to recognize when to make navigation and tasking easier for a user by bringing the starting point of a main task up a level, possibly even to the home page, thus making it more accessible. Food.com had a tracking system in place that monitored all major visitor activities on its site. Through examining user feedback and site logs, the internal team was able to track where visitors were having difficulty and decided to move the primary action on the site — ordering food — from a first-level page and put it smack up front on the home page. Subsequent monitoring of the site's activity showed a sharp increase in orders immediately after the feature was implemented. The team tracked steady improvement over 15-, 30-, and 60-day periods — and an approximately 30-percent increase in the first month! It was all about listening to the site's users and making the primary task (in this case, ordering online) intuitive, easy, and fast.

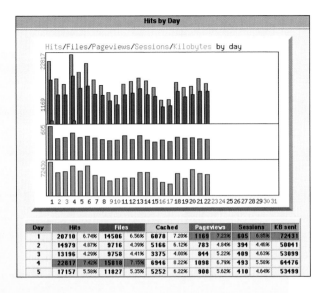

Hits by Day

Hits/Files/Pageviews/Sessions/Kilobytes by day

Day	Hits		Files		Cached		Pageviews		Sessions		KB sent
1	20710	6.74%	14506	6.56%	6078	7.20%	1169	7.23%	605	6.85%	72431
2	14979	4.87%	9716	4.39%	5166	6.12%	783	4.84%	394	4.46%	50041
3	13196	4.29%	9758	4.41%	3375	4.00%	844	5.22%	409	4.63%	53099
4	22817	7.42%	15818	7.15%	6946	8.22%	1098	6.79%	493	5.58%	64476
5	17157	5.58%	11827	5.35%	5252	6.22%	908	5.62%	410	4.64%	53499

< 7.12

What are the most popular pages on your site? Can you define user behavior and patterns? This sample graph was generated by a simple server log and shows top pages by visits.

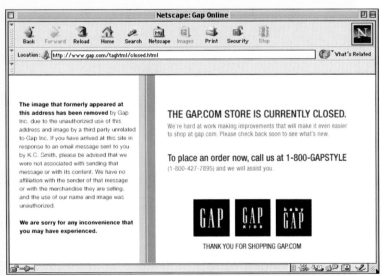

< 7.13

In December 2000, a hacker broke into The Gap's online store and caused enough damage to force the online store to close while the problems were fixed.

pages of barely comprehensible user logs. Unfortunately, it is not easy to decipher this raw data and turn it into meaningful summaries. Few companies actually allocate the time and resources to do it. An alternative would be one of the many software packages that specialize in gathering information, tracking results, and coming up with methods to increase usage [7.12].

Confirming Site Security

Security is usually not the responsibility of the external web development team because no one on the team typically has that expertise. It may, however, be the responsibility of the in-house team — whether they like it or not. If so, hopefully there is a security specialist on staff to protect against hacker break-ins and to go into damage control after security is breached.

The unfortunate reality is that hackers are plentiful, relentless, and invasive. They are the internet equivalent of thugs who spray paint buildings and cars, break into houses and shops, or cause general noise nuisances. Hackers steal personal information, cause chaos, and are nearly impossible to bust. But whatever their reasons, *you* lose credibility and revenue when hackers force you offline [7.13].

What we present here in this section is very rudimentary; it should not be mistaken for a comprehensive how-to on site security. Rather, use this section as an overview of items to think about.

< P H A S E 5 : L A U N C H A N D B E Y O N D >

< T I P S >

A Few Tips to Consider as You Plan for Your Redesign's Security

- Install a firewall — a configured mechanism that enforces a policy of admittance or nonadmittance — in your internal server.

- Protect yourself by outsourcing hosting to a larger service provider, one that has firewalls and aggressive monitoring and response systems.

- If you have an internal team and you host in-house, hire an information technology (IT) person to monitor and understand server complexities and troubleshooting solutions including security. This is probably a full-time position.

- Avoid easy passwords. Use a combination of numbers and letters. Don't make the password ridiculously easy to figure out like "2000" or "1234." This is not called security. Hackers may be craven vandals, but they are rarely stupid.

- Change passwords frequently, especially after any layoffs. Disgruntled employees are always a risk.

- Make it especially hard to get to high-security information. Set up multilayered protection.

- Restrict physical access to your equipment. Lock your doors.

- Pay attention! If you know the warning signs, you have a much better chance of protecting yourself. Monitor your site and its activity. Check server logs. Be aware!

Hacker Alert

How will you know if your site has been broken into? It might be glaring: You have no site, or all your text has been suddenly replaced by gibberish. It might be offensive: All your site images have been replaced with pornographic material (true story, actually happened). It might be more subtle and subversive: A sudden, unexplained increase or decrease in regular traffic patterns could indicate infiltration. The more you monitor your site, the better you will be at noticing when something is amiss. Stay aware!

< C H A P T E R 7 >

PHASE 5 CHECK-OFF LIST

Delivery

☐ Complete the Production
    Style Guide

☐ Create the handoff packet

☐ Track and archive
    documentation

☐ Conduct a postmortem
    meeting

☐ Schedule maintenance
    training

Launch

☐ Prepare an announcement
    plan

☐ Register with search engines

☐ Launch the site

Maintenance

☐ Assess maintenance team
    capability

☐ Develop a maintenance plan

☐ Measure the success of
    the site

☐ Confirm site security

PHASE 5 SUMMARY

Congratulations! Your redesigned site has been launched and transitioned from development into maintenance. If you are an external team, maintenance is a weaning time. Hand off and evaluate the success of the project. Did the Core Process work for you? Where did things run smoothly? Where were there hiccups? Assess, adjust the Core Process to fit your own developing workflow, and move on to the next project. Is it a redesign? No problem — you are now seasoned in doing it right. You've successfully completed the five phases of redesign site development: Defining the Project, Developing Site Structure, Visual Design and Testing, Production and QA, and Launch and Beyond. Don't stop here. The next two chapters, Chapter 8: Testing for Usability and Chapter 9: Analyzing Your Competition, contain extraordinarily helpful processes to add into your workflow if time and resources permit. We highly recommend them.

If you are an internal team and are just receiving the redesigned site for launch, you have a significant ongoing responsibility ahead of you. Regularly registering with search engines and continued analyses of site success are up to you. Maintaining standards and incorporating new content will be a daily/weekly/monthly job. The redesigned site is like an engine that has been rebuilt using many new parts. Knowing how that machine was built, however, is always insightful.

Maintenance, when it comes right down to it, is really just the regular introduction of new content. Why make such a fuss and spend so much time developing guidelines and plans? Shouldn't it all be straightforward? Maybe, but probably not. The fact is that a significant percentage of sites launched grow stale through lack of good upkeep. Having a plan always helps. Whether starting out in the defining stage or wrapping up and preparing for maintenance, whatever the task, we always recommend taking the time to define goals, outline methodology, allocate budget, set a schedule, and identify responsibilities. Winging it rarely works. In fact, many sites slated for redesign stagnated in "No-Plan Land" before the decision to redesign was acted on. Keep your redesigned site healthy and growing with iterative relaunches that smoothly introduce improvements and changes that respond to user needs.

Then you won't have to redesign again for years.

< C A S E   S T U D Y >

Food.com

Client: Food.com
URL: www.food.com
Design Team: Idea Integration, SF
Creative Director: Kelly Goto

Art Director: Serena Howeth
Designer: Eunice Moyle
Production Lead: Chad Kassirer
Production: Rachel Kalman

Food.com caters to the food-delivery customer by providing restaurants with online takeout and delivery services. Although the business continues to expand into different food-related industries, the foundation for Food.com remains being "The Internet Takeout and Delivery Service."

< P R E V I O U S >   < C U R R E N T >

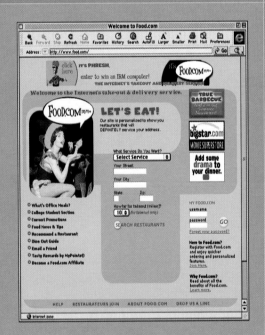

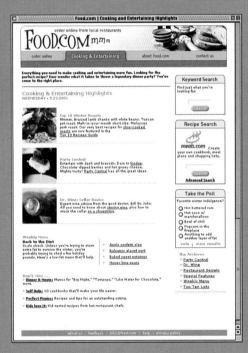

FOOD.COM [OLD] presented itself in the colors and theme of its marketing campaign and a 1950s campy style. Quirky and humorous, yes, but the download was long and the usability poor.

FOOD.COM [REDESIGNED] evolved into a food portal with additional sections (dining, cooking, and news) and a new, clean, and simplified brand image. Redesign goals focused more on audience, a change from the old restaurant-centric and technology-driven approach. (2000)

Result: Improved usability through clear messaging and a directed user path. Online ordering increased.

> Focus groups are what users think they *might* do. Usability testing is what users *actually* do.

Testing for Usability 08

< C H A P T E R 8 >

Testing for Usability

Why does a site get redesigned? Often, a group of people will sit down together and brainstorm: "We need this on our new site," and "This aspect about our current site doesn't work." Unfortunately, this type of idea generation is based entirely on speculation and the personal opinions and prejudices of the people running the company.

Why does a site need to be redesigned? One reason is that it may not be fulfilling user needs, and users are not able to find what they are seeking. A web development team *must* think about usability — once a site is redesigned, will it function as planned? Will

the client/designer desire for the coolest site possible backfire when tested on actual users? What are the stumbling blocks and problematic areas?

We believe strongly in the value of conducting usability tests. Understanding usability testing is important, and this chapter will help orient you. It is designed give a quick overview of the basics so your team can determine the best solutions for obtaining direct user feedback.

Many companies think they are already conducting usability tests, but actually they are running focus groups or online surveys. These are not usability tests. Although all feedback can be valuable, the results are radically different.

For a comprehensive and meticulous look into usability, Jakob Neilsen's book *Designing Web Usability* (New Riders, 1999) is about as complete a tome as exists, and his online articles are top notch (www.useit.com). We are not going that deep into the subject of usability. Instead, we are setting theory aside and are simply explaining how you can fit usability testing into your daily workflow.

WHAT THIS CHAPTER COVERS	
UNDERSTANDING USABILITY	**CONDUCTING USABILITY TESTS**
> Getting Started	> Plan and Prep
> Usability and Redesign	> Find Participants
> When to Test	> Conduct the Session
> Costs of Testing	> Analyze Data and Make Recommendations

< T E S T I N G   F O R   U S A B I L I T Y >

UNDERSTANDING USABILITY

Usability is defined as ease of use. How easy is it *really* to make something work? Operating a can opener is easy. Operating an airplane is complex. Operating a VCR should be easy but usually isn't.

Website usability is the measure of how an individual user actually navigates, finds information, and interacts with your website. Note the word "actually." Usability is not about how you *think* users will navigate, search, or interact. Unlike surveys or focus groups, usability testing is a one-on-one process that incorporates a watch-and-learn approach. One moderator observes one user. Results are immediate and indisputable. If users click the wrong link, they're not wrong... the design is. Usability testing displays how users actually use the site.

Getting Started

It's easy: You need a pen, paper, computer, and browser. You need a plan, participants, and possibly some simple legal forms like a nondisclosure or consent to videotape. You can add a video camera and a testing facility, but often you can conduct tests on a more modest scale, even within the user's own environment. The hard part is finding the time. Having a printed version of the main paths through the site is helpful for note-taking. Be prepared to be surprised; usability testing is never predictable.

The Little Site That Could

Once upon a time, way back in 1996, Carl Smith of Husk Jennings Advertising received a call from a large media company inquiring whether Carl and his team could build them a website in two weeks. Carl assured them he could make their deadline. After all, they had a budget of $8,000.

The site was delivered on time. It was a very simple, clean site that had brief text with a single custom icon on each page. Carl and his team did what was reasonable with the given time and budget. They kept it streamlined and within user-download capabilities.

A few days later, the client called and read Carl the riot act. It turned out that a different department of the client's company had hired another (now absorbed/defunct) web agency to build the site as well. It was beautiful. It blinked! It flashed! It actually had sound! The other design firm obviously knew how to build a site. Husk Jennings Advertising obviously did not.

A week went by and Carl got another call from the client. Suddenly the client loved him. "You're brilliant," the client said. "Your site rated #1 in usability testing. It is easy to use and straightforward. Not at all like that complicated other site."

And the lesson here is?

< EXPERT TOPIC >

< CHAPTER 8 >

JAKOB NIELSEN ON THE VALUE OF SMALL-STUDY USABILITY TESTING

The web development situation now is different than it was in the mid-nineties before usability became a real factor in web development. Now many redesign projects are, in fact, driven by usability needs. Many existing websites are poor matches with user needs, and much too difficult to use. People are finally starting to realize this. I predict that once enough websites are truly driven by usability, they will become so superior that competing websites will see a significant reduction in traffic, and therefore business. The result will be a real impetus to redesign with usability in mind.

Unfortunately, while it seems that most people know they should test for usability, the reality is that they don't. The barrier for many is the false notion that usability testing has to be an elaborate and costly project. If you always wait until you have the budget for the perfect study, you will never get anything done.

If you, as is common, find yourself with no budget or time, you may be tempted to view testing for usability as an expendable step. My

standard advice is still to test but on an abbreviated scale. A very small study with just three or four people — really just a day's work and requiring a very small budget — is incredibly valuable. Focus on just one of the top three core things the site does and test that. With small-study testing, there will be a richness that is lost — you will not be able to test the secondary features, nor will you be able to start obsessing about audience segmentation. But the difference between no testing at all and some data… That difference is immense.

Never say, "We can only afford a small study, so it probably is not worth doing." That's one of the biggest mistakes. I regularly emphasize the notion of many small, fast tests. What almost always happens is that the results of those first simple tests are so valuable, so revealing, that you will get the budget for future studies because everybody realizes how very helpful the testing is.

You can conduct these small studies all along the development process. With redesign

projects, one of the most overlooked testing opportunities is right at the beginning, with the outgoing site itself. Here are two reasons not to pass up testing the outgoing site:

1. What's Wrong?

There are probably a lot of opinions within the company as to what's wrong with the outgoing site — everybody has their own theory. But without empirical insight from real users, any analysis is based in myth. What if you consider an aspect of the website to be wrong, but in reality it is not a big problem? You would be focusing your resources in the wrong place. There is substantial benefit to actually *knowing* what is wrong with the outgoing site before redesigning it.

2. What's Good?

The old site is bad, granted, but it probably is not *all* bad. It likely has some elements that are good and should be preserved. It would be a shame to lose those benefits in the redesign process. Look for what is working in the outgoing site. The old site is, by definition, trying to achieve some of the same goals that the redesign will have. Recommended usability methodology has always been to test several versions of a prototype as it evolves. Testing the old design will give you insight into how users behave with the type of features and content the site offers, as well as the types of products being sold.

Of course, just because people redesign and improve their websites does not mean that they will get a perfect website. First of all, no perfect website exists. Secondly, there is the real-life factor that, as a development team, they have to get the project done in a specified timeframe. Think of web development as a never-ending process — every two years or so you have to go over this again and redesign. There will always be substantial room for improvement, and usability is always a great place to start analyzing.

Dr. Jakob Nielsen (www.useit.com) *has been called "The world's leading expert on web usability"* (U.S. News & World Report), *"The smartest person on the web"* (ZDNet), *and "Knows more about what makes websites work than anyone else on the planet"* (Chicago Tribune). *His most recent book,* Designing Web Usability: The Practice of Simplicity *has about a quarter million copies in print in 13 languages, and his Alertbox column about web usability — published on the internet since 1995* (www.useit.com/alertbox) *— currently has about 200,000 readers. Dr. Nielsen holds 53 United States patents, mainly on ways to make the internet easier to use.*

Why You Haven't Tested

Usability testing: We know we should be doing it, but we tend to push it aside in favor of what may seem to be more important issues. It's like New Year's resolutions (I will work out, eat organic vegetables, and drink eight glasses of water a day). We know we *should,* but we don't often follow through. More pressing issues always seem to demand our attention because the consequences do not seem immediate.

What a mistake. Don't test and the consequences can be dire, regardless of tight development schedules and budgets. Make testing a priority instead of making excuses.

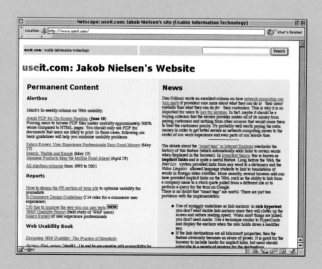

Hire Experts Whenever Possible

Usability as an industry long pre-dates the web. Although in recent years many individuals have spe-cialized in web usability, human fac-tors specialists and ergonomic engi-neers have long studied user needs as they pertain to a wide range of products and situations. The data to draw from in the field is substantial. Consider bringing a pro on board. A web usability expert has experience not only in conducting the testing, but also in analyzing the results and making recommendations.

Usability and Redesign

Test your current, about-to-be-redesigned site. Test-ing the current site for usability will yield valuable results (see this chapter's expert topic with Jakob Nielsen) and give pointers as to where to begin with site improvements. You are probably already well aware of areas that need improvement, whether through complaints or lack of sales. Draw on exist-ing data for your tests.

Here's a prickly point in testing redesigns: Testing new looks and navigation on your current site's reg-ular users will almost always yield skewed results. As a rule, people dislike change. If a site is changed, many regular users will have something negative to say, even if the redesign is easier to use. Don't test solely on your existing audience.

When to Test

It is difficult to determine when to test within the workflow. The obvious time to test is at the end of the production phase, while you're Q&A-ing but before launch. However, this is also a difficult time to test, primarily because the focus is on getting the site live, not adding more processes. Also, just before launch, the schedule is already tight, and what if testing forces the team back to the drawing board when there isn't time to do so? But what if the site goes live and is flawed? It is a mistake to leave the site until the last minute without having someone *besides* the development team or client take a look.

When should you test? The earlier the better. A cliché… but true. Conducting usability tests early in the process not only is cheaper in the long run, but

One-On-One Testing

- Testing duration is one to two days with four to six par-ticipants each day but only one participant in a room at a time.

- Individual session length is approximately one hour.

- Tasks performed are predetermined.

- Tasks test specific areas or user paths, not the whole site.

- Tasks to be performed are pretested by a member of the development team to make sure they are feasible.

- The test moderator watches, keeps quiet, and takes notes. One test moderator can test all participants but only one participant at a time.

- Sessions can be videotaped.

- Sessions can be watched by the development team. Formal testing environments often incorporate a one-way mirror to avoid making the test subjects uncomfortable.

- Results show what is working and what is not working.

also is easier on the schedule (and on the team and on the budget). When you test early, you can quickly identify problems and make changes before you build structures on top of fault lines. If you are too far along in the process to change things, the tendency is to simply launch and hope for the best. But note: No business school trains its MBAs to go forward with a flawed business plan and "hope for the best."

We recommend testing at as many critical junctures as possible. A little bit of testing at the wireframe or paper prototype stage requires little time or budget. And yet, it puts your project in a far better position to move forward into visual design than if you didn't test at all. Testing visual design flat screens or an HTML Protosite also brings potential issues to light. And again, start early enough in the process to avoid having to backtrack too far.

Costs of Testing

Informal testing is one-on-one testing with friends and colleagues who closely fit the specific user profiles and who are not directly involved with the project. The cost for this is usually minimal. Semiformal testing raises the bar to the next level; outside participants are recruited and paid. A makeshift testing area is often set up. Formal testing can take many forms, but it is common to have a paid usability consultant who is a human factors specialist, as well as rent a testing facility. Hence the higher budget.

INFORMAL, SEMIFORMAL, AND FORMAL COST COMPARISONS

All levels of testing are valuable. Mixing levels of formality at different points of development is also valid: perhaps semiformal testing at the outset on the existing, to-be-redesigned site; informal testing at several stages during development; and then formal testing upon launch. It depends on the budget, the timing, and the client's dedication to make the site user-centric.

$0	**Informal testing:** Use friends/co-workers as unpaid subjects.
$500–$1000	**Informal to semiformal testing:** Find outside participants through postings and pay them $35 to $75 each.
$2,000+	**Semiformal testing:** An outside company finds and prescreens participants.
$5,000–$20,000+	**Formal, professional testing with experts and a laboratory or formal testing environment:** Use impartial and consistent specialists trained in human factors. They should be trained to plan, set up, conduct, analyze, and report results.

FORMAL VS. INFORMAL TESTING

In addition to budget and time (formal testing generally takes additional time to prepare for sessions and to analyze results and develop recommendations afterward), the biggest difference between formal and informal testing is expertise. Formal testing requires an expert in human factors engineering and/or cognitive psychology who has experience in the testing-and-analysis process. This person or team should also have experience in conducting and analyzing test results.

Informal Testing	Informal testing usually takes place in the participant's own work environment or in a casual office setting. Participants are often friends, family, or co-workers. A simple test plan and task list is prepared and is observed and noted by an impartial moderator (usually not a human factors specialist).
Semiformal Testing	Semiformal testing, like formal testing, may or may not take place in a formal facility. Participants are prescreened and selected from a pool of applicants. Moderating is usually conducted by a member of the team.
Formal Testing	Formal testing usually takes place in a formal facility with a human factors specialist moderating and running the testing process. Participants are prescreened and selected from a large pool of applicants. There are viewing facilities through a one-way mirror, and often intricate video-monitoring practices are used.

< C H A P T E R 8 >

CONDUCTING USABILITY TESTS: A FOUR-STEP PROCESS

Throughout this book, we focus on core processes. This chapter is no exception. Usability as a topic is extensive. In the interests of discussing simply how to fit usability into your workflow, we have distilled the process of usability testing into an overview that incorporates these four key steps:

Step 1: Plan and Prep

Step 2: Find Participants

Step 3: Conduct the Session

Step 4: Analyze Data and
Make Recommendations

Each of these steps can be applied to any of the three levels of formality: a simplified, informal approach; a semiformal, more expanded plan; or a formal, expanded, full-blown production. The main difference between the levels is in the expertise involved.

Step 1: Plan and Prep

Your tests don't need to be complex, but they do need to have specific goals. The point here is to stay focused. Your time while testing is limited — you only have about an hour for each session. You will need a plan.

Test Plans

A test plan should be the overview and guide to your version of the testing process. Your test plan [8.1] should contain at least the following:

- **Overall goals/objectives**

- **Methodology (testing procedure, equipment, facility, and so on)**

- **Target audience profile (whom you will be testing)**

- **Testing outline (orientation, check-off lists, test questions)**

- **Specific task list**

- **Final evaluation (analysis of data)**

- **Reporting structure (how you plan to submit results and recommendations)**

A test plan allows you to align expectations and goals. Make sure you are focused on specific tasks; you will not have time to test everything. Remember that the testing plan is a work in progress and may vary from session to session.

Task Lists

Choose straightforward tasks to test potential problem areas. For instance, if you are not sure about your login, plan for a series of testing tasks to cover the whole login process. Your users should be prompted to do something that requires a login so

< T E S T I N G   F O R   U S A B I L I T Y >

that they discover *on their own* that they need to log in. How easy and intuitive was it for the user to figure it out?

Create a list of tasks that a general user can (hopefully) finish in about an hour. Have additional tasks prepared in case the tasks take less time than you predicted. Make sure the tasks are neither too simple nor too difficult to accomplish within the set timeframe — either defeats the purpose of the session. Pretest the tasks to weed out the problematic ones.

When developing your list of tasks, keep in mind that the usability test session should be casual, informative, and low stress. Let your subjects get comfortable and confident, as they would be in their own environment — usually their home or office. Developing the proper site-specific task list takes both time and practice.

Tasks should obviously relate to the site, but make them as real world as possible. Have one task relate to the next in a comprehensive manner — like a real user experience. But while you don't want to combine tasks that might skew results, neither do you want the user to perform random tasks. Keep the individual on a flow. Here are a few examples:

- **If the site you are redesigning is for a national housewares chain, one sample task could be to have subjects order a gift off of a wedding registry. Then have them request a catalog.**

8.1 >

A sample test plan: Test plans should outline basic requirements, including overall testing goals, the audience profile, the methodology, and the testing outline. Note that this plan is an example — your user profile (for example) will likely differ from this semigeneric example.

Usability Testing Plan

Overall goal: To provide specific feedback on search, login, and e-commerce features. To determine expected performance on the current site and identify serious problems prior to the next phase of production.

Specific questions that need to be answered:

1. Are the basic search features intuitive for a new user?
2. Are the advanced search features intuitive to use and learnable?
3. Is the purchasing process clear?
4. Are user login and member requirements clear to the user?

User profile: Participants will fit the target market profile of being versed in current internet practices and adaptive technology. The target market is internet users ages 25 to 45 with moderate to high internet experience. To qualify, participants should access the web at least once a week, purchase products online at least twice per month, and be familiar with basic search and e-commerce functions.

Methodology: Usability testing of six to eight individuals will be held at an outside testing facility. Each session will take approximately one hour. The test monitor will greet and orient participants. Participants are asked to fill out a basic questionnaire and background information, and nondisclosures will be signed.

Testing outline:

I. Orientation

II. Background: Testing Site

III. Begin Task List

IV. Fill Out Post-Test Survey

V. Debrief Participant

Summary of results: All participant testing notes will be compiled. Observations and specific findings will be summarized. Other data (time taken for each task, ability to complete each task, post-testing information) will be summarized.

Recommendations report: The report will include the complete testing plan and task list, result summary, and findings/recommendations. All notes and participant comments will be included.

<CHAPTER 8>

- If your redesign is for a bank, have the subjects check their balance or investigate mortgage applications. Next, have them sign up to pay bills or make a transfer.

- Is it a site that indexes restaurants? Have your participants save three restaurants to their favorites folder (which they will have to create). This would require a login as well. Next, have them locate an Italian bistro that delivers to their neighborhood or a medium-priced restaurant with live jazz. Then have them make a reservation.

- If the project is for a bed-and-breakfast, have them attempt to reserve a room, find directions, and then inquire about large parties or large dogs.

Sample Test Script

The moderator needs to keep the flow of the test moving. Getting chatty with your test subject is an easy trap to fall into, but it wastes valuable time. To aid you in staying on target and to make sure you don't miss anything during the actual test, have a test script on hand [8.2].

A test script should cover the following: introductions, the test-session schedule, and a brief explanation of methodology. Put the test subject at ease when you explain the testing setup and expectations. When orienting your participant on the day

---

Orientation & Greeting

Greet the Participant — Orient to testing and expectations:

"Hello, my name is John, and I'll be working with you in today's session. I would like to give you a brief idea of what you should expect and what we are trying to accomplish.

"Today we are testing the online ordering process and determining how effective and intuitive it is to use. Your experience here today will help us evaluate our website. Remember, you are not being evaluated in any way — we are simply trying to see how users navigate through the site. Do your best, but don't be concerned with the results. While you are working, I'll be watching and taking notes. Feel free to talk aloud as you go through the site. You may ask questions, but I probably won't answer them, because it is important for you to go through the site as if I were not present.

"Afterwards we will have some time to talk about the site and your experience. I will also have a short survey for you to fill out before you leave.

"Do you have any questions?"

(Give the NDA form if applicable, and begin the testing.)

Begin Task List

< 8.2

A sample test script: This is a sample of what you might say, based on a test script developed by Jeffrey Rubin in Handbook of Usability Testing. *Remember: Don't read the script word for word.*

of the test, you need to cover the following important points, so make sure to include them in your test script:

- **Introduce yourself and your role as a moderator.**

- **Explain that your role is as a silent observer. You shouldn't answer any questions directly; you're just here to observe and take notes.**

- **Give an overview of the testing goals.**

- **Assure participants that *they* are not being tested in any way. It's the site that's is being tested.**

- **Encourage participants to "talk aloud" during the testing process.**

- **Get an NDA signed (if applicable) and ask if there are any questions.**

Step 2: Find Participants

Finding potential participants is one of the more challenging aspects of conducting usability testing. For informal or most semiformal testing, you can enlist people you know — they just have to fit the profile. You can recruit the easy targets: your mother, your neighbor, the kid who delivers the Friday staff pizza… but regardless of their convenience, they are only good choices if they match your target audi-

ence. Select with care. If your site is B2B auto supply and your mother couldn't identify a carburetor if world peace depended on it, she is not a good test subject.

Drafting co-workers may seem convenient, and although they may be adequate for many informal tests, we suggest recruiting outside your office. Testing with individuals who are not associated with your company or your site will give better results, and gathering an ongoing user base for use both in focus groups and usability tests is valuable for any web development team — whether in-house or not.

That said, co-workers and friends are great candidates for a "dry run" of the usability testing session. Since co-workers or friends are familiar with you, they will feel comfortable providing feedback on your methods and processes. Plus, this kind of preliminary run-though provides the moderator with an opportunity to work out bugs in the script.

Setting up sessions and tracking down ideal candidates can be a formidable time investment. Depending on available methods of advertising in your local area, you can secure ideal candidates in less than a week's time. First, determine your best methods for reaching your target users. Would they be responsive to the local weekly? Is there an online resource for jobs and postings? Would posting a flyer at a college work? Post an ad in the local job listings ([8.3] and [8.4]). You will see quick results.

Test Often!

Small-scale testing at several points during development is arguably more beneficial than testing only once. Develop methods of quick, iterative testing to allow for feedback on specific issues throughout the development process. In design meetings, whenever there is a question or discussion regarding navigation, functionality, or user response, cheerfully add it to the list for the next round of testing. Use testing to settle arguments — nothing speaks more loudly than the actual user.

< CHAPTER 8 >

Earn $50 for an hour of surfing the web!
Participate in an online usability study.
Contact information@_____.com

< 8.3

A sample job posting for usability testing subjects where the target audience is wide. Note that you may have to pay a participant more than the going rate if the session is on super-short notice.

Looking for women over 45. Earn $50 for an
hour of surfing the web! Participate in an
online usability study.
Contact information@_____.com

< 8.4

A sample job posting for usability testing subjects where the target audience is narrower.

Screen Participants

One of the differences between informal and formal testing procedures is the professional screening of participants. Professional testing facilities and companies are paid up to $1,000 per participant (usually targeting a group of 8 to 12) to locate, screen, and recruit participants for usability-testing purposes. The value of this service lies in the opportunity for a precisely targeted group to be selected according to specific demographics determined by a usability expert. Furthermore, it allows for screening and recruiting to be conducted in other cities (if testing is to be done in several locations), which allows for a wider sampling.

The more closely targeted the participants, the more viable the results. Specific profiles may include CEOs, day traders, or long-distance truckers — none of whom might be readily targeted using traditional posting or advertising methods.

Test Subjects for Intranet Sites

Testing a typical user in an internal audience can be tricky. On the one hand, you absolutely know who your users are. When it comes to testing for usability, however, you may have a problem finding good participants. Actually, the problem may be that your participants are *too* good. Often, when you contact a department and request that someone be sent over for usability testing, they send you a "star." Departments want to shine, so they send their absolute best: "Rudy is the biology department's resident internet whiz" or "Pamela knows computers better than anyone else in the human resources department." Congrats to Rudy and Pamela, but they aren't typical. When you request participants from departments, request "typical" users, not whiz kids.

<TESTING FOR USABILITY>

Profile Test Subjects

Direct potential subjects (from ads, postings, and re-ferrals) to fill out an online or faxed form that asks for basic demographic information as well as inter-net usage patterns [8.5]. On any form you distribute that asks for personal information, note that all in-formation is confidential and that no information will be distributed.

The reasons for wanting this information should be obvious: When you test for usability, you want your test subjects to match your target audience as closely as possible. Otherwise, what's the point? Compile your collected information into a grid or some other easy-to-reference format and sort [8.6]. Narrow your results. Schedule a few more than you need in case someone cancels. These extra partici-pants, called floaters, should still get paid.

Send an introductory email to applicants who fit the desired profile. Explain briefly when they should expect to be contacted and what they will be doing, but don't get too specific. Follow up with an email or a phone call closer to the confirmed date [8.7].

8.5 >

This online test subject pro-filing form gives you the information you need to identify potential test sub-jects as aligning with your target audience. It can also be faxed, but since you are testing online habits and usage, most subjects will have access to the internet.

< CHAPTER 8 >

ID	Sex	Occupation	Salary	Web Experience	Time Online	Online Activities	Purchases Per Month	Types of Purchases	Computer	Browser
5	F	Partner development	70K–100K	web savvy	daily	email, news, research, stocks, shopping, travel	1 to 2	books	Windows	Netscape 4, IE5
6	F	Marketing	50K–70K	web savvy	daily	email, chat, news, research, banking, stocks, shopping, travel	3 to 5	books, furniture	Windows	Netscape 4, IE5
8	M	Music therapist	15K–30K	intermed	daily	email, newsgrp, news, research, music, shopping, travel	3 to 5	books, music, services, equipment	Mac	Netscape 4
9	F	Teacher; director catalog content	30K–50K	web savvy	daily	email, chat, newsgrp, news, educ, research, shopping	1 to 2	airline tickets, books, gifts	Mac, Windows	AOL, IE4, IE5
18	F	Housewife/ mother	70K–100K	web savvy	daily	email, chat, newsgrp, games, news, research, music, stocks, shopping, travel	1 to 2	books, toys, clothes, airline tickets, collectibles	Mac	AOL
30	M	Employee operations	30K–50K	web savvy	daily	email, chat, newsgrp, news, educ, research, banking, shopping, travel	3 to 5	books, computers, flowers, groceries	Mac	Netscape 4, AOL, IE4
46	M	Interior designer	50K–70K	intermed	daily	email, newsgrp, educ, banking, stocks, shopping, travel	3 to 5	makeup, CDs, DVDs, electronics, groceries	Windows	AOL
75	M	Student	15K–30K	techie	daily	email, newsgrp, news, educ, research, music, banking, shopping, travel	1 to 2	anything	Windows	IE5
87	F	Office manager	30K–50K	web savvy	daily	email, chat, games, news, research, music, banking, stocks, shopping, travel	6 to 9	movies, groceries, books, body products, travel tickets	Mac, Windows, UNIX	Netscape 4

< 8.6 >

This sample grid of potential test subjects shows the information collected from the online profile form [8.5]. This data has been poured into an Excel file. Out of 400 responses, 40 were selected for client review. Eight were eventually selected as participants.

< T E S T I N G   F O R   U S A B I L I T Y >

Step 3: Conduct the Session

Begin each session with a pleasant and patient attitude. Introduce yourself and explain the process — that the user will be asked to perform a set of predetermined tasks. Take care with your choice of words; don't prejudice your results by telling the test subject the number or length of tasks. Explain your role as an observer. Make it clear that you are an observer, not a helper. Have an NDA and any other paperwork prepared in advance. Keep the formalities light and make the user feel as comfortable as possible. Refer to your test script to keep you on track.

Remain neutral during the testing process. As a facilitator, you will be a silent observer, speaking only when giving a new task and taking notes throughout the process. If the participant asks you a question, respond only if necessary and in a very nonspecific manner. Do not give any hints, verbally or by eye or hand motion. You might be tempted to "rescue" the individual, but this would defeat the purpose of the testing. If the participant becomes frustrated, read the level of frustration and note "Failed task" only when all other options have been taken. Do not consider a failed task to be a testing failure. It's quite the opposite. By uncovering site flaws, you should diminish the number of users who click out of websites in frustration (that's lost business and perhaps a permanently lost customer). Videotaping the session is also helpful for later review and to show to other members of the development team.

Initial Contact

Hello,

Thank you in advance for your participation in our usability testing. You have been selected based on your online profile. We will contact you via email to confirm the testing dates and your availability. Currently we are scheduled for the 17th and 18th of this month. Testing will be held at our offices downtown, located at 1200 24th Avenue, Suite 100. That's between East 12th and East 14th on the south side of the street. The entire session should take approximately one hour. You will be paid $50 for your participation at the end of the session.

If you have any questions, please do not hesitate to contact us via email or phone.

Thanks!

8.7 >
A sample script for contacting participants.

"Two distinct advantages to formal testing: It provides feedback for site development, and it is an educational opportunity for designers and engineers, allowing them to see firsthand the decision-making process of an average site visitor."
— Jupiter 1999, www.jup.com

<TIPS>   <CHAPTER 8>

Know When To Quit

If a participant becomes too frustrated or goes too far off track, it is time to have him quit the task. Make it clear that if he does not or cannot perform a task to completion, he has neither ruined the test nor demonstrated incompetence (except perhaps the development team's!). Flustered test subjects will not perform well.

Make sure to have everything you need before starting. Here is a handy check list:

- **Have an NDA ready for signing.**

- **Make sure your internet connection works.**

- **If you are videotaping, have batteries charged for your video camera because cords can be problematic. (Note: We do not recommend videotaping for informal testing.)**

- **Have a printout of the site handy for easier note-taking (pages associated with the task).**

- **Have your list of sequenced and predetermined tasks.**

- **Have the survey form ready for post-testing.**

- **Have the site bookmarked and ready to use.**

Basic Data Collection

Take meticulous notes during the testing process. A blank form to write notes on is always helpful [8.8]. Use the same form for all test subjects. This streamlining will be handy for compiling notes and comparing findings.

Make certain to note all of the following points for each task:

- **Could the test subject complete the task?**

- **Did he need help? Did the task fail?**

- **How much time did it take?**

- **What stumbling blocks did he encounter? Describe problems and obstacles.**

- **Note overall observations. Add commentary. Did the test subject mutter in frustration? Did he say, "Cool!"?**

Moderating Do's and Don'ts

DO introduce yourself and your role as a silent observer.

DO explain that they should think aloud as they feel comfortable. Keep the session relaxed, use humor when appropriate, and stay impartial.

DON'T describe the tasks in advance. Say only that participants will be performing a certain number of tasks in one hour's time.

DO make it clear that they are not being tested and that there are no wrong answers.

DON'T set expectations. Don't say, "This is so easy you'll have no problem."

DON'T rescue the participants when they struggle.

DO recognize when a participant is getting really

< T E S T I N G   F O R   U S A B I L I T Y >

You don't need to write down absolutely every click or hesitation, but make certain to be thorough when you report problem areas. Follow closely enough to track a task's flow. You will base your conclusions on the data you collect.

After the Session

Keep an eye on the clock. A few things need to happen before the test subject is finished and can leave. First give the participant a brief post-test survey, then conduct a quick debriefing interview, and finally pay the test subject for his time.

Prepare the post-test survey in advance [8.9]. It should contain questions about the person's overall impressions and experiences with the site. Offer the participant the opportunity to rate each question/component on a scale of 1 to 10. The survey should take no longer than five minutes to complete.

Debrief the participant. If you have allocated time, let him say whatever is on his mind and then ask him questions. Begin with overall, high-level issues and move on to specifics — the areas you marked in your notes. Have the payment ready for the participant once the session is complete. Don't forget to thank him. Be sure to keep the door open

Participants may have suggestions for how to improve the user experience. Make a note of any suggestions, but don't get involved in a dialogue. As a moderator, you should not be interacting with participants.

8.8 >

Use this sample observation form to help take notes during a typical session. The form is available for download at www. web-redesign.com.

Participant ID#		
Date:	Site URL	
Time	Task Description	Observations/Comments/Notes

< CHAPTER 8 >

Post Session Survey

Please fill out the following questions based on how you are feeling overall about the site:

Name: (First Name, Last Initial) _____
Date: _____

1. Able to complete tasks as requested
Frustrating   1   2   3   4   5   Easy

2. Able to navigate through the site
Confusing   1   2   3   4   5   Very Clear

3. Overall look and feel of site
Not pleasing   1   2   3   4   5   Pleasing

4. Relevance of site images to content
Not relevant   1   2   3   4   5   Relevant

5. Relevance of site content (text)
Not relevant   1   2   3   4   5   Relevant

6. Overall ease of use
Confusing   1   2   3   4   5   Very Clear

7. Overall page layout and organization
Confusing   1   2   3   4   5   Very Clear

8. the site inviting to use?
Not inviting   1   2   3   4   5   Inviting

9. Were the naming and labeling of links clear?
Confusing   1   2   3   4   5   Very clear

10. Would you recommend this site to a friend?
Never   1   2   3   4   5   Absolutely

Please list any additional comments about the site and your experience:

_____

_____

_____

_____

< 8.9

Have the participant complete a survey like this one after the testing is finished. Post-test feedback and comments are an excellent basis for understanding user preferences. This form is available for download at www.web-redesign.com.

for further correspondence and further testing — maybe on the same project, maybe on a different project down the road.

After the participant leaves, if you have time before the next test subject comes in, prepare a short summary of the session and the results. Outline specific problem areas and surprising results. Include personal observations if appropriate. Some test sessions schedule subject after subject, and there isn't time between to summarize. Take good notes; you won't be able to remember many specifics after three or four test subjects.

Step 4: Analyze Data and Make Recommendations

Here is where experience will show. Understanding how and why a user fails a task or seeing where problem spots exist — this is easy. Determining how to fix the problem takes expertise. Even if you aren't an expert, however, you can still make educated recommendations for improvement.

Gather data as you go — this is obvious. Compile and summarize this data while the test is still fresh in your mind and don't forget to transfer handwritten notes to a digital file. Summarize all data in one format — a grid works well for this — showing the results of each test, problem areas, comments, and user feedback from the post-test survey.

When calling out problem areas, note why there was difficulty. If you can determine it, indicate the source of the problem — even use a screenshot. This

< T E S T I N G   F O R   U S A B I L I T Y >

will help immeasurably when thinking up ways to improve these areas. Identify user interaction with specific factors such as navigation, text, graphics, and so on, as well as global issues such as consistent logo placement and branding or inconsistent naming and labeling. If there was a particular problem in the course of carrying out a task, note the issue in detail. Rank all these problems in order of frequency and then prioritize. Concentrate on high-level functionality first: issues with global navigation, text links vs. graphic links, page layout, and so on. Then focus on specific areas and recommendations for improved user experience.

After all sessions are complete, compile your findings into a final report. Translate the collected data into recommendations; much of the information may validate thoughts you already have regarding your site. Divide recommendations into short-term and long-term goals. Determine an implementation plan for putting your findings into action and adjust your site to better fit the way it will actually get used.

The Final Report

Putting all of your findings into a final report provides a concise reference for your client and your team [8.10]. Unless you selected prejudiced or inappropriate test subjects, usability testing results are incontrovertible. Report these findings; any recommendations based on them will have to be taken seriously. An improved site is almost guaranteed as the result.

8.10 >

For the final report, recommendations are shown here using screenshots and caption callouts to emphasize specific points. Not all reports need to be this detailed.

Food.com   Usability & Recommendations

RECOMMENDATIONS FOR IMPROVEMENT

1. Pathways to order completion are too long.
The sheer number of pages and clicks the user must navigate is burdensome and confusing. Users have a difficult time moving between the menu, menu options, and the checkout procedure.

Recommendations

• Create a "pop up" for the options page; it simplifies the flow for the user. The secondary window isolates "Add to my Order" and "Cancel" from the "Edit/Remove" and "Checkout" buttons.

• Extend "Your Order" to span the entire page. Information like the delivery or take-out can be represented along with the delivery address, alerting the user as to what criteria has been specified and what has not.

Refer to www.web-redesign.com for useful links.

Educate Yourself

For some projects, hiring an outside consultant might be overkill. In these instances, do some reading. Besides Jakob Nielsen's *Designing Web Usability*, there is also *Don't Make Me Think* by Steve Krug (New Riders, 2000 — this one is funny!) and *Handbook of Usability Testing* by Jeffrey Rubin (John Wiley & Sons, 1994). Although you will not become an expert overnight, you will undoubtedly benefit from some research before you embark on your own informal usability testing. Refer to www.web-redesign.com for useful links.

Usability Testing...

... settles disputes with data instead of guesses.

... provides real feedback from actual users.

... is low cost for valuable results.

... shows that what is obvious to the developer might not be obvious to the user.

... minimizes risk prior to public launch.

A final report should contain the following:

- **Executive summary.** A brief synopsis of major findings, recommendations, and suggestions of areas on which to focus. Overview what is working and what is *not* working on the site.

- **Methodology.** A description of the nature of the research, how it was set up, user profiles, data collection methods, and so on.

- **Results.** A clear, comprehensive display of all test results, survey feedback, and so on.

- **Findings and recommendations.** A presentation of general and specific information, short- and long-term changes recommended, and the type of changes suggested (for instance, graphic only, text or backend programming, and so on). Include information about the given task, the reason for the problem, and the recommended solution.

- **Appendices.** Raw data, notes, samples of test materials, background data (no names) for participants, and so on.

CHAPTER SUMMARY

Although usability testing will neither create nor perfect a website, it will yield a more usable, more successful site. It can identify disaster so you can avert it. Feedback is valuable. Observation is critical. Once you remove yourself — switching roles from developer to observer — and watch a typical user navigate through the site — attempting to click on graphics, finding his way back to the home page, executing fairly simple tasks — you quickly realize that a little observation goes a long way toward knowing what makes for a positive user experience.

Have tangible goals. It is impossible to test all aspects of a site's design, architecture, and navigation. Break down your site's needs. With specific goals in mind, it is easier to tailor your tasks to a particularly questionable area. Sometimes when upper management finally agrees to a budget for usability testing, they expect to be able to test the entire site in one fell swoop. Test often, and — to quote Jeffrey Veen from the foreword of this book — may all your user feedback be good.

Casey Claybourne

Client: Casey Claybourne
URL: www.caseyclaybourne.com
Design Studio: Waxcreative Design, Oakland, CA
All Project Roles: Emily Cotler

Romance novels constitute 58.2* percent of the popular paperback fiction purchased in the United States, generating $1.35 billion in sales. Casey Claybourne, an award-winning romance novelist, saw her ninth novel, A Thing Of Beauty, garner rave reviews. Like many authors and creative professionals, she is her own small-but-thriving business.

< P R E V I O U S >   < C U R R E N T

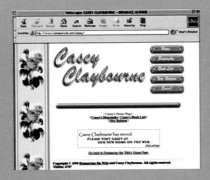

CASEYCLAYBOURNE.COM [OLD] was a clunky, cookie-cutter design reminiscent of the countless amateur sites on the web that so often become the fate of small businesses and professional individuals whose kid/husband/cousin knows some HTML.

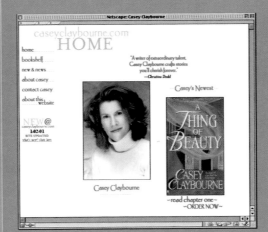

CASEYCLAYBOURNE.COM [REDESIGNED] uses imagery created specifically to reflect Casey's sophisticated style. Employing a clean, simple, and elegant design, it matches the level of professionalism she has attained in her writing career. (2000)

Result: Better industry positioning. Romance readers, tired of the stigma attached to the genre, applauded the upscale design in plentiful fan mail.

*Statistic: www.rwanational.com/statistics.stm

> To become better partners with our clients we must understand the client's industry online, against its competition. What are the goals of the company, product, and market as they relate to the web?

Analyzing Your Competition 09

< CHAPTER 9 >

Analyzing Your Competition

A competitive analysis should be part of a web re-design process no matter the level of approach — and the levels can get very lofty. With large, fiercely competitive industries such as commercial airlines or personal computer hardware, there might be both the need and the budget for a formal industry analysis. In these situations, plan on spending up to six figures for an outside marketing or research company to deliver an exhaustive document the size of Tolstoy's *War And Peace*. For projects without mammoth budgets, we recommend conducting an informal features analysis.

What's the difference between comparing industries and features? Expertise, budget, and approach. A full-blown formal industry analysis is conducted by marketing- and strategy-focused teams with solid research methodologies driven by experience. It focuses largely on markets and business positioning in a broad competitive landscape. A features analysis, whether formal or informal, focuses on comparing the actual customer experience — primarily online but sometimes offline as well. It provides a snapshot view of the competition's services and features from a user standpoint.

The results generated from this analysis will be used by both the web development team *and* the client. The team gains the invaluable experience of being able to simulate the user experience within the client's industry. The client — whether external or internal — receives data that helps them see what their online competition is offering in the way of content, features, and services. Through conducting a features analysis, the team and the client each gain

WHAT THIS CHAPTER COVERS		
DEFINE	**CONDUCT**	**ANALYZE**
> Defining the Process	> Performing Individual Analysis	> Creating a Features Grid
> Build a Plan for Analysis	> Conducting Informal Usability Testing	> Making Overall Evaluations
> Defining the Competitive Set		> Creating a Final Report
> Categorizing Your Competitive Set		
> Creating a Features List		

< A N A L Y Z I N G   Y O U R   C O M P E T I T I O N >

a better understanding of what is working and — just as important — what is not working for users.

When the client's site was first built, the client probably surfed extensively to see who was doing what in the client's field. The client leveraged ideas from some competitors and rejected others. Now that the site is being redesigned, it is time to take another, updated look. The industry has likely changed — even if it's only been a year since the site was originally built. Significant industry change may even be the primary reason why the site is being redesigned. Include the existing site in your analysis. Looking at the existing site alongside its competition enables you not only to compare features and user expectations, but also to look at how the existing site measures up (or doesn't measure up) against the competition. This will help to establish redesign goals.

Throughout this book, we advocate hiring experts whenever possible. Conducting competitive analyses is no exception. Expertly gathered information is always incredibly worthwhile and usually hits on points that non-research types may not even consider. But conducting an informal features analysis is valuable for a different reason — it enables the team designing and developing the redesigned site to engage in the information-gathering process. Part of the value of conducting an informal competitive analysis is that it helps the team begin to think like a user within the client's industry, and that type of thinking is priceless.

FORMAL INDUSTRY ANALYSIS VS. INFORMAL FEATURES ANALYSIS

Understand that the informal analysis we recommend in this chapter involves online features and customer experience, not marketing or branding or product analyses of the company's current or future business position. These other analyses may have already been developed by the company and may provide an understanding of where the company has been and where it is going — especially as it relates to redesign goals. Gather as much information from the client as you can during this Discovery process.

FORMAL VS. INFORMAL COMPARISON		
	Formal Industry Analysis	**Informal Features Analysis**
Team	An independent research team with expertise and background in marketing, communications, research, and/or strategy.	Members of the web development team who will be re-creating the user experience online.
Approach	Formal analysis of industry, market segmentation, trends and forecasts, and customer needs.	Informal analysis of competitive sites focusing on features and user experience.
Results	Quantitative data–driven, market- and research-centered focus.	Feature-driven, qualitative information; show what is working and what is not working.
Report	A huge book of information.	5 to 20 pages, short and sweet.
Budget	$20,000 and up.	Lunch to $20,000.
Goals	Provide comprehensive, detailed, strategy-based recommendations on changing marketplaces, evolving business models, and customer habits and segmentation.	Gain firsthand view of customer experience. Provide relevant documentation and industry information to the client.

< T I P S >

< C H A P T E R 9 >

Obscure Industries

Unless the client's field is so technically obscure that you cannot understand even the basic terminology (for example, genetically engineered livestock food supplements, FAA-mandated commercial jet engine maintenance, or Shih-tzu breeding), you should be able to use and review several sites right away and form solid opinions. (Note: If you *are* redesigning a jet engine maintenance company's website, you should plan on a crash course in aeronautical terminology, hire yourself a jet engine expert, or better yet, have the client give you a detailed tour of their plant.)

The ultimate goal of a features analysis is quite direct in that it answers this question: What are competitors doing to provide services and content that is positive and meaningful to users? For the purposes of this book, we focus primarily on online competition, though the brick-and-mortar world should not be ignored. Sometimes most, if not all, of your competition is offline and just a phone call away. But to analyze the entire industry is outside the scope of what we suggest. The job of the web development team as it embarks on a features analysis is to look at the goals of the company, product, and market *as they relate to the web.*

Becoming an Expert User in the Client's Industry

The process of becoming an expert user begins much the same way as you might begin online research for personal reasons — with a search at Yahoo! or Google or the like and then visits to several competitor sites. Perhaps one of the client's products is fingerless fleece gloves. By plugging those three keywords, "fingerless fleece gloves," into a search engine, you will get a dozen or more online catalog sites specializing in sporting wear or outdoor clothing. All these sites are in the same industry and therefore make up a competitive set. Perhaps some of them are even on the list of perceived competitors

Gaining a User Perspective

A small design group embarked on a complete redesign and rebranding of an online food delivery website. "Make it a better experience," was the goal. "Increase customer usage." It was a straightforward challenge: Take a site and identify what needed to be changed and how the experience could be improved.

The team started by looking at other sites within the industry. Online food delivery, online grocery delivery, online dining guides, offline food delivery, cooking sites, and so on. What worked with these sites? What didn't work? The only way to find out was to become actual users. The team compared site features. They went through checkout ordering processes. They registered and became members. They searched for restaurants and

ordered food — a lot of food. They called customer service to complain when food was delivered late or the orders were incorrect. They felt the pains of a user when a particular menu couldn't be found or a restaurant was closed. They quickly saw what was successful and why.

In the end, they became experts by *doing*. Not just observing or researching but being real users. What did they learn? The design needed to be simple and straightforward. The ordering process needed to be as easy as picking up the phone — even easier. They knew the site needed to do more, think faster, and perform better than the main competition: the offline, phone-in delivery services.

The upshot? The redesigned site wasn't just useable; it got used.

< A N A L Y Z I N G   Y O U R   C O M P E T I T I O N >

the client provided (from the Client Survey in Phase 1: Defining the Project). By looking through many of these sites, you — a typical user for that industry — become better versed not only on the specific product, but also on the industry itself.

A big theme throughout this book is to THINK LIKE YOUR USERS. The competitive analysis is no exception. Approach this task with the mindset of a typical user and "shop" through the client's industry much the way you "shopped" for fingerless fleece gloves. Compare competitors. Use the competitors' sites to complete transactions and find information. It takes time, but by being a typical user on site after site in the competitive set, you quickly become an expert customer in your client's industry. Be reasonable, of course. If your client sells cars, you certainly don't need to purchase several of the newest models. But take it as far as possible without committing serious dollars.

Analyzing the competition from a user perspective enables you to remove yourself from your web developer's get-it-done, make-it-work point of view. Making decisions based on things that matter to users — ease of use, likes and dislikes, and other fickle attributes that users with little patience or aptitude might apply to their actual online experiences — helps immeasurably in understanding the client's industry online.

CONDUCTING AN ANALYSIS

Conducting a features analysis is a basic, easy-to-follow process that can be expanded or decreased depending on time, resources, and budget. Whether 20 hours or 200 hours, the process contains the same four steps: define the process, create a features list, conduct analysis and usability testing, and lastly, create a report. Use the accompanying chart as a guide. Modify as your time, resources, and industry dictate.

In-House Expertise

If you are part of an in-house web development department and are therefore inside the client company, chances are you are already exceedingly familiar with your industry. Most likely, you have spent considerable time browsing through competitor sites... but how long ago? If your research is more than a year old, your industry's online landscape has probably changed. Perhaps your competition is no longer in existence. Perhaps you have new competition.

Perhaps you are too close. Internal teams are often biased and would benefit by having an outside team's vantage point. Regardless of circumstance, being at the brink of redesign is a critical juncture at which the competition should be looked at closely.

< CHAPTER 9 >

STEP 1: DEFINING THE PROCESS	
Build a Plan for Analysis	Outline basic goals, process, and deliverables. Establish team, timeframe, methodology, allocated hours, and deliverables.
Define the Competitive Set	Using client-provided information, search engines, and research, identify a range of companies that fall into the competitive set.
Categorize Your Competitive Set	Break the defined competitive set into categories within the overall industry. Note that each site should fall into only one category.
STEP 2: CREATING A FEATURES LIST	
Create a Features List	After initial evaluation, create a list of features that apply to most or all sites within the competitive set. Include relevant offline features. Break these features down into individual categories.
STEP 3: CONDUCTING ANALYSIS AND TESTING	
Perform Individual Evaluations	Each person working on the analysis should conduct an individual study of each site, answering basic questions about overall experience, perceived company objectives, and types of services provided. They should also add to the features list as they get deeper into the site.
Conduct Informal Usability Testing	Determine key tasks that can be conducted on most or all sites. Perform informal usability testing (see Chapter 8: Testing for Usability) and record observations and effectiveness from site to site.
STEP 4: CREATING A FINAL REPORT	
Create a Features Grid	Using the features list, create a comprehensive grid showing all sites and the categories and listing features that exist within each.
Make Overall Evaluations	Create final report (in short, executive summary format). Outline the main findings and indicate how they apply to the company's direction and business goals. Follow with screenshots, evaluations, and summaries about each site in the competitive set. Include a features grid that lists main features within each site. Overall evaluations rank each site for overall use, usability, and likeability.

Step 1: Defining the Process

Clearly identify what information you intend to generate. Specifically, who will be using the final results? Is this primarily to benefit the design team? To generate ideas for content? To better understand the industry? Have clear goals. Whether it is a budgeted deliverable for the client, an exercise for the team as part of the Discovery process, or both, define what you hope to gain from this analysis.

Build a Plan for Analysis

Create a plan for analysis that details overall objectives, methodology, deliverables, schedule, and budget [9.1]. Competitive analyses differ widely in size and scope, depending on the details sought. Analyses should be conducted by at least two people because this allows for different perspectives. Depending on time and resources, this process can take a week (for small to mid-size budgets of 20 to 70 hours) or up to a month (for budgets of larger scale). If you can charge for this work, do so. Many firms conduct exactly this type of analysis and charge a meaningful fee for it. If you can't invoice for the competitive analysis on its own budgetary line, build the cost of an abbreviated analysis into the Define the Process step as part of the Discovery process.

< A N A L Y Z I N G   Y O U R   C O M P E T I T I O N >

Define the Competitive Set

The goal here is to identify two things: Who are the key industry players — the heavy hitters, the ones to beat? Who are your client's direct competitors — the sites the target audience might visit in lieu of your client's?

First, choose broadly. Gather information the way a user might: using search engines, marketing influences (what billboards have you seen lately?), and other resources like the phone book or referrals. Collect as much information as possible. The client already provided the team with a list of its perceived main competition (from the Client Survey). Now is the time to really look at those sites. Look beyond the client's list as well; the client might have a biased or narrow view of the industry or might have forgotten some key players, especially in the offline arena. This last bit might require extra sleuthing and research on your part.

9.1 >

This is an example of an analysis plan that outlines overall goals and objectives, basic methodology, and deliverables. In a more detailed version, include specifics about team and project scope (with schedule and hours allocated) and details about both the user and general tasks associated with the company's site and industry.

Competitive Analysis: Overview

Overall Goals and Objectives

Provide a comprehensive industry analysis and comparison of competitive sites. Evaluate features, technology, content, usability, and overall effectiveness. Compile a list of features in a matrix format to establish detailed site offerings and simple comparison methods. Generate a report of what works and what doesn't work within each site, individual site analysis and comments, and final recommendations for possible implementation into the redesigned site.

Methodology

The analysis will be conducted and compiled by team members including the Creative Director, Marketing Analyst, and Information Designer. Individuals participating in this analysis are classified as potential users, and will be conducting several task-oriented tests for each of the sites with a user-based orientation, instead of a developer's point of view. This analysis, though informal, will allow a range of observations, input, and overall use of each site.

The analysis will be conducted in three phases:
1. Individual Analysis (Heuristic)
2. Informal Usability Testing (Task-Oriented)
3. Features Comparison

Deliverables

The report will contain a detailed overview of each site, including screenshots, specific features and differentiating factors, and ratings which will include usability, ease of use, and overall rating. Also included will be a comprehensive features grid, which shows a breakdown of the competitive sites into specific industry categories, and specific features divided into graphic, technical, content, and site-specific categories. The final report will also contain overall recommendations for the possible implementation of specific features that were highly rated and should be considered in the site's redesign.

(Note: The information compiled in this report is not statistically significant. It is based on general use and informal opinions and should be taken for recommendations only.)

<TIPS>

<CHAPTER 9>

Hours and Budgeting

At the barest minimum, allocate at least one hour to analyze each site in the competitive set, including testing, tallying features, and making recommendations.

It's simple math: A 12-site competitive set equals a solid day and a half of work, at minimum. Obviously, more time per site will yield better results; if you have the resources, several hours per site is advantageous. If you don't have the resources or budget, limit the number of sites you are analyzing or limit the time you spend analyzing each site.

Are there any sites that match your client's to a T? Select the primary ones. Also choose several others that are only partial overlaps. Here's an example: The redesign project is an online travel agency. Look at direct competitors' sites — other travel agency sites — as well as at portals like Expedia.com or Travelocity.com, and at airlines like southwest.com or ual.com. Also consider more specialized travel sites, like one or two of the many and widely varied adventure travel sites such as away.com, and don't ignore brochure sites like lonelyplanet.com or letsgo.com. Keep in mind that there are also offline competitors, such as 1-800 numbers, 24-hour customer service lines, and (gasp!) actual travel agencies with storefronts or phone-in customer-service representatives.

The client's site? The existing, getting-redesigned site? Make sure to include it in the competitive set. The redesign goals will become more focused if you can clearly see what needs attention alongside competitors' sites.

Now narrow your competition. Limiting the analysis to 12 sites or fewer can be a difficult task. There are bound to be dozens, even a hundred, depending on the industry. Choose roughly 20 for starters. Sorting them will pare that number down. You should have as many sites as necessary to give you a broad yet focused perspective on your industry. Have at least five but no more than a dozen. Presented here is an example of a competitive set within the travel industry ([9.2] to [9.7]).

< A N A L Y Z I N G   Y O U R   C O M P E T I T I O N >

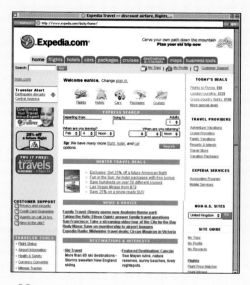

< 9.2 >

Expedia.com (Category: portal).

< 9.3 >

Travelocity.com (Category: portal).

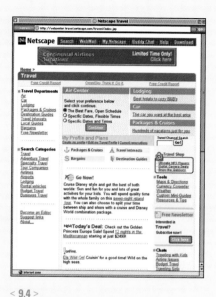

< 9.4 >

*Netscape Travel Center: webcenter.travel.netscape.com
(Category: search engine portal).*

< 9.5 >

away.com (Category: adventure travel).

< 9.6 >

lonelyplanet.com (Category: brochure site).

< 9.7 >

United Airlines: www.ual.com (Category: airlines).

< C H A P T E R 9 >

Categorize Your Competitive Set

You have your list; now quickly evaluate each site (a five-minute evaluation, nothing intensive) for category placement within the industry. Start with the existing site: Where does it fit into its industry's big picture? These are broad categories; don't get too specific. Looking back at the travel industry example, categories might be eco-tours, adventure travel, travel portals, airlines, and so on. All are definitely travel sites, but each specializes. If you are working on something as specific as Shih-tzu breeding, make sure you look at sites that focus on other small breeds. Be imaginative. Investigate related categories such as purebred dog shows or veterinary obstetrics.

The idea here is to sort and categorize. Although you may have a category with several sites in it, each site should be in only one category. This limiting factor will help clarify true market segmentation and will undoubtedly simplify the total process. Determine industry relevance. Make final cuts.

Step 2: Creating a Features List

No, this is not a rundown of what is playing at the local megaplex. A features list is a concise inventory of what each of the selected sites has to offer ([9.8] and [9.9]). Content, graphics, media, functionality, things to do, things to see, actions to take... List them all. Take all elements into consideration. Identify the download speeds and graphic weight of the different competitive sites. Include features such as

Scarcity of Choices?

What if there aren't even five sites for your comparison? You may have been the first in your industry to go online, or perhaps you found a niche with essentially no competition. Much of the reason you are conducting the informal features analysis is to get deep into the company and to discover what it is like to be a user in this particular industry. Get creative. If you are unable to find more than three to five sites to compare within your industry, or if most of the competition is offline or traditionally functioning (brick-and-mortar types), try to find areas of similarity with other sites and companies. Look for similar information, similar choices, similar e-commerce functionality. Begin to test functions against your site. If need be, assess the offline competition in greater depth. How? Explore, purchase, and contact offline competition through traditional means. Locally, this might mean driving to a facility or store. Nationally, it might entail contacting the company by phone and requesting a catalog or other information.

< A N A L Y Z I N G   Y O U R   C O M P E T I T I O N >

< T I P S >

Graphic & Content Comparison	Competition A Brochure-site	Competition B Interactive	Competition C Dynamic
Company Name			
Company URL	samplea.com	sampleb.com	samplec.com
Site Classification	brochure	destination	portal
Frames based	x		
Use of animation	x		
Splash screen	x		
Scrolling on homepage		x	x
Scrolling content on sub-pages		x	x
Graphic buttons	x		
Text/HTML links		x	x
Ad on homepage			x
URL on homepage	x	x	x
Printable homepage	x	x	x
Global navigation on subpages	x	x	x
Sitemap/Site Index		x	x
Dynamic content (changes daily)			x
Rollover navigation	x	x	
Email or feedback ability	x		
Pull-down menus		x	
Download less than 50k		x	x
Total # of features per site	9	10	10
Rank Effectiveness:	*	**	****

< 9.8 >

Here is a generic example of graphic and content features that might appear on competitive sites. Note that this example focuses on graphics and functionality...

Feature Comparison	Competition A Brochure-site	Competition B Interactive	Competition C Dynamic
Company Name			
Company URL	samplea.com	sampleb.com	samplec.com
Site Classification	brochure	destination	portal
Search Function		x	x
Contests/Games	x	x	x
Email	x	x	x
E-Commerce	x		x
Ad Banners		x	x
Chat			x
Press Releases	x	x	x
Company Information	x	x	x
Video/Music Clips		x	x
Web Links	x	x	x
Contact Information	x	x	x
Press Releases	x	x	x
Client List	x	x	x
Feedback	x	x	x
Message Boards			x
Flash Animation		x	x
Other	x	x	x
Total # of features per site	11	14	17
Rank Effectiveness:	*	**	****

< 9.9 >

...And this example is content oriented. Your features list should be likewise grouped.

Categorizing

Make categorizing easier by using self-stick notes. Spread out on a conference table or use a big, white, dry-erase board. Draw a grid and create initial categories. Print out the company logos and URLs and tape the information to the notes. Place the companies in the appropriate categories on the grid. Rename categories if you need to split them (the dry-erase board is handy for that) or move sites to other categories if it becomes appropriate (self-stick-note mobility makes this a snap). Remember, each site should fall under only one category. Some, like portals, will logically qualify for more than one category, so select the category that best fits.

< CHAPTER 9 >

search, registration, and message boards. Determine the best navigation methods. Customize your features list to best fit the industry. Keep it feasible and within budget; an exhaustive list is not necessary. You can get a comprehensive view of the online competition without listing every last feature on every last site.

While evaluating a site, rank the importance of each feature. Determine how it applies to the overall site goals. Decide as a user if you like it or hate it, or could take it or leave it. Be as diligent and as detailed as possible in the time allowed. In the final competitive analysis report, you will compile these features lists and create a grand master grid for an ultimate comparison experience.

Step 3: Conducting Analysis and Testing

With the competitive set defined and the features list created, you are ready for the actual "doing" part. Gathering data from each site in the competitive set is the most laborious part of the entire analysis. This is the step, depending upon the depth and complexity of research conducted, that can quickly blow a budget.

We present two approaches here: individual evaluation and informal usability testing. Each will work on its own, or you may determine that your budget will only allow for one approach (individual evaluation). Again, determine what your goals are for the analysis and testing, and be realistic with time and resources.

Brainstorming for Features

When generating a features list, begin by logging every feature (graphics, content, functionality, and so on), then narrow down to specific categories, and finally hone in on features that repeat across several sites. In the end, the features listed and compared should cover as many sites as possible but need not go across the board. The final number of features compared will depend on resources and detail desired, but a target of 20 to 30 after narrowing down is a good goal. Here are some things to look for as you begin your features list:

- **Graphics.** Splash screen, Flash animation, GIF animation, frames, ads, etc.

- **Media.** Audio clips, video clips, etc.

- **Content.** Press releases, a description of products/services, a company description, bios, a client list, whether the content is static or dynamic, etc.

- **Functionality.** Search, login, community boards, online chats, registration, online purchasing, security, etc.

< A N A L Y Z I N G   Y O U R   C O M P E T I T I O N >

Cheat Sheet

Don't have the time to perform an online competitive analysis? If your project falls into one of the 22 web-oriented industries listed at www.gomez.com, then much of the work has been done for you ([9.10] to [9.12]). Providing an at-a-glance scorecard that rates an industry's top 10 to 15 sites for overall performance, Gomez.com breaks its analyses into helpful categories such as ease of use, customer confidence, on-site resources, relationship services, and overall cost. Gomez.com updates its data quarterly.

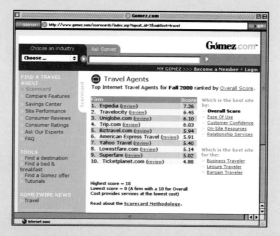

< 9.10 >

In this example (for the travel industry), Gomez.com highlights the top 10 and ranks them according to an overall score.

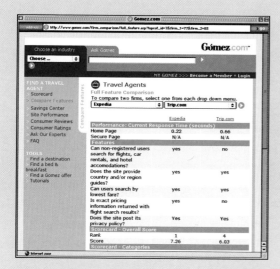

< 9.11 >

This features list (from Gomez.com) is a side-by-side comparison of two sites within a defined industry. It lists the major attributes/features of the site (starting with home page loading time) and is very specific to the industry.

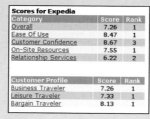

< 9.12 >

Gomez.com also scores each site for overall ease of use, customer confidence, on-site resources, and relationship services.

< CHAPTER 9 >

Competitive Analysis   Site: _____

Date:
Tester name:

1. What is your initial response to this site?
   _____
   _____
   _____

2. After a brief examination (less than five minutes), please describe your
   impression of this company's purpose.
   _____
   _____
   _____

3. List the services that this site provides.
   _____
   _____
   _____

4. Using a rating of 1–5, 1 being poor, 5 being excellent, rate the following
   aspects of the site:

   Ease of use: 1   2   3   4   5
   Look & feel: 1   2   3   4   5
   Navigation: 1   2   3   4   5
   Overall: 1   2   3   4   5

5. Additional comments:
   _____
   _____
   _____
   _____
   _____
   _____

< 9.13

This individual evaluation worksheet outlines some of the basic things you should think about when taking a look at each website during the individual analysis.

Perform Individual Evaluations

After all sites in the competitive set are appropriately checked against the features list, each evaluator should give his or her opinion on each site from a user perspective. Prepare a simple document [9.13] to fill out for each site in the competitive set. Take a look at each site in detail. You did so while checking for features; do more now if time and budget allow. The more you investigate the competitive set, the better versed in the industry you will be.

Conduct Informal Usability Testing

Informal usability testing takes the evaluation a step further. If you have the resources, we highly recommend testing a feature or two across the competitive set for ease of use. Identify some basic tasks that can be performed within the set of competitive sites. If there is more than one audience for your redesign project, choose tasks aimed at each audience.

Consider again the travel industry. How hard it is to find and book a trip for two to Tokyo? To check on flight arrival times? Try to find a motel in Madagascar, a rental car in Reykjavik, or hiking trails in Helsinki. If you are doing an analysis on the lighting industry, order some light bulbs. How easy or difficult it is to find the size, type, and brightness you want? Now wait a few days until your order actually arrives. Return a few items. How easy is that? Call customer service for assistance. Complain. Be an actual user.

< A N A L Y Z I N G   Y O U R   C O M P E T I T I O N >

Depending on the objectives of your redesign project, these tasks might be very simple or highly complex. For the most part, this type of testing will be more in-depth than what one user can accomplish in one hour. You will want to analyze tasks from start to finish, and in some cases, that will require actual purchases. Invest a little time and money. The results are worth it.

Step 4: Creating a Final Report

Putting your findings and information together in official report format is the final step of competitive analyses, regardless of formality. The final report will be most effective if it is put into an "executive summary," easy-to-read (easy-to-skim) format. In one or two pages, convey your top findings and recommendations. Get straight to the point. What were the most surprising results? What made the user experience a positive one? What was infuriating? The rest of the report should explain methodology and process and should include screenshots and overview pages of the sites reviewed, along with the comparison grids you so painstakingly produced (and checked and double-checked) [9.14].

Obviously, the formality of the final report depends on whom it is for: the web development team or the client? Most often it is for both. Primarily, the entire competitive analysis is for the team to wrap its collective head around the project. However, this exercise can be extremely valuable as a deliverable to the client as well — especially if the client is starting

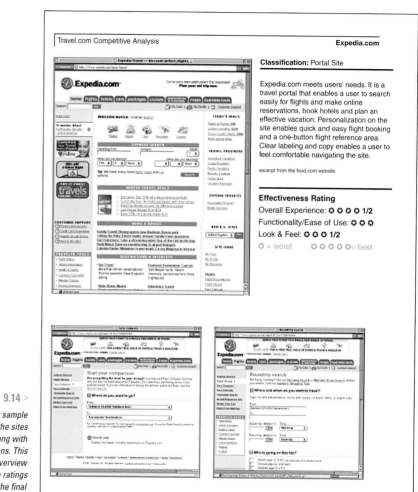

9.14 >

This final report sample page shows one of the sites being analyzed, along with several subscreens. This page will have an overview and will take the ratings (from the bottom of the final grid) to give an overall ratings score.

< C H A P T E R 9 >

to evaluate its services and features for a redesign. This report can show what other industry leaders or competitors are offering, which is important in evaluating what content should appear on the new site.

Create a Features Grid

Before completing the report, we highly recommend taking the time to compile the gathered information into a visual grid. Take the features list for each site analyzed and merge them, putting features down the side and sites across the top. Put the existing site first. Add your usability-tested tasks into your features grid. Chunk the features together into comprehensive categories such as "Search" and "Personalization." List subcategories if further definition is necessary [9.15]. This grid will probably be several pages long, but the more detailed and specific the features list, the more comprehensive the report.

The Final Report Should Contain at Least the Following:

- An executive summary (a one- to two-page overview)

- Findings and recommendations (can be included in the executive summary or expanded as necessary)

- A description of the methodology/process/approach

- Screenshots and an overview of each site (two to three screenshots, final ratings from the grid, a brief overview of collected experiences)

- A features grid (created next)

- Overall ratings (included in the features grid)

- Notes and raw data

< A N A L Y Z I N G   Y O U R   C O M P E T I T I O N >

Site Name	Travelocity	expedia	travelnow	Yahoo/ Travel	Netscape/ Travel	Lufthansa	Icelandic Air	Southwest	Alaska	United	Away.com	LonelyPlanet
CLASSIFICATION	Portal Sites					Airline Sites					Adventure Travel	
GENERAL FEATURES												
Search for Flights									●	●		
Make Online Reservations												
Search for Hotels	●	●	●	●	●		●				●	●
Make Online Hotel Reservations	●	●	●	●		●	●				●	●
Search for Rental Cars	●	●					●				●	●
Search for Vacation Packages	●	●					●				●	
Customer Service 1-800#	●	●				●	●				●	●
Customer Service Online Chat												●
BOOK FLIGHT FEATURES												
Search for Flights			●									●
By City			●									●
By Date	●	●					●					
By Price	●	●	●	●	●	●	●	●	●	●		●
Sort Flights		●				●	●	●			●	●
By Airlines	●	●									●	●
By Lowest Fare											●	●
By Non-stop											●	

< 9.15 >

This is a sample features grid for the travel industry showing the 12 selected sites in three categories: portals, airline sites, and adventure travel. The features (listed on the left) are then compared across the board for a direct side-by-side comparison.

Note: This is a sample used for display purposes only and should not be considered actual data.

< C H A P T E R 9 >

Ratings								
Overall Experience	✪ ½	✪ ✪	✪ ✪ ½	✪ ½	✪ ✪ ½	✪	✪ ✪	✪ ✪ ✪ ✪ ✪
Functionality	✪ ½	✪ ✪ ✪	✪ ✪ ½	✪ ✪	✪ ✪ ✪	✪	✪ ✪	✪ ✪ ✪ ✪ ✪
Look & Feel	✪ ✪ ½	✪ ✪	✪ ✪	✪	✪ ½	½	✪ ✪	✪ ✪ ✪ ✪ ✪
Homepage Download (graphics only)	54K	10K	30K	120K	8K	24K	18K	110K 2nd page

* = Recommended feature
(•) = Hidden feature

< 9.16

Ratings for overall experience, functionality, and look and feel are shown here. Also included is the K size for the home page download for comparison purposes.

Effectiveness Rating

Overall Experience: ✪ ✪
Functionality/Ease of Use: ✪ ✪ ✪
Look & Feel: ✪ ✪

✪ = worst   ✪ ✪ ✪ ✪ ✪ = best

< 9.17

For individual site overview pages, relist the ratings information next to screen-shots of each site [9.14].

Make Overall Evaluations

At the end of the analysis, prepare two evaluations. First give an overall rating for each site in the competitive set. Select at least three main areas to evaluate and use a standard rating system of one to five stars ([9.16] and [9.17]). Get feedback from all involved — one team member may have had a horrible experience with a site, and another may have had major success. The main areas for rating might include the following:

- **Overall experience.** What was the general experience when using the site? Favorable? Frustrating? Did you feel the company was responsive to your needs as a user? Were you able to complete tasks successfully? Would you want to return to the site?

- **Functionality.** From a functionality standpoint, was it easy to complete actual tasks, or did you hit dead ends? Was registration and ordering problematic or smooth?

- **Look and feel.** Was the site visually appealing? How did it make you feel about the company or the brand? Did it appear professional, targeted, and clean? Did it seem dated, overloaded, and badly executed?

Another form of evaluation is a more comprehensive, written piece summarizing the experiences, pros and cons, and overall impression of the site from a collection of user responses. This summary should be accompanied by screenshots, be brief and to the point, and outline the most relevant findings about that particular site.

< A N A L Y Z I N G   Y O U R   C O M P E T I T I O N >

CHAPTER SUMMARY

Out of a need to become better partners with our clients, conducting analyses like the informal features analysis described in this chapter is a valuable part of the Discovery process. Although the final report is often surprising and sometimes enlightening, understand that the process itself is as important as the results for one big reason: It enables both the client and the development team to see the client's industry from a user's perspective. Yes, you are evaluating the industry's current online and offline competitive landscape and are making pertinent comparisons. And yes, those results go a long way toward understanding how the client's company fits into its competitive set. But as a web development team, the ultimate point of this analysis is to achieve a better understanding of the client company's site that's slated for a redesign, the overall industry, and the user experience for which you are ardently aiming.

Index

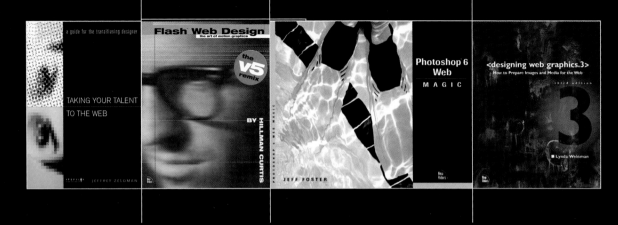

Taking Your Talent to the Web
Jeffrey Zeldman
ISBN: 0735710732
$40.00

Flash Web Design: the v5 remix
Hillman Curtis
ISBN: 0735710988
$45.00

Photoshop 6 Web Magic
Jeff Foster
ISBN: 0735710368
$45.00

<designing web graphics.3>
Lynda Weinman
ISBN: 1562059491
$55.00

The Art & Science of Web Design
Jeffrey Veen
ISBN: 0789723700
$45.00

<creative html design.2>
Lynda Weinman and
William Weinman
ISBN: 0735709726
$39.99

Don't Make Me Think!
Steve Krug
ISBN: 0789723107
$35.00

New Riders

The Authors. The Content. The Timeliness.

What it takes to be a classic.

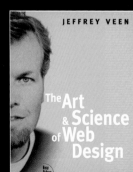

COLOPHON

We wrote this book using Microsoft Word® (which we cursed regularly) on several machines, including Kelly's generic Dell PC Pentium, super-fast, organizational behemoth and Emily's Apple Macintosh G4, as well as three Apple Macintosh Powerbooks — two G3s that crisscrossed the Bay Bridge and the country often enough to warrant better carrying cases for each, and one antique 520C that met an untimely (and heretofore unsolved) death in a hotel room in Seattle.

This book was laid out using QuarkXPress™ 4.1. Illustrations were completed using Adobe Illustrator® 9.0, Macromedia FreeHand™ 9.0, and Adobe Photoshop® 5.5 and 6.0. Also used: Macromedia Dreamweaver® 4.0, Macromedia Fireworks™ 4.0, and Inspiration®. Fonts: Sabon (body copy), Info, and Univers Condensed (headers and captions).

The pages of this book are printed on 60# Mead Web Dull. The cover is printed on 12 point C1S. The book and cover were printed at Graphic Arts Center/Indianapolis.

Mascot support was provided unconditionally by Malcolm The Wonder Kitty.

Malcolm The Wonder Kitty.